War – Pride – Vi

1930 – 1965 in Germany/Poland

Only Partially Fictionalized

Composed in America

By Anna Louise Haman

with David A. Froebel

Newvo Peace Publishing Santa Fe, New Mexico

Many Vietnam Veterans and Old Hard Core Hippies and
Others helped make the book.

Copyright 2007 © War Victims
ISBN 978-1507682685
Day of publication: 04,26,2011
Anna Haman's birth date March 6,1952, 6:00 AM
Anna's translation/death 2005
David A. Froebel's birth date Oct. 20,1944

War – Pride – Victims may be downloaded for free at
http:www.newvopublishing.com
Newvo Peace Publishing Post Office Box 23450 Santa Fe, New Mexico
87502 (david@newvopublishing.com) Distributor: Baker and Taylor,
2550 West Tyvola Rd.# 300, Charlotte, N. C. 28217, 704-998-3100
Wholesaler: Ingram International
International Agent: Blessingway Authors' Services, Santa Fe, NM USA

Library of Congress Cataloging-in-Publications Everybody Loved Anna :
a German family's story of confronting social normalcy / Anna Louise
Haman with David A. Froebel.

p. cm. 1. Haman, Anna Louise. 2. Haman, Anna Louise-Family. 3.
Germany-Biography. 4 Poland-Biography. 5. Germany –History20[th]
century. 6. Haman family.
I Froebel, David A. II. Title DD247.H2516A3 2009 943.087'092 QBI09 QBI09-700049

Acknowledgments

This book would have been impossible if it were not for friends, *Vera Timofeeva* (Anna's beloved girlfriend) piano composer, diversified sprit of nature; *Sandra Smith,* Master of Arts Composition and Communication Central Michigan University; *Catherin Pond,* Master of Organizational Behavior (Brigham Young University); *Robert Grogan,* 1966 Special Forces Viet Nam, a dear buddy beginning in high school 1961; *Constance Albrecht* grant writer, writer, farm girl and burned-out activist; *Dennis Smith,* (Corky), two years First Cavalry in Viet Nam, disabled-translated/died Sept 08, War Victim, Silver Star, by synchronicity he lived next door to me, and oh about every day he was there listening to me piss and moan about publishing and to teach me the physiological effects of a soldier to be in a war zone for two years; Mark Wenneborg, literary professor and *Jack Spratt,* who has published in every major newspaper and magazine in the world. He has worked for forty-four years as a free lance photo-journalist for the New York Times.

Bob, Joyce and Bobby Bentley, Dave Yount, Shawn Miller, and Allen Maples where I worked as an automotive technician at Diagnostic Auto Repair when Anna translated, AA, ACOA, NA, Nicotine Anonymous, *Old Hard Core Hippie and Viet Nam Veteran Friends,* Anna's Sufi Camp friends especially *Laura Wills*; Mesilla Valley Writers especially Louis Meissen who served in the American infantry in World War Two in Europe; Ted Specker (City of the Sun); Helen Polley whose deceased son had three tours of duty in Viet Nam; Lionel Colbert BSME Louisiana State 2000; Kenni Gottlieb who has sort of devoted his life to friends in distress (on U tube Woodstock, he was filmed tripping but he no longer does drugs or alcohol); Venny Garke (from India) who gifted a computer with guidance from his Guru that Anna had previously gifted him, Yoga teacher and stress management consultant; (female name omitted) Physic Medium; Philip Madrid USMC sergeant, 3 tours Viet Nam, farmer, Pueblo Indian, published writer, main timing advisor for book; Mitral Benton author and holocaust (concentration camp) survivor; Tiresas Stoughton Zen Teacher; Touchstone Yoga Center; John Waugh BA Sierra Club; *Mike Quinn*, main proofer, world wanderer, published author in South Korea and his brother Will Quinn 1969 Viet Nam; Mrs. Karole Skeen and proofing by *Mr. Mack Skeen* purchasing manager; John Ingress survivor and aspiring law merchant; Pablo Nuanes, (Turtle), Apache Indian / Hispanic; Bel Canto Writers Group, Barry Dunleavey, editor/publisher Heights Inward Manhattan, N.Y.C. and actor and creative writer instructor, Bette Waters, RN CNM author / publisher, Dr. Esther Bohuslov, retired English professor and published author, Jonathan Fackler, artist, Executive Director, Main Street Program, Deming New Mexico; Attorney and author Edward DeV. Bunn; Jessie Orta engineering and part-time professional musician; Estella Floras professor/teacher; Paul Bringman author/farmer ACLU state board, Iowa; Dale Sluter sweat lodge coordinator, one of the original founders of the huge Brotherhood of the Spirit Commune; Margret Bertelstein artist/writer, coordinator; Maggi Rodriguez-Anna's sister a very gifted French potter; Richard Polese, was executive director New Mexico Book Association, consultation on the book; Brian Secovnie (Moish) apprentice book binder; Alisa Blake Sufi Homemaker; Debbie, Transvestite - dance specialist; Ben Sheets Christian/Native American Spiritualist; Dr. Jose Del Moral psychiatrist; Pette of France; Ethan Froebel, Anna's step son, author of (Tai Chi, Yoga and Eastern Mysticism) and painting contractor; Julian Rivers Froebel, my grandson, (finder of Oak branch for book signature); Michael Madrid; (female name omitted), US Army

Julian Rivers Froebel, my grandson, (finder of Oak branch for book signature); Michael Madrid; (female name omitted), US Army independent contractor, counselor of women and children; Cynthia Simonson, dry cleaning manager, my link to hiphop world; Ellen Kleiner, Blessingway Authors' Services - Santa Fe, New Mexico; Cynthia Vandermark, personal care attendant; Josh, (Waffles T Clown) architect, dedicated activist; Bret Berman, artist, musician, writer, community facilitator; Manus Kowitz proofreader, serious activist for Native American Indian rights; Dr. (female named omitted) German/Israeli/American Psychologist; Claudia Hadley business advisor (from Columbia, South America); Dr. Bob Worthington, my SCORE business advisor etc., retired Clinical Psychologist, army commander in Viet Nam and the author of two books and a movie; Robin Pierce; Parker Clevland many years of dedicated experience with intentional communities; Barbra Ballou, smoke jumper (parachutist), United States Forest Service, associates fine arts sculpture, physical therapy–message 1969, BS Geology, Agriculture 1975 U. of Minnesota; Suzy Beaver aka Harley Davison Lady, spelling bee champion; Ron Donaghe, editor-owner Two Brothers Press; Linda Jackson proof reader, educator; James R. Blaisdell; Jack Rokowski Jack@A-VideoGrapher.com from Poland; Anita Frietz school cook; Roger F Beckmann member of Eckankar; Michael Ransom photo graphics, Beirut Veteran, Comanche Native American; Dave Chapman, jokester, proof reader, partially Blackfoot and Cherokee Indian; Nicole Daddona MA Sociology, computer assistance, proofing, my half Jewish neighbor; Cris Johnson, (Yuki – his Japanese name); Greg Sherman substitute teacher; Arrowhead Center NMSU; Dottie Beaman partially American Blackfoot Indian; Ingrid Richardson, RN, MA (detox nurse) from Germany; Alishia Jones proofing; Randy Harris, proofing, coordinator/leader for "The Great Conversations" Southern N. M.; Pierre retired Unity Minister; a couple of people did not want to be listed because of their positions in society. Also, pertaining to some listed people, there is nondisclosure about metals from Vietnam their choices. And my Apache Indian –Anglo friend

Doug Cody for watching/overseeing the office/residence day and night when I go out of town, 1964-1965 Vietnam Veteran E5 Combat Engineers.

My grandmother/grosmutter was born in Germany and had had family members on both sides of the world war. I was her last grandchild to mature whereby she gave me a lot of one-to-one attention in our close-knit family. She was one of the key women leaders in Central Connecticut, USA for the woman's right to vote; her brother Freedle was one of Mark Twain's (Samuel Clemens') inner circle of friends. Actually saw her on National Public Television marching down the main street of Hartford, Connecticut, for the woman's right to vote. Excuse me for getting a little carried away; well, I had the wonderful experience of saying good-by when she was in her last hours of life. As a small child, sitting on her bed with the door closed, one-too-one. Well, she said "I am going to a good place and I want you to be happy and look your mother and aunts are going to [freak out (my wording)] but I want you to be happy." Near the end of Anna's life SHE LOVED to hear that story!

Contents

Preface

Anna Haman invites and conducts the reader through authentic experiences of herself and family through historical cultural growth expansion starting in the beginning of the 1930's. There is a saying that from the life story of one person we can learn more about the historical epoch than from many historical books. She invites and leads the reader to experience events promoting cultural growth with an expanding broadness of views before her birth and as a child growing up in a small town in Germany. She has a memory going back to being a toddler unlike the vast majority of us. The factual stories were passed down by her family. Her family had a profound caring about Jewish people during the war.

INTRODUCTION

Anna Haman had the rare ability to pierce through the fears / paranoia of people and connect with their true selves. In her writings she states about herself: "I am not of the talking type. I digest feelings, like cows digest grass, chewing the cud in silence." No matter whether someone was three years old or seventy-three years old she was able to penetrate her love into that being; it used to amaze me watching her do that. One night I asked her about it after she had done it with a young convenience store clerk, and she said, "I have been doing it all my life."

Her family were story tellers, demanding, for whatever reason, that she learn about family members' past tremulous problems starting before the war and during the war. For her the teachings began as a little girl.

Her going into the psychological depths about people in her family shows what she had learned about mental anguish; even when at a young age she did analyze, in her own way, why her great aunt went insane, explaining what a horrible mess she was in, especially with her husband. Oh yes, Anna exposed the situation for what it actually was. She left no family secrets uncovered except for one, as far as I know.

Some people say that the title of the book should have been "War Victims"; maybe it should have been. Anyhow, the psychological after-effects of war she wrote about are very heavy: the social mechanisms of a post - war society, Anna's family going through painful changes that she wrote about in her journalistic style. She had been a writer for a newspaper after graduating from high school in Germany pertaining to rock and roll musicians.

The historical research she did in America, and she visited Germany for her writings. She wanted to get the job done right; it was her purpose in life.

She has shown in her writings her personal path of -being raised in a small German town. That some people would call thick headed, having a herd mentality way of functioning as a society.

Was Anna a well-behaved girl growing up? Nope. Her mother once told her, "But maybe you have an ancient soul inhabiting your childlike body. I've often wondered about your wise old eyes when you were just a newborn." And later, in her teen years, her father was, shall we say, perturbed about her sexual freeness.

Soldiers are trained and taught to be fearful of everyone, especially in a war zone as some say, and the population of Germany had this after-effect of World War Two. As a result, the women of Germany developed their womanly skills such as how to cut to the chase and communicate with men; her writings bring a understanding of this. Anna had experienced being exceptionally daring from a very young age; how as a woman she lived in the after-war culture, and later as a young woman moving away from Germany.

As a whole, her close relatives before the war and during the war had prominent positions in society with strong non-racial, socially liberal attitudes towards Jewish friends and others: they were liberals overall and Presbyterian. Later they were suppressed mentally and physically over the years by the powers that were.

When Anna started the book in 1993 she was in a Masters program working towards a degree in Creative Arts Therapies specializing in Movement and Psychodrama from Lesley University at Cambridge, Massachusetts. When she had lost her dissertation paper-work on her computer, she started her book so that she would have paperwork to turn in to get her Masters degree.

Once, Anna tried to establish her own counseling business in New Mexico. For awhile, she focused on Astrology and Yoga to help her clients. The business was short lived. Seeing that her degree was from a very liberal college in Massachusetts, the State of New Mexico shut her down. She tried to fight the ruling but gave up on the endeavor before exploring all of her options.

Anna made many moves in New Mexico, all over the state, after being divorced. Someone once told her that in a past lifetime she had been a Native American Indian suicide counselor throughout this area of America, and she believed it.

Having ample money, she lived quite frugally but not always. She had gone through extremes from staying at a high-dollar Santa Fe resort to living at a very economical hot springs complex elsewhere in New Mexico. When it came to living in new-age intentional communities, the same applied there also.

Near the very end of Anna's life one day when her inner physical being was in horrible shape, I sat down and watched her walk down the sidewalk, and then, at the end of her short walk, she came right up to me with a very perturbed look on her face and said to me forcefully point - blank, "What were you looking at?" and I said, "I was watching you walk." Instantly, a huge happy smile came over her face. Anna once said she really hated going into big truck stops; well, with her permanent yogic wiggle walk etc., it is pretty evident, and very easy for me to understand.

Once she told me how she sped down the highway in the open desert to Albuquerque, New Mexico at 110 miles per hour in a high-dollar sports car without getting a speeding ticket. So, I asked her, "How did you do that Anna?" Her reply was, "Flattery". She had her gifts of life to use in different ways and that she did.

After Anna died, I called up different friends of hers and, oh yeah, some cried; one neighbor, a retired lady, cried in my arms. Hell, I was grieving also. I suppose one of the disadvantages of being a male is not being allowed to cry when need be.

Newvo Peace Publishing's business policy is <u>the truth comes first</u> and the fuckin' (please pardon my rash word; it's the best that I could think of) <u>money is a secondary issue</u>. This policy started from the very beginning of learning how to publish.

The book may be downloaded for free at www.newvopublishing.com

Chapter 1

Before Beginnings

I was the first baby born alive in my family. However, I was not my mother's first child. In an alien environment, during the upheaval of World War Two, while Father was on short military leave, Mother had conceived during their honeymoon.

The weather was dismal. Dirt roads around the house had turned into mud pits. The winds swept with a chilly razor's edge across barren fields and bellowed arctic air into every crevice and fissure. Temperatures plunged way below freezing, even though spring had already marked its entry, on the calendar at least.

It was far from the warmer climates of his family's previous rambling spread near Odessa, Russia, on the Black Sea, where Willy Haman my father, could have entertained his bride Margret, my mother to be, in grand style with sailing, hunting excursions and wine tasting. He and his wedding party were stuck in this depressing place in Poland where sadness draped the rich antique furniture. In the pantry, endless rows of jars with jams, preserved vegetables and meat that stared at the new tenants with labels that were written in a foreign language and indicated that this was once a Kosher household. It must have obeyed altogether different culinary laws than the more Dionysian tastes and indulgences of my father's family.

When Dad sauntered into the well-appointed pantry or descended into the root cellars brimming with potatoes, carrots, and cabbages, he felt cold chills waft across the back of his neck. Inevitably, he thought of the former proprietors. Did they exhale their grief into his nape? Were they upset that he had opened the blackberry jam and heaped several spoons on the still-steaming white bread his mother had pulled from the oven just minutes ago? The thought of meddling with spirits who might be still attached to to their worldly goods made him shrink back. He closed the lid on the jar, wheeled, and left. This cornucopia had fallen into his lap because of the mysterious misfortune of those who had cultivated the land and laid up the fruits for the winter that they never came to experience in the glow of their own hearth.

When he walked by the yard where a chicken roamed, he tossed the blackberry jam sandwich in front of the mother hen who gobbled it up eagerly with her flock of little chicks. His hands felt free and easy again, and he relaxed.

Each member of the Haman family approached the inherited forbidden fruits of this place in his own way. Some of father's numerous siblings coped better than he and freely helped themselves to Brazilian cigars they found in hidden recesses in the secretary. But when Mandel and Emo puffed blue grey smoke curls into each other's face, inevitably they talked about the former residents of the place and speculated about their tastes and vices.

Outsiders who came to visit immediately noticed that the Haman clan was not truly at home, even though they had come into possession of an impressive estate. It is not surprising, therefore, that during and after the wedding celebration, bride and bridegroom, *in fact, the entire family*, and a small circle of friends felt vaguely apprehensive. Everybody seemed to have a complaint. The roast was undercooked. The whipped cream on the dessert was too runny. The band only knew how to play polkas, and on and on. While in reality such superficial complaining only camouflaged a state of discomfort. But nobody found the words or had the gumption to address that nagging feeling lodged somewhere between the gut and the solar plexus.

Bride and bridegroom were aware that their wedding party was a lackluster affair, but were at a loss to know how to remedy the situation. Especially Willy, my father, who was accustomed to the high life, missed the bright and lively entertainment and company he so easily engendered in Bessarabia, South Russia. In these more southern latitudes, whenever he and a group of friends got together, a party happened without any effort. The warmth of the sun and the expansiveness of the land buoyed them into spontaneous capers that filled the pages of photo albums that have yellowed with the passage of much more sober times. Wild escapades were almost routine in his life then. Admittedly, that was before the war, when his facial lines were drawn into a permanent grin and laugh wrinkles radiated from the outside of his eyes like sunbeams.

As much as he tried to ignore the shadows that were upon his heels, the new homestead in Poland bore down on him like a leaden weight.

"I swear this is a jinxed place my son. I feel like I'm drowning in a sea of invisible tears," Anya, his mother, had whispered to him while handing him the plate of assorted cheeses during the wedding feast. The entire wedding party felt like a bunch of hostages held under the spell of a malevolent environment. Everybody did their best to extend their heartfelt wishes for a bright future to the bride and bridegroom, in spite of the fact that nobody had the vaguest idea of how the future would unfold.

By no means was this location the kind of place the Haman clan would have chosen as a home had anybody asked for their opinion. They found out with great sorrow freedom of choice was one amenity the war blasted into smithereens.

This was particularly difficult for this enterprising family since their expansive sense of freedom, had accustomed them to venture into the thrills of technology before anybody else even thought of it. My Grandfather Manfred Haman built the first power plant in the region and supplied the whole community with the magic juice. He sped away with the first car when everybody else still trotted along hitched to horses or mules. When any of the brothers got into trouble with the law, one of the more senior siblings would invite the town chief of law enforcement over for wine tasting, cheese sampling and target shooting. Promptly, any record of the infraction would disappear in the town marshal's waste basket.

In his early thirties Willy managed three separate grist mills with relative ease and a sense of humor. Later he and his parents and eleven siblings, had been uprooted from their sweeping home base and tossed like small pieces of driftwood into an angry ocean where the tides of war carried them into this gloomy place to settle into property that was tainted by violence.

Hitler's brooms of racial cleansing had scoured this Polish estate and left no living soul behind. Even the livestock had been ransacked. Possibly Polish neighbors, who as soon as the manor was vacated, embarked by night - like pirates, and divvied up horses, cows, sheep, pigs and poultry by throwing the dice. Rumors ran that these same neighbors orchestrated a slaughter orgy. Butchering men waded with rubber boots in blood pools and women hung the skin of pork entrails on the washing lines in preparation for stuffing them with congealed blood, ground up liver, stomach heart and kidneys spiced with sage, and garlic.

As soon as the Haman clan moved in, some of the spokesmen among these neighbors came up to the front door and offered the new tenants pork sausage links as a goodwill gift.

One of these guys winked while handing my grandmother Anya a basket with sausage and said quizzically with a broad peasant grin on his weather beaten tawny face, "The swine roamed in the oak woods that belong to your new estate and it only makes sense for us to offer you this neighborly favor. As you know yourself, everything returns, by the will of God, to its place of origin."

Nobody among the Haman's openly broached the topic of what had happened to the former proprietors, especially not in the bride's presence. My mother Margret quickly picked up on an uneasy charge that emanated from every piece of furnishing, including the four-posted oak bed that she and my dad Willy occupied during their honeymoon. Moreover, she noticed that the new occupants moved about in this household more circumspect and restrained than their own domestics.

Even the bridegroom - otherwise thrilled to have the opportunity to finally be intimate with his bride - entertained Margret gingerly. If it hadn't been serious, it could have passed as slapstick. He moved awkwardly like a waiter who expects to blunder any moment and spill the sauce into the lady's lap or trip with a tray of glasses over the ripple in the carpet. In fact, when he handed her a glass of wine, his hands trembled and the wine did spill on her hand.

What prompted Willy to behave more like a klutz than his usual quick and smooth feline nature was the nagging feeling that he was a thief and impostor. Starting with the finely etched crystal glasses and vintage Beaujolais that he and Margret held in their hands to toast their united future, all of these things were not really his own. But, in reality belonged to the former owners of this estate, Polish Jews. They lived here no more because of circumstances that remained in the dark of fear.

Dad's inquiries, "Did you, by chance, know the family that owned all this land and the house where we live now?" fell on deaf ears. They pretended not to understand, but more likely still, nobody dared to talk about the ominous place where Jews were taken, for one could easily end up being deported for any indiscretions. All the neighbors of Jewish descent had been removed from their homes in the blue-grey anonymity of the pre-dawn hours. Uniformed men herded them to the railroad station where SS officers (in their black leather coats, imposing boots, with blood thirsty German shepherd dogs at their sides, and their demur Polish and Russian prisoners of war) packed the human cargo like cattle into windowless cars. Then the long train slithered like a poisonous snake toward its destination that was not listed on the itinerary of the platform bulletin. Judging by the cautious silence of those who had witnessed the twilight spectre, it was an unnamed or rather unspeakable destination.

Only children risked to take a whack at the truth. "Don't you know that all the Jews are being cooked in giant ovens further east!" is what a handful of Polish street urchins jumping rope told Willy when he asked them concerning the whereabouts of the people who once lived here. Then they broke out in raucous laughter and dispersed like seed pods in the wind. Willy dismissed such gossip as blatant exaggeration.

Granted, he had heard rumors of Polish Jews being killed wholesale in camps. But even that was far too outrageous to believe. Back in Bessarabia, Dad knew Jews who lived in luxury and sophistication surrounded by grand pianos, looming libraries, and numerous Russian domestics. Many of them - like his friend Samuel Sackmann - had ventured into manufacturing. They excelled in the textile industry and were expert merchants in men's and women's fashions. Every item in his large wardrobe he had bought from Jewish shopkeepers who prided themselves on having the best quality silks from China, hats imported from Paris, and shoes from Milan. As dad was a connoisseur of fine quality clothing, he held these enterprising people in high regard and respected their savvy.

Surely-so he assuaged his rumbling conscience-the former owners of this place were given another homestead, just like his folks. It all amounted to one huge real estate swap a cruel re-shuffle. Stalin's and Hitler's bureaucratic henchmen didn't give a hoot whether those who were uprooted would have preferred to stay on and wait out the ravages of the war, at least surrounded by the comforting familiarity of their own homes.

Wherever Willy turned, he saw people tossed into a void, mere pawns in the jousting match of two power maniacs. Hitler - who in dad's eyes looked more like a Turkish jailer than the Savior of the Master Race - was determined to remake Europe. And Stalin was equally callous in his power game. Individual lives that were bonded to the soil and shaped by a strong sense of belonging, did not enter into their megalomaniac ambition. That's how Willy appraised the prevailing gale winds of change, knowing all too well that he, like the rest of the uprooted lot, did not count, they were miniscule specks of dust caught in a relentless whirlwind.

In and out of Willy's consciousness, his concern faded for the fates of those who had slept in the four-posted oak bed under down comforters and Portuguese sheets before Willy and Margret cuddled and snuggled and made love repeatedly every night. While their vanishing was a vexing issue, his own precarious condition was more immediate cause for fitful sleep and nightmares that left him drenched in sweat. Dad's life was on ransom. Like a puppet on a string, he had to perform tasks that went against every grain of his magnanimous personality. Worst of all, he had to fight a war that pitted him against the very people he loved most. Furthermore, he had to acquiesce to whatever domicile he was granted since war fugitives had no negotiating leverage.

Like it or not unless they preferred to roam the war-torn land like vagrants, Willy and his family had to accept the keys that were handed to them in the hush of Nazi secrecy. Raising any objections would have been folly. Opposition to these forces was suicidal. Therefore, they feigned demure complacency in the aftermath of wholesale confiscation of Jewish property. Gritting their teeth, but asking no questions they set up quarters in a once stately but now ghostly home that Hitler's territorial meat carvers had assigned to uprooted Germans like Willy as a gesture of recompensation for the loss of all their property and the eviction his folks had suffered when Hitler invaded Mother Russia.

Willy's current living conditions as a hostage housed in seized property was a direct outcome of the tit-for-tat laws that rule in wartime. Once German tank columns pierced the sacred skin of Mother Russia, Stalin, in the mean spirit of instant retaliation, kicked with his left foot out of bounds those of German ancestry who - like the Haman clan - had peacefully lived among Russian peasants for many generations.

Russian maids had fed Willy a daily diet of superstitious tales that featured witches who entangled horses' tails beyond repair, so they had to be cut off. "Malevolent ghosts lurk everywhere," plump old servant babushkas told him and shifted their head scarfs further over their forehead. More than a thousand miles to the North in Poland, encased by the walls of wrongly seized property, the Old Russian teachings rebounded with a vengeance. Ghosts lurked behind the green curtains and hid in the cherry wood cupboards among the stoneware. Dad suspected their omnipresence. Being watched all the time, he couldn't relax. Even in the warm glow of the open fireplace while flames flickered in Mother's deep brown eyes as she lay soft and voluptuously on the sheep skin to receive Dad's embrace, he felt modest and reluctant. The thought crossed his mind that their intimacies were being staged in front of a jealous audience.

Finally, when carnal desire overpowered his doubts and hesitations and he gave of himself with abandon, a nagging voice whispered into his ear. "*You're not alone*," with lightning speed he became aware of an ethereal presence. The presence of those who had dwelled there before. They patently ignored his need for privacy and hovered like sticky cobwebs around him. They closed in on him when, at the height of excitement, he thrust himself into his new bride. Disquieting thoughts kept creeping up when he wanted to climax and dive into the oblivion of their embrace. Would they have disproved of us copulating on the floor of their drawing room? All this internal jabber detracted from the intense physical chemistry that Willy and Margret enjoyed in those first nights after their vows.

In a slightly different way from her husband, Margret also felt orphaned in these wintery flat lands where the wind wailed about recent injustice and coming doom.

For the first time in her life, she left her home and parents left behind. They had sent a suitcase full of warnings with her on that long train journey that she undertook all by herself. Her mother and father pleated their faces into deep frowns during the last good-bye hugs, for they instinctively disapproved of this wartime nuptial that seemed to be thrown together with such alarming urgency and haste. Unsure how Margret would cope with a man fifteen years her senior one who never read a book aside from technical manuals about milling and generating water power they reluctantly parted giving her their blessings.

Both parents harbored unsettling questions which made them look with great ambivalence at their daughter's betrothal. Was the bridegroom afraid he'd be killed soon on the Russian front and therefore want to rush matters along? And still more disturbing to my Grandfather Herbert and my Grandmother Louise was the suspicion that a soldier like Willy, deprived of intimacy during service, made haste of this major lifetime decision, because he itched to be sexually intimate with Margret?

Consequently, Margret was loaded down in a big way when she stepped on the train. Besides her tangible luggage, Margret took with her on the trip the heavy burden of her parents' misgivings. On top of that, Mother had been deeply disturbed by an experience that turned her journey into trauma.

Gray haired, bespectacled, with impeccable dress, this man at first glance appeared so trustworthy, particularly when he told her about his career as a university professor of Slavic history. And just when she relaxed her reserve and opened herself up to him, confiding that this was her first long train trip in her life and that she was getting married in two days, he flicked the light switch off and pounced on her. He dropped the cool academic composure like a glove and dove into his beastly sexual identity which was more like that of a wrestler than of a learned man. Her insistent pleadings, "Please, Sir. No Please, don't do this to me!" fell on deaf ears. Instead of letting up, he ripped into her sheer silk blouse as if it was sandwich paper. To her great alarm, this man had a weapon of a penis. With one expert move he lifted her marine blue fitted wool skirt and ramroded his prick between her legs that she held like twin pillars glued together. Like a voracious moray, his eel-like organ darted into soft spots on her thighs and her abdomen. Blind and feverish it probed for the orifice that Margret protected by crossing her legs. The incessant rubbing and thrusting nauseated her. And she was at the point of vomiting her disgust upon his prick. His breath further aggravated her nausea. It steamed like that of an angry stud and came down hot and moist against her exposed breasts. He fondled her nipples. In response, she elbowed him in the solar plexus.

It was high time to fall back on her animal defenses. She remembered what had worked miracles when she was a rough-and-tumble tomboy, pitted as the outlaw against the King's knights in never ending re-plays of Robin Hood's adventures. And it was rough play indeed, for everybody else in the cast was male.

She inhaled strength from surging memories of her own fierce fighting. Fully resolved to get as mean as she could, she took a deep breath and imagined digging into the bone marrow of this double-faced creature. Her head plunged down like that of an eagle and without further hesitations she bored her incisors and canines into his upper arm until she tasted blood.

It stunned her that in spite of the deep gash she had bitten into his biceps, his erected organ kept on rubbing and thrusting with undiminished vigor. It appeared like this prick of his had a life on its own and that the pain of her sharp incisors did not register in the flushed redhead. Her assailant was beyond the stage where pain creates a pause. On the contrary, her teeth carving into his body seemed to drive him into heightened states of ecstasy. Like the steam engines that pulled this long train through the night, this man drove with inexorable desire for that one orifice that - so far - she had successfully withheld from him. The question arose for Margret who had never gone beyond hugging and kissing and allowing a man to caress her breasts, whether she was faced with an onslaught of sexual desire or political vengeance. Did this animal behavior spring from the need to punish and defile a female specimen of the German master race in answer to the subjugation and disgrace that this man's country had endured. Did he purge with his penis the demeaning treatment he had received from the Nazis who regarded Poles as second class citizen?

She focused all her visceral strength into keeping those thighs clamped shut like an impenetrable vise. All the while, she still fought him off with elbows, fists, and nails. A mouthful of his blood had tasted so repulsive; she gave up on biting him. All to no avail, her physical resistance only further excited the old buck. But when she finally screamed full throttle for help, the man ran out of the train compartment which they had shared for the past two hundred miles. He slipped past the conductor who rushed to see what was going on.

"He slipped away like a weasel", Mother told the conductor in a state of shock. The uniformed railroad official came up closer than felt comfortable to her and insisted that she tell him the details of the sexual assault. Mother couldn't though. It felt like engaging in yet another exploitation of her body. While the conductor probed for her full account, she just gazed blankly out of the train's window into the blackness of a rainy night that enveloped what Mother had gazed at for most of her passage across Poland, a dreary-grey landscape that swished past in its remarkable flatness. Clumps of wind-swept barren trees, were the only relief to this flatness. "He slipped away like a weasel that makes its escape from the chicken pen," Mother said in a bewildered, nearly demented tone of voice. The conductor, aware that he wasn't going to press any juicy details out of this crazed woman. He shrugged his shoulders and turned away.

Since, as an act of rebellion against her disapproving parents, she had embarked on this train journey two days earlier, and nobody was waiting at the train station to pick her up. Mother was dazed when the train finally came to a stop at her destination. When dad's bride arrived a day earlier than planned, she found out what it felt like to be mistaken as one of the uprooted people who roamed the countryside in search of a rind of bacon or cheese and some bread.

Mother looked defeated when she arrived at her destination. Her head hung low, and she kept her eyes cast downward after the humiliating experience on the train where she had been preyed upon. When she stepped down from the train, her head almost exploded with the images of her recent experience. Still under the impact of her close encounter with a man who intended to rape her, Mother walked the couple of miles from the train station to the estate where her future husband was waiting.

She walked like a defeated beast of burden. Two suitcases in each hand took their toll, and she had to set them down every few minutes. She had to ask for directions many times over because her mind was buzzing like a beehive and would not hold the instructions she had received minutes ago. Her head was feverish with rapidly churning thoughts. Why, for God's sake, had she decided to come two days early? So far in life, it had been her experience that instigated surprises tend to backfire badly on the one who cries, "Surprise!"

Then her thoughts hurdled back to the scene of assault. Had she dressed too seductively on the train? Was she showing cleavage? What if he had succeeded and penetrated her? How would she explain to her future husband that she had lost her virginity two days before the wedding during the night on a train ride across Polish potato and turnip fields? Would he believe her? Would he forgive her? She set down the suitcases and felt her forehead. She must have run a temperature. Her temples pulsated wildly, and her head felt close to bursting.

When Margret arrived at the estate with her once shiny now dirt-clodded black shoes through the mucky dirt road, she overheard one of father's sisters yell, "Hey, Mother, come to the door and look, another woman is walking into our yard. I bet she's one of those homeless fugitives, desperate to find a safe place to hide her identity." Seeing Mother (who looked dark like a gypsy or even a Jewish woman) who was wrapped in a modest woolen coat, Dad's sister Inge had cast her as just another vagrant woman, flotsam of the war, looking for a domestic position in return for shelter and food.

Inge had forgotten though that all of the Haman family were fugitives also. Granted, they were privileged fugitives since they were part of the Aryan race. But they also had to leave their home behind and were assigned by Hitler's territorial planners to a home that still breathed the conversations, laughter, whispers, and prayers of people who mysteriously disappeared.

Still, in spite of the political earthquake that sent tremors through his wedding ceremony and mud-logged honeymoon, Dad had in his mind fantasized about this wedding for years. Only now did he feel safe enough to confess to Mother, that years earlier when he had first laid his eyes on her - she being just a thirteen year old bashful girl - he had imagined her as his future bride.

During that innocuous first meeting of theirs, Margret's black hair was braided and curled like cinnamon rolls around her ears. Self-conscious, like most girls her age, she thought that this debonair man dressed like an Italian movie star, was staring at her odd hairdo rather than the whole person.

Oh, how she hated this peculiar hairdo, but her straight laced governess insisted that these monkey swings - so she jested - were most becoming for a decent, young, upstanding lady. This governess was Herbert's sister Ruth and because of her close relationship with her brother Herbert, she ruled with the authoritative command over anybody related to Grandfather. However, there was doubt within the family clan, whether Ruth was sired by the same burly butcher, Herbert Senior, as the other siblings. She was too devout a Protestant, too averse to the world of sensual pleasure, and far too conventional in her outlook to fit in with the rest of her more maverick siblings. Many suspected that Herbert's mother had entertained a secret tryst with the village pastor, and Ruth was the, result of this clandestine romance.

Still Aunt Ruth had her brother's unquestioning endorsement to rule as she saw fit in her role as governess; and, therefore, Mother had no chance at having it her way. Freedom for mother meant to sneak away from the house and Inge's surveillance and to play in the drainage ditches, culverts, and other hidden places where nature impinges on the town's landscape. Places Aunt Ruth would avoid because she found them far too hostile and unbecoming for a woman. Places where Mother could be her own wild self.

The epitome of rebellion for Margret in her teenage years revolved around having her own way with her hair. Daydreaming, Mother entertained a bold fantasy. She envisioned scissors sailing down straight from heaven, at God's behest, coming to her rescue. Snip and snap these scissors cut off the dreaded monkey swings. In her smartest dreams, Mother would wear her hair in a short sporty bob, like the women athletes she had admired in the papers who competed in the first Olympic Games that year - 1936 - in Berlin. She too wanted to be as uncomplicated and cropped in her appearance and to reflect her love for outdoors adventure and rough-and-tumble games.

Yes, Dad remembered the monkey swings, but only marginally. He was admittedly amused by the unusual touch. But much more so than the strange hairstyle, he was taken in by Margret's gaze. Her big brown eyes left an indelible imprint in his memory. He had never experienced anything like it before. Pleading and soft like a doe's eyes, and then like flicking a light switch on, Margret's gaze would change completely turning fierce like the eyes of a dangerous predator.

In fact, so Willy found out during their reminiscing sessions on their honeymoon, her eyes were asking questions that remained mute at the time, for she was shy and withdrawn in social matters, but fearless when it came to solitary pursuits like climbing trees and exploring dark and forbidden places.

While Dad cradled his new bride in his arms and the endless rain pattered against the window panes like the tears of those who had to evacuate their cozy home, Mother told Dad the questions that were burned into her mind when they first crossed each other's threshold into consciousness.

The most vexing question regarded this stranger's identity. Who was this man who dressed with the aplomb of movie stars? What made him leave behind a generous trail of lavish gifts and tips? And how could he laugh so readily and show his feelings so freely, when the people in her surroundings remained most of the time emotionally distant and undemonstrative. What made him hug people easily and firmly. While everybody else in Mother's environment abstained from physical contact or touched only cautiously, as if bodies were highly polished pieces of antique furniture?

Uncle Willy! She called him then, although they were not related by blood or any other kinship. She respectfully called him uncle, for he was more than twice her age. This man so suave in his manners that he created something of a whirlwind in Mother's hometown and immediately won himself the reputation of being a ladies' man, looked with curiosity at this teenage girl that had more the appearance of a gypsy than that of the pampered daughter of an entrepreneur and respected local politician.

Willy heard the voice and dismissed it like many other promptings that speak to us in distant echoes and make no sense. He was an eligible bachelor with a splendid career in his homeland Bessarabia, Russia, and wherever he went, women took note of his suave manners. In fact, Helga an aunt to this teenage girl was seriously infatuated with him and hedged high hopes in her big bosom for a more permanent relationship.

Dad had engaged his generous side toward Mother's family as a way to repay them for the favors they had lavished on his favorite and most trusted brother out of eight male siblings. This was *Erich, the silent, pock-marked young man, who had enjoyed room and board at Aunt Dora's house while he studied electrical engineering in Stuttgart. Aunt Dora was Herbert's oldest sister who had married successfully into middle class society. Her husband ran a house painting business, and in her large home she could entertain guests with grace.

Among her father's six sisters, Mother loved Aunt Dora best. In fact Dora's daughter, Edith, often came to Seiffingen to visit with her wild and outdoorsy cousin Margret. By serendipity, it so happened that they always wore identical clothes. Edith even enjoyed styling her thick chestnut colored hair in the dreaded monkey swing fashion.

And, indeed, to the great delight of those who had barely heard of the boarding student Erich Haman, Dad treated everybody with the name Spenzer as if they were royal family.

Flower bouquets of roses for the ladies and silk ties for the men. He'd take Spenzer clan members out to dinner and found out to his dismay that neither aged French wines nor dry champagne from select regions of the Rhine valley managed to unbutton the protestant propriety of the Spenzer clan. For this clan was sworn to uphold sobriety. The family embraced abstinence as a counterbalancing measure to Wilfred Spenzer's virulent alcoholism. As if to atone to the Gods for their brother's excesses, all of Wilfred's siblings, including Aunt Dora and Herbert, abstained from spirits.

Dad remained unflappable even though he had never entertained such straight-laced folks. Seated with baked trout and other delectable entrees to follow, Dad sipped his Burgundy by himself and fell into the role of merrymaking while his guests looked at him in staunch Protestant sobriety.

Like the visitor from foreign shores in an operetta, Willy's spendthrift ways and slightly exotic manners of dress-nobody wore white linen and silk suits in the whole of the Swabian countryside, possibly not even in all of Germany-remained the topic of many conversations long after he had left the Spenzer's to go back to the sandy shores of the Black Sea where he could sail in pajamas and nobody thought anything of it, where women lovers waited for this big spender to take them to lavish dance parties, and romantic picnics in his family's vineyards.

One day between dove hunting, wine tasting, and chess games with friends, Dad received something unexpected. A postcard from that mysterious looking teenage girl Margret, the one that looked at you and through you, like a wise soul far beyond her worldly age. Mother had written him a thank you note, at the behest of her father and mother. "Dear Uncle Willy", she had written duly. But to the man who held the card in his hand it was more than a polite gesture. The unexpected contact re-awoke that mysterious voice, the oracle which had spoken to him of his future marriage to this girl with the gypsy manners and penetrating gaze.

He answered the postcard with a friendly letter calling Margret, "His little wild dove," and other terms of endearment. While she read the words, her cheeks blushed and her heart beat noticeably faster. For nobody ever had called her anything else but plain Margret.

Like a primed pump that spurts out water on its own, their correspondence continued, fueled by festive occasions like birthdays, Christmas, and New Year.

Then the war created the biggest occasion of all. Nazi propaganda enticed the young women in the Reich to do their fair share to bolster the morale of the German Reichswehr fighting at the seams of Europe. Letter writing and sending care packages to the front was one way for the German woman back home to support the war effort. Mother didn't need an anonymous soldier assigned to her so she would write to him; all along she had been corresponding with Uncle Willy.

Under the pressures of the war, the words in their letters went beyond the niceties of, "My dear little wild dove," Christmas greetings and birthday wishes. The words now became vessels of feelings. Particularly for Willy.

With no choice of his own, or so it appeared to him, Father was drafted to serve with the Cossacks, cavalrymen who aligned with Hitler's forces to topple Stalin's communist rule. But fighting the Russians made no sense to Willy, who spoke Russian more fluently than German and who counted Russians among his very best friends. True he was German as his ancestors were all German. But he was born, surrounded by Russian peasants. For more than two centuries his ancestors, had tilled Russian soil and demonstrated to their Russian fellowmen more productive ways of making use of the rich black soil that the Danube had deposited in this wide delta land.

For all he knew, he had shared benches, mash notes and spitballs at grade school with Russians and always deeply enjoyed the soulful ways of his Russian comrades back home between the rivers Prut and Dniester. The folk wisdom and superstitious tales of the Russian maids in his home had seeped deeply into Dad's beliefs. He had assimilated the Russian lore onto horses, and when Erika the black quarter horse he rode across minefields and past enemy lines, bucked and balked at the sound of exploding shells, he would whisper the lyrics of Russian folk songs into her perked ears.

The Russians, so Dad told me later, play, drink, and sing harder than any German, Rumanian, Turkish, or Jewish friends of his. "With a Russian soul you commune from the center of the heart," he told me. "Where as with Germans it's all up here in the head."

Since Willy, steeped in Russian culture, could easily pass as a Russian himself and because of his fluency in Russian and German, he was sent as a spy into partisan holdouts. The order was to find out the militant villagers' next move and duly report back to his commanding officers. The mission to infiltrate peasant villages and pretend to be a Russian compatriot caused Dad great quandaries. He felt torn by wildly raging conflicts of divided loyalty and obedience.

In those moments of great doubt, when he thought of deserting and joining the ranks of the so-called enemy, or when he gave serious thought to the pros and cons of turning double agent, a letter from Margret in his hand was like God-sent. He would read her words over and over, memorize them and put the letter into the pocket of his uniform, next to his heart. He had so much faith in everything that had touched Margret's hand, he actually believed her letters would shield him from bullets and shrapnel. And indeed, the three bullets that entered his body in the course of five years fighting on the Russian front, all entered on the right side, lodged between bones and muscles of his rib cage, where they did not rupture any vital organs.

Here in dismally grey Poland in February, with his bride nestled like a puppy in his lap, her head next to his heart, he thought of the precious little time he had been granted to consecrate the most important decision of his life. At least he was out of earshot of gunfire and advancing tanks.

Unlike in his fantasies, where he would wed in his beloved Tatarbuna in an Orthodox Church, sacred Russian chants mingling with the scents of myrrh and frankincense to endow their marriage vows with the earnest tradition of Russian Orthodox religion. Then he would show his bride the good life within the vast spread of the family estate. Cellars filled with new and old vintage, pantries where large chunks of cured ham, loaves of bread, shelves with rows of pickled vegetables and spicy stews (made of hot peppers, onions, garlic, eggplant, tomatoes and herbs) sat ever so ready for those who came with knife and a jug of wine to indulge in a snack under the shade of the grapevine arbor.

This dream fantasy did not come to pass. Instead, the wedding ceremony took place in German occupied Poland. Mother found herself sleeping with Dad in a house that was completely furnished and even stocked with canned food and other preserved edibles. It appeared to mother as if the former inhabitants were still living in the house too. She felt their presence when she was cooking on their range as if they were looking over her shoulder. Guilt tainted Mother's romance with Dad. Here they were making love in the marital bed of another couple. People they had never known and would never see. The down comforter had warmed a war-anguished man and woman who were by the whim of political fate torn out of the comfort of their comfortable country home and farm.

Former residents of this home were relocated further east in Poland and Russia, so read the official explanation that was handed by the Third Reich propaganda machine to German fugitives who fled war invaded Russia and were routed by Hitler's bureaucrats to re-settle in vacated homes in Poland. Some believed the official line, so as to sleep with a calm conscience at night in someone else's bed. Mother, however had learned from her father - who regularly listened to the British Broadcast news - that the German government's version could not be trusted.

It is in Poland where at the time - unknown to most Germans in the Reich - Polish Jews, children, husbands and wives, uncles and aunts were herded into concentration camps like animals are driven to the slaughterhouse. Here, in the house, still breathing the family spirit of those who were extracted from their legitimate homes like virulent teeth, mother got pregnant for the first time in her life.

Back in her hometown, she found out. For several months she bore the fruit of the war, as she saw it with ambivalent feelings. She was going to have a baby while the father was on duty on the most dangerous war front. The prospect of having a child in these times where death hung like the Sword of Damocles over every able German man drafted into the Reichswehr that was invasive all over Europe, shoring up a cancerous growth that was already starting to fray, was grim indeed.

In the sixth month of her pregnancy, she started to bleed like the women in the neighborhood whose grim stories she had heard many times. Not wanting any more mouths to feed at the table, these women, uneducated and short of means, gouged their cervix and dug into their uterus with knitting needles, knives and other household weaponry, desperately trying to kill a growing fetus.

When Dr. Wassermann the older, came and saw mother bleeding like a stuck pig, he shook his head in disbelief. "I wouldn't have thought that you would do something as stupid as that Margret!" he said. Then he rolled up his shirt sleeves and tended to mother lying there in sheets soaked in blood. He retrieved from her womb two premature twin babies that were dead. Mother dimly saw them being disposed of into a paper bag. Later she found out that the miscarried fetuses were dumped into the toilet. "I never even got to look at them," She told me later. I detected a sense of grief and disappointment in mother's voice. Without her even telling me, I understood right away though, that she had never inserted any pointed or sharp object into her vagina to abort a child.

Nonetheless, the story virtually repeated itself. This time with Dr. Wassermann Junior when my brother, her youngest and last child was born. Bruederle, as we all called him from day one with much affection, arrived in this world amidst much bloodshed. Again mother had soaked the sheets of her bed with her blood. When Dr. Wassermann, the younger - but even more aristocratic in airs - arrived on the scene. He raised his eyebrow and told mother with a tinge of contempt in his voice, "This was way too late for you to try and abort the child." He tended to the blood loss as best as he could though by changing her position so the legs and abdomen were raised. Once Bruederle pushed his head through mother's womb, the flow ceased miraculously. Here he was, a mirror blood image of herself when she was a baby: Black hair on his head, dark complexion, brown eyes, and chubby like a cherub. Mother didn't waste the glimmer of a thought on the doctor's unwarranted accusation and contempt, too great was her delight in this brand new being that was carrying on her bloodline being so much more similar to herself than of her two girls, she just had to hold him close to her breasts and kiss his cheeks and nibble at his fingers. It was like a halo of love enclosed mother and child to the exclusion of the rest of the world.

Chapter 2

Toilet

Herbert Spenzer, Mother's dad, was a powerful man by anybody's standards. He made sure his business and home, which he had conveniently merged into one, was a beehive of activity. And better yet, he enjoyed the sight of many people including his wife, sisters, and only child working for him. Since he regarded his business as a civic calling, anybody involved, so he presumed, would share his heightened sense of purpose. Those who labored hard for him in a selfless way stood a good chance of gaining a slice of Herbert's recognition, a tip of his hat, a friendly pat on the shoulder. More than anybody else, Mother craved her mighty father's recognition.

Mother, his only daughter, often volunteered for jobs that no hired hand would touch. Similar to Cinderella, she sensed that dignity can be found even in the meanest of chores. However, while Cinderella had mean stepsisters and a downright wicked stepmother who held her in bondage, it appeared that, more than outside pressure, Mother had internal voices that made her get down on her knees and do the dirty work.

Looking humbler than any cleaning maid, Mother, starting in her lateteens, would take on the job that everybody on staff passed on to the most recently hired personnel and, if you were stuck with the toilet job, everybody else wrinkled their nose in contempt and sneered at you for being stuck with the meanest job of all.

Like her father who wouldn't tolerate inequity, Mother cut right into this habit of not passing the buck, and decided to take on the job as a sign of social equality. It was a symbolic gesture inspired by her father's egalitarian ideals. She meant to say that we're all the same, no matter what job we do. Whether her message got across is doubtful though.

People who saw her get busy in the toilet stalls didn't understand her motives but they admired her humility and exacting standards of hygiene. To the outsider, mother acted as if God almighty had decreed that she should get down on her knees and scrub every inch of the toilet stalls. She bore her yoke willingly and never complained.

Hers was a service not only to her much-adored father, but to the community at large. People off the street would wander in frequently and use the toilets. The Lange Stange, a former inn and Grandpa's base of various business ventures, buzzed with public traffic and was situated conveniently for public use and abuse, opposite to the town's principal church. The Lange Stange stood face to face with the church devoted to Saint Martin. They combined and blended in a highly meaningful pair of saintly figures.

To Mother, the Lange Stange was synonymous with self-sacrifice and Saint Martin parted with half of his coat in cold winter and gave it to a freezing beggar. Both Herbert and his daughter, who wanted to live up to his near holy image, incorporated these principles of self-sacrifice and unconditional sharing into their daily lives.

While common people were drawn to Herbert and his daughter, they also kept a respectful difference, for they sensed the high principles that operated in this man and his daughter; principles of social equality and fair play drove Herbert often to radical, if not extreme, behaviors.

Even though people around them thought such principles venerable, such socialist values did not exactly engender the kind of bawdy and raw intimacy that exists between blue-collar buddies. Grandfather dressed in unassuming blue cotton working suit and cap, the uniform common among skilled labor. His highly educated ways bled through, no matter how much he tried to be like the common guy.

I never understood why Mother, out of her own free will, had subjugated herself to the filthiest job and taken it upon her shoulders to maintain the cleanliness of all the toilets in the Lange Stange, when paid staff looked on and snickered behind her back. Nonetheless, she had a different, more inspired view of her cleaning days. As it regularly happened with her, mother immersed herself in her job. *The "I" and the "It" became one*, as artists who claim that they become the dance or the song that flows from their body. She

She also connected with her powerful father through her work. By performing even the lowliest job, she felt a connection with God, the father above her father.

As any work was godly in Mother's eyes, so was the toilet stint. The grimy tiles and stained urinals became Mother's laboratory. Here she learned her first lessons in human psychology and the chemistry of human excretion. Years later, almost with a sense of enthusiasm, she would share with me the various insights, many of them uniquely hers, all garnered while working on soiled floor and wall tiles and stinky toilet bowls. She had intimate glimpses into the nature of man, while performing her pariah job.

During her toilet assignment, Mother had developed a dog's nose for different types of smells and what they could tell you about the patron who left them behind. When she hovered over urinals scrubbing the inside and outside of urinals, she found out that drunkards who mainly indulged in hard liquor left behind the most pungent odors. Milder smells originated from patrons who preferred beer over schnapps. On top of that, Mother distinguished between the more acrid smelling urine and feces of heavy meat eaters and the much fainter, more benign odors of those who abstained from meat. "It's the same with animals," She enlarged the topic. "You know yourself how rotten the cat's feces smells, compared to that of a cow."

Paradoxically, Mother was exposed to the vocational hazards of stinging and caustic smells of human excrement, even though her father ran a strictly non-alcoholic restaurant that attracted many vegetarians. While the paying, health-conscious clientele left behind non-obtrusive smells and clean toilets seats, people off the street who freely took advantage of the Lang Stange spic-and-span toilets filled the air with clenching odors, spattered the seat with fecal matter, and took aim at the wall tiles when pissing.

Still, no matter how scroungy you looked and how bad you smelled, Herbert Spenzer, widely known as the good samaritan, the social-minded benefactor of the community, would never turn away any street bum. On top of that, his only daughter had taken on Cinderella's calling and would clean up any mess that a drunkard or hobo off the street left behind.

Armed with sponge and brush and a bucket of water, Margret would attack stains, odors, spills, spit, and spatter as valiantly as an Arthurian Knight. With generous sprinklings, she saturated the stalls with disinfectant and bleaching cleansers. Nothing would deter her, no matter how repulsive and nauseating in nature.

No chitchat with passing employees or nosey patrons. Mother believed in merging with the task at hand, virtually becoming one with it. She wasn't squeamish either. As if she were meditating the layout of tiles, she kept her eyes down. To the observer, her activity looked like a vigorous physical workout. Bristle brush in hand, she rubbed in quick succession widening and constricting circles around the dregs of human elimination, applying the considerable strength of her upper body.

Invariably, her efforts bathed the toilet stalls in gleaming freshness. However, the germicidal chlorine makeover would last but briefly. Even while she cleaned, a couple of street customers usually lounged outside the stalls waiting to relief the burning itch between their legs.

True humility radiated from Mother's concentrated activity. People who passed by this unassuming young woman on her knees sensed her single minded commitment to the basest of jobs. Instinctively, they paid their respects to this cleaning lady who had taken on the meanest yet, in many ways, also the most important job of the Lange Stange and still maintained an air of dignity.

Once she had that toilet shining again, she would step out into the daylight with a serene expression on her face. She would take in a deep breath of the fresh air in the yard and greeted with equanimity newcomers to the Lange Stange who had that awkwardly twisted walk that betrayed urgency of bladder or bowels. With that same evenness of mind, she would greet those who left the Lange Stange with a satisfied burp, zipping close their fly, sliding suspenders over their shoulders, spitting into the gutter, and pulling their hats deep over their eyes. In some roundabout way (so she thought) she was doing godly work indeed.

Even after Mother was no more in her father's employ, she would still get down on all fours and scrub the floors. Not surprisingly, her knees were the only landmark on her body that was unsightly. Scuffed and worn down by so much cleaning mileage, Mother's knees had turned a somber grey and looked prematurely aged compared to her otherwise youthful appearance. I do not know whether Mother's extended exposure to the nauseous stench of toilets in the Lange Stange had an effect on her pregnancy when I was a tenant in her womb. To this day, the question remains whether it made me feel uneasy, possibly sick, when she inhaled the foul air.

Chapter 3

Beginnings

Church bells chimed loud and clear to greet the morning hour when I was born. And astrologically, planet Venus which bathes the world in a soft pink light of beauty and affection rose as the *morning star* on the *eastern horizon*. Venus sent her twinkling light right into my crib and from then on, the love chemist among the goddesses would be my guiding light in search for love and attraction.

Pluto, on the other hand, not visible to the human eye, was descending in the west, exactly opposite Venus. In myth Pluto is known and feared as the ruler of the Hades. This most outer planet has the infamous reputation of putting those who have a birth connection with him, and I sure did, through trials that abduct the soul into Hades, the realm of death. Pluto's gift to the initiate is that of total change or obliteration. By the prominence of Venus and Pluto during my birth, Pluto had definitely put designs upon my soul and thus I was born one of Persephone's sisters.

Dr. Wassermann, a tall handsome man with a distinctly aristocratic air, which some people mistook for arrogance, was our family doctor. It was he who ushered me from my dark passage into the nascent light of Thursday, March 6th, at exactly the sixth hour in the morning. It was the year 1952 and as mother would often tell me later that Stalin, the power monster to the east, who had played heavily in my father's destiny, was still alive. I had resisted the birthing journey and delayed my arrival a whopping two weeks past Dr. Wassermann's calculated probable date of my birth. Moreover, I was a restless babe, one that liked to kick and jerk. Altogether, Mother had to endure fourteen days of intermittent labor which, in later years, she would hold against me whenever I upset her with my renegade ways. "From the beginning when you were in my belly, you already acted the part of a rebel and God knows how much you've upset me ever since."

When Mother let forth with her indignation, I just sat there, defenseless like a mutt with tail clamped between its legs. Thus I bore Mother's aged rage. It was her way of purging pain that *by now* had crept into her bones, where painful memories fester in the marrow like small dosages of venom.

Every time Mother compared me to Sister, I had a sinking sensation. I did not truly belong to her, so I imagined. In fantasy I saw myself an adopted child, or better yet a foundling, the offspring of royal parents. Never mind my fantasy, Mother would serve up the birth trauma I had caused her at times when I least expected it. She'd put it right under my nose, like the slimy oatmeal gruel I so much detested. "What did I know about pain until you were born! Compared to your sister's, your birth was testing me to the breaking point. I don't know why, but her delivery was easy. I mean *EASY!*"

My Sister arrived on Advent Sunday. It was an auspicious time. Mother was in a festive mood and marked the beginning of the holiday season by lighting the first of four candles on the red ribboned evergreen wreath. She was in high spirits that day, expectant of a holiday baby which was due any day now.

With no pain to speak of, other than the slight ache in the lower back that she usually had during her period, Mother was busy preparing lunch. She was in a peaceful and contemplative mood. She prepped the ingredients for a sumptuous Sunday lunch and paid her customary attention to every detail. Yes, she felt strain on her knees, ankles and feet, but once she got to pinching and rinsing tender rosettes of rapunzel for salad, she was so drawn into the center of these delicate swirls of lettuce, she totally forgot about those sore feet.

This particularly tasty variety of lettuce is named after the delectable greens in the ancient tale Rapunzel where husband and wife pledge their still unborn child to a witch just so the pregnant woman can feed her cravings with unlimited portions of the scrumptious greens that beckon from the witch's garden.

Mother was just halfway into the colander dripping with sparkling green rapunzel rosettes, when the amniotic sac burst and the water ran down her legs.

Sister had arrived with a big splash! Surprised by this painless onset of her delivery, Mother ran to her bedroom. One hour later, just in time for lunch, the staunch and stern midwife Hartmann, tough as iron, which her name already suggested, held sister in her strong spade hands. She bathed the babe and found her to be about perfect.

A bit stiff in her arthritic bones, she handed the bundle of flushed pinkness over to Mother. This she did with a touch of ceremony, much like a waiter would serve lobster in a four star restaurant. Delighted by rapunzel baby, Mother, too, found her second girl close to perfect.

Her fingers caressed a whorl of baby hair, dark like hers and she stroked the babe's skin that radiated a bronze luster, an echo of Mother's own dark complexion. Clearly, this girl was made in her likeness. And she would bear her name for all this likeness, and because Dad insisted so.

As she gazed deeply into rapunzel baby's eyes and saw herself so wonderfully reflected, Mother pondered the future of her infant. Would this baby of hers grow up in the likeness of Rapunzel in the fairy tale who grew luscious long hair as fine as spun gold? Would her daughter Margret speak and sing with Rapunzel's enchanting voice so beautiful that it would attract the attention of a prince? Would she share Rapunzel's confinement in the tower that had neither entryway nor stairs? And Rapunzel's banishment to the woods? Baffling questions that crossed mother's mind.

Sister's birth connection to Rapunzel became family legend, whereas my kinship with Venus and Pluto slowly revealed itself only as my life was shaken by cataclysms.

I often wondered why the circumstance of Sister's and my beginnings ranged as far apart as night and day. Was there something inherently wrong and difficult about me to have caused such trauma to my mother and father? So I asked myself many times until one day, Mother, in a congenial and talkative mood, handed me the key to understanding. She cued me into the history that pre-dated every one of her birth experiences and therewith I found an exit out of my self-imposed guilt.

The main change that transpired between the two births was a slowing down of Mother's workaday buzz. When the second baby came around, Mother was content to fill the role of homemaker rather than slave at her father's bustling business. She still was within his influential orbit though, as she lived with Dad in the grist mill that was his property. The three goddesses who decide upon human destiny made it seem inevitable that my parents be glued to my Grandfather's real estate and thus subject to the whims of this family patriarch until his violent death. In due time, they would pay dearly for their dependency.

After years of self-imposed indenture to him, Mother enjoyed the more sensual and relaxed pace of teaming up with Dad. Willy was glad to run every decision by his wife and grant her the last word, for he greatly respected her insight. Both of them still felt much like newlyweds, even though it had been close to three years that Dad had returned from prisoner of war camp.

More so than Mother, Dad was madly in love. No matter what she wore, he looked with desirous eyes at this voluptuous woman. To him she was a trophy he had earned during a decade of patient waiting. He had yearned to be reunited with his wartime bride, during five years of active service on the Russian front. He had buried her picture in the frozen soil east of the Ural Mountains where he served another five years as prisoner of war in Siberian lead mines. This portrait smile of hers was his most precious possession, his lifeline to all he held dear. It was his greatest fear that one of the Russian prison guards would tear her image away from him and defile his war bride or worse yet, rip her into shreds.

He had waited more than ten years between his draft into the Equestrian Cossacks, who allied with Hitler's troops to fight the Bolsheviks, and the end of his imprisonment in Siberia, for that one delicious moment when he could wrap his arms around his wife. Even though he had been with her now for a while, her presence still had a dreamlike quality. And he treated her most tenderly, as if she was his queen.

Indeed, she did feel like a queen of sorts. But whenever she surveyed her new kingdom, it loomed so big and unpredictable. As Mother's eyes slowly swept across the building expanse that she, Dad, myself and the baby in her stomach now occupied, she felt a gnawing sensation in her stomach. *"I dare you,"* the grist mill spoke and towered six stories high above her. Looking all the way up to the gable gave her a crick in her neck.

Nobody ever went through the actual pain of measuring the total spread of space that encompassed this whale of a place. Except for factory buildings, this was one of the five largest historically significant buildings in town, two of which belonged to her Father.

Compared to the ramshackle shed where we had lived the first year of my life, our new home was breathtaking. But exactly what took her breath away Mother couldn't quite figure out. Was it the overwhelming dimensions? Or perhaps a contributing factor. More so, she felt choked by the vast stretch of history that dwelled within these walls. The place had burned down three times according to the town chronicles. In its foundations though, it reached back to the early Middle Ages when it was part of a castle. All those many generations that were born and gave birth here, who played, toiled, celebrated, ate, fucked, and finally died! The thought alone gave Mother shivers.

Surely there must have been violent deaths, so she wondered. Her gaze scanned the rocks of the foundation as wide as a full grown man's two arm span. Her psychic sensibility told her that the ghosts of former tenants hovered around her. They lurked in dark corners, under stairwells, behind beams. Their presence was as palpable and frigid as the cold spray that misted her bare arms when she stood within a stone's throw of the ancient water wheels.

Still in the clutches of this chilling embrace, Mother had a premonition. The layers of past lives, many of them lived with resentment, hatred, and guilt, could turn into a ghostly ménage. They could steamroll over the unwary and snag innocent children.

Despite the shadows of the past and an amorphous feeling of doom, Mother remained fearless. She felt like a frontier woman who would dare push further the boundaries of civilization regardless of the real possibility that primitive man would pounce on her.

Unlike some women adept at hiding their true age, this peculiar home had the wrinkled and parched countenance of a crone outside as well as inside, the mill appeared dilapidated and neglected.

Everywhere she looked, the house whispered "I need fixing up." Until it swelled like one of Wagner's opera choruses and hounded her with the line "I need fixing up." It became painfully clear to Mother how badly this old venerable crone needed a facelift. Surely her looks would improve once she and Dad would get down to it.

For the time being, and for the benefit of the second baby in her belly, Mother reined in her feverish workhorse nature and distanced herself from the mill's spell. Instead, she turned to the garden. In her white socks and leather sandals she strolled leisurely, a slight sway in her strong hips, toward Dad. He was busy digging deep and wide holes to plant a phalanx of willow and popular trees along the Ortzan stream. The planting was to celebrate the coming of the second child.

Mother approached Dad without a sound. He still noticed her and dropped his spade to come up close and hold her. In a familiar gesture, he wrapped his arms around her, right beneath her large breasts, whispering, "How are we doing?" into her ear, as he stroked her belly tenderly. She relaxed visibly and leaned into his body. She and Dad stood so close; from afar they looked like one. Mother tilted her head back and rested it on Dad's shoulder. Both of them squinted and gazed into a blindingly bright autumn sky, where cloud castles formed and disintegrated, puffed up and bulged, and then were shred asunder by a quickening breeze.

These structures were so much lighter and less complicated than the fortress Mother and Dad were intent on making their family residence and source of income. Almost simultaneously, a sigh escaped from this expectant couple and neither one of them could tell you the exact sentiment that prompted such a sigh.

Dad's embrace loosened and he turned back toward his tree project, Mother continued her leisure walk and strolled through the tall grass of the mill garden. She passed by the brown chicken which pecked and dug for food in small streamlets of water that meandered through the knee high sweep of grass that thickly carpeted our orchard garden. At the clothesline a willow basket of freshly laundered linen was waiting to be hung in the blazing fall sun. As she picked up the sheets, Mother exhaled and inhaled deeply every time before bending and straightening. Baby must not be disturbed, she thought to herself.

Mother had undergone a conspicuous change since moving into the mill. Visible even to outsiders, Mother's rhythm had slowed down. She now moved peacefully and unhurried compared to the frenzied activity when she had slaved for her father.

Unlike the idyllic days in the mill when Sister tenanted Mother's womb, my experience of growing up as a fetus was tinged by Mother's relentless dedication to hard work. At the time when I sprouted limbs in her belly, she had the raw ambition to outdo her father's truck loading crew - all brawny men with hardy quantities of beer, liverwurst, and rye bread in their bellies.

Even into the last trimester of her pregnancy, Mother meant to show to everybody that she had the work morale and prowess of Hercules. Despite the prominent swelling of her pregnant stomach, which made it hard for her to bend over, she would not let up. Self-appointed foreman at her Dad's business, she made sure that her Father's three delivery trucks were stacked high with cases of mineral water and fruit juice in record time.

Except for her feverish work pace, immaculate sense of organization, and ripe state of pregnancy, she behaved humbly. More than you would expect from the only child of the big boss.

Dressed in plain work clothes, loose fitting denim work pants, flannel shirt and denim work jacket, Mother heaved slatted wooden cases of carbonated and mineral water, as well as cases of her father's famous apple cider. "I had stomach muscles like steel ropes," Mother commented with a tinge of pride, when she told me the story.

Her pregnant stomach felt so hard to the touch it could pass as a turtle's carapace. Dr. Wassermann ruffled his forehead in consternation when he examined Mother during her pregnancy. He found abdominal muscles the like only weight lifters and professional athletes have. When he learned about her excessive work routine, he had strong doubts whether Mother really wanted to have this child. Truly, she behaved in a most irresponsible manner toward the unborn baby.

However, in his detached aristocratic air, he didn't voice any of his concern. Especially since the Spenzer clan had a longstanding tradition with the Wassermann family. It was orally passed down from the elder Wassermann to the younger not to contradict any of the members of the Spenzer family for, like the rock of Gibraltar, they were intractable. His Father had been called into the Spenzer home at critical times and told his son of his showdown with Herbert and how he got all blood spattered when Margret Spenzer was born. Now Margret was pregnant herself. And her tight belly on which the younger Wassermann laid his long piano-loving fingers had all the makings of another bloody ordeal, so he thought to himself.

When the due date set by Dr. Wasswemann passed and Mother had gone in and out of contractions without any result, she decided to accelerate the process. Together with Dad, she went on strenuous walks. Dad could barely keep up when she scaled Mount Remmer. Legend held that this mountain was home to a sleeping tree. Of all the mountains surrounding my native town, and there were half a dozen of them, Mother thought it most auspicious to hike Mount Remmer, because she and the fairy princess shared the predicament of prolonged waiting.

It was then the tenth day past the boldly-encircled date of my prospective birth. Snow tumbled in large unhurried flakes which graced the earliest spring flowers, snowdrops and crocus, with peaked gremlin hoods. Despite the wintery weather, Mother and Dad headed up the mountain. After every dozen steps, Mother stopped and sucked in a deep breath all the way into her swollen belly. Dad did the same. He would do anything in those days to alleviate her suffering.

When she spotted a solemn spruce tree, Mother unlinked from Dad's supporting arm hold and walked right up to this mountain sentry. As a last resort, Mother hugged the tree fervently. She held tight to the trunk. She murmured pleadings for quick relief into the rough bark. Dad stood by, a silent witness. In this moment, he became aware that his seed had brought on to her a state of unspeakable distress. And overcome by a sense of helplessness, he watched Mother teeter on the very brink of madness.

The business of delivering babies on my Mother's side of the family was one of plain torture. Giving birth meant self-sacrifice, tremendous blood loss and the crucifying decision whether mother or child should live.

Louise, my Grandmother, gave birth to Mother when she was in her ripe forties. This being her first child, it was quite an eyebrow raising event in those days. Her tall, willowy body was not meant by nature to produce children. It was hard to imagine this detached and intellectual woman cuddle and coo with a baby.

In preparation of Mother's birth, Dr. Wassermann the elder, examined my Grandmother Louise's abdomen and arced his eyebrows. A slight but sharp whistling sound escaped through his lips. Clearly he was about to divulge bad news. The outlines of the still unborn body gave him much concern.

In all likelihood this baby suffers from hydrocephaly, he told Grandfather Herbert with a grave expression. In this condition too much fluid presses down on the brain. Chances run high that the newborn will be a retard. Herbert didn't flinch. An idiot, you know, Dr. Wassermann said to make himself fully understood. And saying this, he looked at Herbert with the cool detachment of those who have the privilege of blue blood in their veins. Grandfather still did not bat an eye.

In the spirit of the time, when men ruled without question over the household, Dr. Wassermann was about to confer with Herbert, man to man. He turned his back to Louise and motioned Herbert to the other side of the room.

In a hushed voice and carefully chosen words, Dr. Wassermann gave his clinical opinion. "I can tell by the abnormally large size of the skull, that this baby will be in bad shape Mr. Spenzer, to put it mildly." Clearly, the doctor was walking a tightrope. Should he safeguard mother or child? Dr. Wassermann favored the mother's side. At least he knew for sure that she was sane.

"Your wife is at high risk" He informed Grandfather and put his large hand in a sympathetic gesture on Herbert's wide shoulder. A shoulder so square, it bespoke of a man used to taking on large responsibilities. Her pelvis is awfully narrow and at age forty three, she's definitely not in prime childbearing condition. So far, Herbert nodded in agreement. While not a medical doctor, Herbert had received extensive medical training to take into the African bush when he was schooled to work as a future missionary in one of the few German colonies on the black continent. But the colony was lost during World War One, and so went Grandfather's chance of saving the black man. After a pause that seemed endless to both men, Dr. Wassermann continued in a grave tone. "I need to intervene in the process in a major way." Herbert stiffened in his imposing bullish frame when he heard the physician propose his plan of action. He said he needed to rush this delivery for it was causing too much strain on an already exhausted woman who had shed way too much blood. In short, he would need to pull the unborn out and use forceps and other gynecological instruments to accomplish any results.

The expectant father, however, thought differently. No matter whether this baby has small brains, large brains, or no brains at all, you're going to do your damn best job and deliver it safely! Gone was the butcher son's deference to patrician noblesse and academic learning. The raw rebel Herbert stood before the doctor, as unyielding as the Ortzan of the Alb Mountains where he was born. It didn't escape the doctor's keen eyes that Herbert's bull-neck flared and blood made the veins in his temples bulge to capacity.

After a moment of locking his steel blue eyes with the more grey-blue eyes of the doctor, Herbert resumed his argument. However, to the doctor's surprise, this time Herbert's voice showed signs of temperance. "You are by far the best doctor in town," Herbert said and his words rung solidly honest. "I urge you, by all means do proceed slowly and gently and take utmost care of the unborn. And, if at all possible, do not use this instrument of torture!"

A deal was struck by silent handshake and the men turned to face the woman who writhed like a snake on cinders. Aware that the mother might not pull through, the two men both held their breath whenever Louise screamed for relief. It must have been too nerve-wrecking for the midwife, for she took a roll of cotton dressing, soaked it in water and put it between Louise's chattering teeth.

Manfred, Dr. Wassermann and the midwife stood in a formidable triangle, positioned in strategic places around Louise's body. They spurred her on like the audience of a wrestling match. *"For God's sake don't let up! Breathe through your mouth. Pant during contraction!"* The doctor yelled. *"Now, press hard! Press harder and breathe! You're doing great! Don't slow down! Keep it coming!"* The cheering team wouldn't give her a second to think twice, not a chance to pass out.

When the baby's head at long last had inched downward in the birth canal and travelled within reach for the doctor to get a hold of it, Dr. Wasserman reached deep into Louise's crotch where contractions rippled visibly. He squinted and cocked his head. God how he would have loved a cigar right now! Almost elbow deep he immersed himself in Grandmother's vagina and blood spurted onto his monocle. "Jesus Christ!" He huffed and the solicitous midwife immediately wiped his forehead off.

When the infant's big head slid through the tightest opening, pubic bones creaked and ached. Ever so reluctantly, with much tearing, the vulva opened wide enough to release the last vital part. Tall as a giant, one question loomed in the room. Just what shape of head would emerge?

No longer could the midwife hold her horses. She screeched in excitement. Dear God, here it comes. Louise, on the other hand, fell dead silent. She was about to be cracked open, much like a walnut. She had a secret yearning to die rather than be pried ajar from the inside out. Herbert's insistent presence however kept her going. She sensed his heightened expectation, the unfamiliar urgency in his steel solid eyes, his silent demand for her to tough it out.

Holy heaven, look at this! The mid-wife yelled. She was thrilled to the marrow that the torment was over. Louise, you did it! The baby's head appeared in full size. Having done her part, Louise passed out, just like a long distance runner who breaks down inches past the finish line.

The midwife now took over with brisk efficiency. She rubbed and massaged the baby's alarming birth purple and slapped it in strategic places, so as to coax its lungs into action. The babe was still an ugly duckling, bloody and mucus covered. Shreds of the uterus lining obscured the baby girl's subtle skin hues of rose and bronze. But looks didn't matter, for the head was well within normal range and the babe took one whopper of a breath and screamed the purple right back into its face.

Meanwhile, the doctor reeled Louise back into consciousness with small splashes of cold water and backhanded slaps across her cheeks.

Completely absorbed into the bundle of life, which he would later call Margret, Herbert was ecstatic that his daughter looked perfectly normal. If anything, she looked wise and precocious far beyond her tender age.

This is how Mother came into this world. Only by a narrow margin of destiny she escaped being pried by force. Still, the head remained throughout her life a part of her body where destiny would strike again and again, like a sharpshooter that takes aim at the most inner circle.

It struck, when she was thirteen years old and the only girl in her grammar school class. Due to peer pressure, she behaved wilder than any of her male classmates. For show she dived from the five meter diving board head first even though vision of the bottom was obscured by algae in this unattended public swimming pool, fed by a stream.

When she emerged from underwater, blood gushed from her skull so profusely, kids hid behind the bushes. Even her Robin Hood classmates, forever pretending to be daredevil outlaws, shrunk back in horror when she approached them and mumbled pleadings for help.

While Dr. Wassermann, put stitches to close the gaping hole in her skull, she told him how, head on, she had hit a nail that stuck out from the concrete floor of the pool. Right then, Dr. Wassermann had a flashback of Mother's delivery and the monster head he mistakenly believed was hers.

Another blow to her head happened when she was twenty years old. Mother was a dark beauty then, but without a suitor. A voluptuous young woman who kept her burgeoning sexuality discreetly tucked away under loose fitting clothes. It made little sense to parade your curves when all the eligible men were gone, defending the homeland on the multiple combat zones Hitler had instigated around Europe.

In those days Herbert listened to British Broadcasting on the wireless. From the very on start of the Nazi regime, Herbert had mistrusted the mustached Austrian who inflated the ego of the Aryan race beyond sound judgment and foamed in the corner of his mouth when talking to mega crowds. In his reliance on the objectivity of news broadcast over Europe by the British, Herbert actually put himself outside the law. Listening in on foreign radio was a capital offense.

His secret soon was discovered. One of the many tenants at the Lange Stange, as Herbert's inn and boarding house was called, monitored Herbert's radio activity. Finally an opportunity to do him in! Herbert was already conspicuous in his defiant ways for he never toed the party line, nor was he ever a member, or greeted anybody with the obligatory Heil Hitler. No swastika or picture of the Fuehrer was to be placed anywhere in his huge house. His daughter was ostracized in school because she didn't join the obligatory Hitler youth organizations. Her Dad had told her to stay away from their indoctrination.

On top of that, rumors spread that early in the morning before daybreak Herbert would go to the train station and actually meet with the outcasts of society. Jewish families, gypsies and misfits of Aryan elite society because of their mental retardation or other abnormality, had been rounded up like hapless sheep by the Gestapo, Hitler's bloodhound police, for transportation to unknown destinations.

Silently Herbert mingled with these folks who looked with anguish down the railroad tracks to that distant point where they all merge together. Where would the train take them? This was the one question that weighed down on these people like a ton of lead. Efficiently, keeping a very low profile, Grandfather handed out woolen blankets and cups of hot cider while the guards snarled at him like pit bulls ready to jump. They wouldn't touch him though, for this man was widely known and respected as a local hero who bailed out anybody in distress.*

However, Herbert had enemies among his tenants. Maybe they just wanted to score brownie points with the local Nazi leadership. When these informants overheard English voices in Herbert's study, they promptly snitched on their landlord. Inevitably, the Gestapo showed up, in the wee hours as they usually did when arresting people. Hitler's policing blood hounds didn't bother producing any arrest or search warrants. They seized Herbert without further ado and took him to Stuttgart the state capital of Baden-Wuerttemberg where he was put in jail in solitary confinement. The outlook was grim for the evidence was plentiful. The snitch had assiduously marked in his notebook plenty of instances when Grandfather had tuned in on BBC front coverage.

Mother was totally distraught. The thought of losing Father was unthinkable. She had heard from inside sources that *the punishment for such subversive activity was death by hanging.* Her reasoning power was temporarily out of order. All she could do is feel a tremendous need to act right away. Driven by the feverish impulse of a young unmarried woman who loves and adores her father more than anything else, she took the train to Stuttgart. She had no eyes for the fashionably dressed women who walked arm in arm with dashing officers who had returned on their short military leaves. She didn't see the elegant window displays of jewelry, luxurious bedding and elegant tableware, things she would normally admire, especially since war time had made such items preciously rare.

Her step, urgent like her taut heartbeat, echoed along the paved cobble sidewalk where she made her way to the court house.

*WWI, Herbert volunteered to walk into his village with a white flag to tell a sniper the war was over.

Her eyes straight forward, hell-bent on making it to the third floor without interception, she passed the guard who had demanded identification at the entrance of the stairway. He blew his whistle but before orderlies could catch up with her, she had stormed up the stairway and now stood breathless before the big shot's office.

With the same impudence she had produced vis-a-vis the guard, she now ignored the inquiring secretary. Thoroughly disturbed by the young woman's brusque behavior, the secretary jumped up from her comfortable chair. When asked for her name and whether she had an appointment with the judge, Mother said glibly, *"No!" She had no appointment and she wouldn't need one she said for she was this big shit's lover.* The secretaries cherry red mouth - glossy with lipstick - fell open. She adjusted her brown horn rimmed glasses and dropped a file of documents onto her desk. Her nerves were visibly in tatters. Stunned into inaction by such infamous behavior, the secretary let the impetuous dark-haired young lady with the gypsy temper pass without further balking.

Not waiting for any *"come in!"* To answer her resolute knocking on the door, Mother burst into the office of the presiding judge in Grandfather's upcoming trial. Only now did she realize the extent of her impudence, she actually had forcefully entered the lair of the man who would judge over her father's life or death.

Three tall looking men looked at mother with utter dismay. Two of them, Mother identified as SS Charges because of their black uniforms and leather boots. The one in the middle was the graying judge. He wore his robe. All of them sat in leather armchairs around the imposing oak desk holding up brandy glasses for a toast that Mother had the nerve to interrupt.

All three men shot up from their seats as is they noticed that they had hot coals under their bottoms. Horrified by the tidal wave of uniformed male menace that approached her, Mother blushed into a deep crimson. However, she mustered her wits for the moment, and gathered the intent of her coming, into three short sentences. The crucial one in the middle. "My name is Margret Spenzer. *You've got to release my father, Herbert Spenzer.* He's an innocent, good man!"

At that moment, the largest of the three men was within an arm's stretch from her. He had narrowed his eyes to slits as fierce as that of a charging lion. He lifted his arm, swung far back and struck mother across her face. Those who witnessed the attack took in sharp audible breaths. That was one wallop of a blow! They thought. And the Judge drew back from his company, he felt uncomfortable seeing a female so bluntly assaulted in the midst of his office.

Mother's knees wobbled, her vision blurred. She lost her balance and reeled backward. The raw violence of this strike across her face, the like she had never before encountered, had knocked her off center and then fully knocked her out, once her head hit the corner of the oak desk. Her unconscious body rippled to the floor.

Orderlies, who had searched for her, arrived on the scene and carried her out of the room. Mother didn't remember how long it took for her to regain consciousness, but once she came to, orderlies put her on her feet and ushered her through the rear exit of the building. The imprint of the man's right hand glowed on her face, turning a grape blue when she returned home to her mother who put both hands in front of her mouth because she was horrified by the sight of her battered daughter.

Herbert Spenzer did gain his freedom shortly afterwards. It wasn't his daughter's daredevil intervention on his behalf that opened the doors to freedom, but friends in high places who knew the indirect ways of skilled diplomacy. They obtained the release of this local hero.

"You were a torture," she later told me, when she gave me the full narrative of my arrival in this earth.

And then there was Aunt Nadine, the third member of the greeting committee who swaddled me into linen. She was an avowed virgin for all of her life and nurse and nanny to British royalty. She fluffed up my soft rosy skin (which was as wrinkled as any newborn babe's), the blinking of my eyes, my tiny curled fingers and toes, the soft lines along my skull where the bones hadn't connected yet to allow my brain to grow. She heard my first cry that breached the silence and found it just as vital and strong as the squeals of Britain's bluebloods.

I was born with no hair on my head. To my mother's dismay my skull was as smooth and hairless as my dad's who had balded even before she ever had met him. I also had blue eyes - like Dad. Altogether she didn't find much of herself in me and that disappointed her.

Chapter 4

Cat

We had a cat from the moment that I was born. The first word I pronounced to the anticipating audience of Mother and Father standing next to my wicker crib was an explosive *"CAT!!"* All the while the little kitten that was my very first pet snuggled like a breathing pompom next to my ears, not knowing that I had dedicated the first word out of my mouth to its fluffy cuddliness.

Cat to me was the world's neatest thing - it purred, smelled good, had the most curious facial expressions, whiskers that tickled, the softest fur, and pink paw pads that felt warm on my skin. Sometimes it projected claws and that was a reminder that Cat had a temper. So when I had my kitten next to me, I was at peace with the rest of creation, including Father who loomed large over the two of us.

Every so often Cat would get up, stretch, arch her back, and yawn. Then she would leap over the rim of my crib and saunter up to her cat dish where Mother had poured some warm milk with bits and pieces of bread. After lapping up her milk, Cat would venture *meow* and beg Mother to let her out into the yard so she could have outdoor adventures. Those moments of Cat's absence seemed endless to me. And then I remember a time when Cat didn't come back from her excursions. It marked the first black void in my infant days.

Mother later told me the story how my little heart got broken because one day Cat would not return. And I had a companion in mourning the loss. It was Prince our unruly and burly German Shepherd dog who was Cat's faithful playmate. Undaunted by his size, Cat would crawl all over him. She would paw his snout, bound onto his back, pounce on his rump and tail, and nuzzle his mane. In return Prince would lather her generously with his long tongue and sometimes he'd pick her up by the skin of her neck and carry her around parading her proudly, as if Cat belonged to the tribe of dogs.

I could see some of their rough-and-tumble games when I lay out on a blanket in the grass. Cat would assault him from every side and he'd just shake her off or grab her by the neck. Watching their antics, I would laugh with delight and reach with clumsy gestures. Mother told me that Prince was exceedingly fond of Cat. He watched her with the protective instinct of a parent.

One day in the spring Cat ventured out into the orchard to chase sparrows. On her last birding excursion. Dad spotted her lunging from behind a mole hill and sending a flock of birds up into the blooming cherry tree.

By sundown on that day, Prince started to miss her. He made whining sounds and reconnoitered every scent track that Cat had left in and outside the house; sniffing the crib, the cat dish filled to the brim, and he sniffed the windows where Cat sometimes sat and watched the birds. Every object that she had brushed against, sat, or walked on he would explore it with his snout; and at regular intervals he would whimper and whine. But by nightfall, I was tossing restlessly in my crib and Prince had to be put outside because he wouldn't stop crying. The next day I refused every spoon of oatmeal that mother put next to my mouth, I kicked and tossed, and threw my baby toys on the floor. Prince was equally distraught. He scurried through the high grass in the orchard and sniffed out every mole hill. He poked his head into every shrub and thicket and even got stung when he sniffed out a wasps' nest. Swollen, hot, and mad he plunged in a menacing gesture into a crowd of chickens and sent them fluttering into all directions. When he returned from his hapless search, he had a dry feverish snout and was covered with a layer of downy chicken plumage.

On the third day without Cat, Prince became gloomy and refused to eat. He wouldn't even touch the soup bone Mother had put under his nose when he lay in the shade of the cherry tree. After a week had passed Prince came up to Mother and whined like a crying baby. He came up close and brushed against her shins and then he would slowly pace away and then stop at a short distance and look at her with his large brown eyes. He repeated this entreating gesture over and over until Mother understood that he meant her to follow him. Prince barked one short woof when Mother had caught on and followed his lead. Always looking back and checking whether she was still behind him, Prince headed for the wood shed. He crawled through a hole just big enough for him, but came right back quickly when he saw that Mother wasn't with him any longer. Mother had to laugh. She told him that she couldn't crawl through that hole and Prince cocked his head and pricked his ears as if he wanted to listen closely to every word she had to say. Then he took a different tack and sauntered around several corners, past a thicket of elderberry bushes overgrown with wild vines and finally sat down in front of a wooden door that was closed with a latch. "You want me to open the door," Mother asked and reached for the latch. Prince looked at her, his big tongue hanging out of the side of his mouth, his bushy tail wagging.

Another short woof and they both stepped into the dark of the woodshed where cobwebs hung like layered drapes and shafts of dim sunlight rested on stacks of construction wood, store counters that once had displayed candy and pralines, and an old arm chair with the stuffing oozing from its arm rests. Mother found herself enshrouded like a mummy by cobwebs and swirling dust. Prince went ahead of her and started to howl in an alarming pitch. When, Mother caught up with him he stood next to a wooden crate. The smell of rotting flesh nauseated her and the sound of Prince's howling penetrated her very bones. She crouched over the crate and pried at the lid to open it up. But the lid was nailed close and as she tried in vain to open it, Prince scoured on his belly, whined, winced and howled in alternation. Mother was about ready to run away from the nauseating scene. That's when she spotted a crowbar leaning against the corner. She picked it up and inserted one end into a small opening in the wooden crate. She braced herself against the wall next to her and with a creaking noise the lid of the crate flung open and the stench of a small cadaver filled the air with a clawing sweetness. Mother looked down and saw a limp furry heap; the calico colors of Cat were still distinguishable. Prince got up and sniffed the cadaver and howled with a piercing wail.

Mother left and called Dad to the scene. He talked to her in a low voice, as if someone might be listening. "Someone knew how to get to us and drive the message home." "What message," Mother asked? "We're not welcome here. I'm a alien, the fugitive from Russia, the misfit." Then he looked over his shoulder in the direction where our neighbors lived. From the shed you could see the high chimney stacks belching black clouds into the June sky, the sawmill operating at full throttle. "This time it was Cat," Father said and turned back to face Mother, "next time it could be something more precious to our hearts." He bent over and picked up the crate and walked into the streaming sunlight of the door. "I'm going to bury Cat under the cherry tree where she liked to chase the sparrows." Mother walked behind him, her head hung low. And Prince followed the last in the procession whimpering small mourning sounds.

Chapter 5

Bloody Nail Trim

Mother was in charge of keeping my nails trimmed. Saturdays, after the once-a-week hot bath in the tub that had the shape of a crescent, she'd fetch clippers, trimmers, files, and a whole case of sharp and gleaming instruments. I sat there on the large wooden table swathed in several towels, a little mummy about to be manicured.

"Scoot back," She'd say, "so I can sit next to you." Mother would wear one of her faded flowery cotton dresses with an apron wrapped behind her neck and in the back of her waist. The apron was usually clean white with some trim that made it appear friendlier than a nurse's uniform. She kept her hair always tied in a bun, but wispy dark-brown strands floated over her large forehead, carried adrift on the exhale and inhale or whatever she spoke. Her eyes were strong and penetrating like that of a bird of prey. And when she had her black pupils trained on my toes, I knew she meant bloody business.

"Why do you have to cut my nails," I would ask. "Cats and dogs don't cut the nails of their little ones." Mother would sigh because I had asked that question many times before and in all truth it was my disguised protest, for I didn't want her to clip my nails, at the risk of ingrown nails, hanging nails, ridged nails, white spots under the nails, nail fungus, and infection, and any of the various other disasters that she had promised would afflict my stubby little toes if she didn't apply careful foot hygiene.

The first utensil she used was a unwieldy nail clipper, with curved blades like the bill of an eagle. It looked way too huge to operate in my tiny toe nails barely the size of half a raisin. "This one just trims off the excess growth that makes you poke holes into your socks," She assures me. I wince and pull back my foot from the gleaming stainless steel intrusion. From former experience I knew it makes a sharp clucking sound - as if you'd cracked a walnut - and bits and pieces of my nail would fly into all directions. Once a piece shot smack into the middle of my eye and Mother had to pluck it out from there while I screamed like a war siren.

"Sometimes blood must flow," Mother said, as she trimmed the corners of my toe nails and dug in with a spatula shaped tool to pull out whitish skin debris, as she calls it. Inevitably her deep probing drew blood. When I pulled my foot away to sop up the blood with the corner of my wraparound towel, she caught it with a deft grip and pulled my hesitant foot right back into her lap.

"I'm not finished yet," she'd say, "the toe will stop bleeding on its own. People don't bleed to death when they have their toe nails trimmed. Only perhaps hemophiliacs." She always liked to throw in some medical science on my toe nails. "So don't worry." She says, "Hemophiliacs are so rare, you'd find maybe five of them in all of Seiffingen." No matter how unlikely, I had a vision of being a hemophiliac and bleeding myself empty while Mother trimmed my cuticles. Little droplets of blood kept crawling down the sides of my toes and gathered in the center of Mother's bleached apron and left a trail of red tears.

Chapter 6

Children's Resort

When Mother was expecting her third child, she and Dad decided it would be best to have Sister and I sent away to a home, a high class nursery. This was a major decision and most notably it was mentioned by, our parents as leaving a big hole in the savings. Father's income as a miller who had to hand over much of the cash to his proprietor father-in-law, was not in the league of those well padded parents who sent their offspring to this luxury establishment so they could go on vacation themselves, or tend to major family business such as the burying of the dead or the delivery of the brand-new.

I remember my awed impression when I first saw the place as advertised in a folded prospectus. It had the airs of a resort hotel, except the guests were short and out of control, all of them kids from infant through kindergarten age.

The main structure was set deeply against a line of black spruce with an ocean of aqua-green lawn stretching out in front of it. I pondered the dark woods that sprawled out behind and to the sides of the structure where by sister and I had felt this irresistible pull toward the recesses of this darkness. The Children's Resort itself, which had the stern and imposing look of a big bosomed governess, made me feel clammy in my palms.

I was four years old then and sister still short at two. My role, as I had taken it upon myself, pretty much since Sister replaced me from my preferred spot of only child, was to be her Guardian Angel or Doberman Pinscher, depending upon the situation.

When the plan to send us off to Children's Resort turned official and our baby-expecting parents encased themselves more and more like honeybees do with-in a shiny crust before they burst forth with wings, I envisioned myself larger than my actual height. In this time of great uncertainty I was bent on playing both parent roles and to be sister's Mom and Dad all wrapped up in one. Me, her spokesperson and fierce stalwart, I'd flash my teeth like a shark if anybody dared to lay hands on her, so I swore to myself and bristled like a fist fighter that anybody at this Children's Resort might just do so. Thus, I mentally prepped myself for this great test and the even greater responsibility that I felt toward Margy, my nickname for sister. It was a peevish thing to call her, since it described the sticky round balls that I would put between the tips of my finger after I mined the nuggets in unwatched moments, index finger deeply plunged into the darkness of my nostrils. But the intent behind Margy was benign mockery and a good helping of love. And there was truth in this name also. Compared to my reedy built and lithe appearance, Sister was still padded by a layer of baby blubber and did indeed look a bit chubby.

In anticipation of our impending departure, Margy and I observed Mother tear off the calendar pages, only the shape of the number of the day would change, but once there were double digits, we knew that the day of saying goodbye was dangerously close.

Surely, it amounted to cruel abandonment, to send Sister and me off to this children's home. In my understanding, any institution was nothing better than a camouflaged hospital. And hospitals I had experienced as a dreadful place to be. In hospitals people lay in bed very ill, tubes grew out of their nostrils and into their arms. It never surprised me that some of them actually died.

The institutional airs of Children's Resort were apparent to me as soon as I got a glimpse of the brochure that Mother and Dad had received. Toddlers sitting on mini toilets, their open stalls were lined up in one straight line, like the cow pens at our neighbor's stable. How could these kids toot and poop in peace when they were being watched by a drill sergeant of a nanny?

Such questions preoccupied me and made for nightmarish expectations. I knew right then that once dropped off at Children's Resort, we would greatly miss our free ranging life at home where sister and I ruled supreme with no competitors other than parents who were too involved in running the milling business to interfere with our reign. Did I know though that sister and I would fall ill at

Children's Resort with a case of terrible homesickness. Neither did I foresee that our homesickness would turn so severe it would scare their fat-assed nannies, prevail over the strict protocol at Children's Resort and even open locked doors.

Our parents couldn't help but notice the frazzled state that we plainly exhibited when we dropped raspberry preserves onto our nice Sunday outfits and broke our milk cups to our cats' delight on the kitchen tile floor, they still would not take the time to sit with us and ease us into this temporary separation. If they had thought about it, Mom and Dad could have parlayed our stay at Children Resort into an adventure trip and thus make it more digestible. Especially Mom had a gift to entrance us with her tales of yore. Like she would do when we curled our nose tips at brussels sprouts or endive salad. "When you eat the brussels sprouts, it will make your mouth so much juicier and the dessert will taste ten times better."

In their defense, neither Mother nor Dad were in a cheery disposition then. Mother, glum-faced, had withdrawn from the outside world and resided mostly in her enormous tummy. Dad looked worried. His arms and legs including toes and fingers were in constant motion, a sure sign that his mind was just as restless. Mother's ripe pregnancy, where her stomach curled over her belt-line in deep sag, threw him off balance. Therefore, he paid only slight attention to Sister's and my acting out. The memories of prolonged labor Mother had experienced before giving birth to me, made her strange withdrawal and preoccupation with her womb a portent of another birth trauma. In his silent fears, he anticipated a repetition of the crisis that four years earlier had made him weary to the point of having worn nerves as thin and brittle as threadbare cloth.

In this slightly dazed state where half of his brain remained with mother while the other half got behind the steering wheel, Dad piled Sister and me into our black Opele, which was our affectionate name for the Opel automobile, our most recent addition to the family. An angular compact car black as a hearse.

Our bags chock-full with neatly ironed clothes for every day we would spend up at the kids' home, Dad tossed them absentmindedly into the trunk. There went Mother's ironing job.

When Mother had packed our luggage, I watched her with the eyes of a hawk. Counting my fingers, I made an effort figuring the number of clothes she stashed into each bag. I simply had to know how many days mother was going to banish us from home, since she herself remained equivocal on the subject. When I would press her for an answer, she'd sound like an oracle, "As long as it takes for me to have your new sister or brother" Subsequently she let out a long sigh, for she remembered that it had taken her two weeks of labor to deliver me.

The vision of having a third one join our smoothly-oiled team of Sister and I was hard to bear. I had dreams of wild animals, especially the big bad wolf, entering in all sorts of benign guises and tenderized voices. Once he got into our hideout, the wolf would drop his mask without further ado and snarl with his fangs and flash his claws. Then he would chase sister and me around the table. For sure he was going to tear us apart. I screamed a lot in those nights and by the morning my pillow was soaked with sweat.

Our actual departure from home must have been a sad sight for our parents to watch. We sobbed goodbyes to our garden playground fully equipped with sandbox, swing, parallel bars and seesaw. We immersed our hands in the Ortzan stream and let the chilly water prick our skin. We sent a passing glance at our secret hiding place under the elderberry bushes where we had buried caches of trophies, such as a magnificent hawk feather and numerous snail shells from the stream. We touched our loft, a bowl shaped indentation in the short and stocky trunk of the most ample willow tree. Even though Sister was not apt to climb into the low branching willow trees nor was she able to jump into the stream, or do flips on the parallel bars because of her tender toddler age, it was still the two of us who enjoyed the play paradise Dad had created out of doors for his two Graces or Heart Beetles, as he would alternately call us.

Then came the hardest farewell of all. Our pets were extended family to sister and me. In fact we were more intimate with our furry pals than with our parents. Particularly with hugs, cuddling and slobbering kisses. Not minding the pungent smell, we hugged our two pet goats Wilma and Derte. They responded by butting us with their knuckle hard brows. Sister and I nearly choked our guardian dog Prince with our fierce embrace and his large pink tongue slavered our faces clean with dog drool. Finally we nuzzled our litter of cuddly fluffball kittens, including their nursing mother. Their little snouts breathed into our noses that sweetest of animal smells, which is the smell of kittens. All this leave taking was too tearful an event to stay in fond colors in my memory.

I do remember distinctly though, how Dad packed us into the Opele and sped away faster than I remember him ever driving in reverse out of the giant and dimly lit garage of ours. I sat in the back seat and clamped my hands in tight fists to hold back the tears that welled up as soon as the mill fell away in the rear view mirror. I didn't want to make Dad's sensitive mission even harder by having my feelings explode. By the sullen expression in his face, his absentmindedness and jerky movements, it was obvious that he dreaded our impending separation nearly as much as Sister and I.

In the small town of Bernau, located at the beginning of the serpentine ascent that would take us to Children's Resort, at a point exactly half way between home and our destination, Dad decided for reasons that remained mute to stop the car and park it next to the curb. Let's take a nap, he suggested out of the blue. Which was perfectly fine with me. I welcomed every minute of delay that would further stretch out our time together. I remember Dad embracing the steering wheel with his arms and placing his head in that cradle. Sister burrowed her head in his lap and I stretched out on the length of the back seat.

I must have dreamed again of wild beasts that broke into the sacred hideaway by the stream where Sister and I dwelled when we needed a chunk of peace. Crashing through the windows, they tore between us, ravaged our smart little home and shattered our dishes and mirror with a vengeance. I screamed, but to my amazement my yelling doubled in volume, a male voice rang loudly simultaneous to mine. I was startled and plunged out of my dream with a sensation of a diving torpedo. How could it be that Dad screamed too? Could he see the beasts in my dreams? It was nothing but a bad dream! Right?

Not so. Dad screamed again. "Are you alright?" Was there something wrong with Sister, I wondered. I lifted my head to peer over the top of the front seat. When I moved into a more upright position, triangles and odd shaped pieces of glass fell from the top of my head. Smaller fragments lay imbedded in my hair. I glanced down my bare arms, the folds and wrinkles of my cotton dress, bare legs and feet in white cotton socks. By golly! I was covered head to toe with broken glass. My going away dress that featured a design of miniature daisies having a turquoise background sprouted vicious spikes.

As so often in my early years, when I found myself in a crisis situation, images of fairy tales sprung to my mind. This time it was the image of Snow White in her glass coffin that appeared before my eyes. Admittedly there was a slight difference: Unlike Snow White, I lay in an Opel automobile and the lid to my coffin had been shattered into a thousand shards and strewn all over my body.

Dad turned around. The anguished expression in his eyes spoke more words than the complete story collection of the Brothers Grimm. "Oh, My God," He said, "You're buried under glass, are you alright?" He gestured with his hands to speak where words failed him. "God Almighty! Anna Louise....! What did I do?" He inhaled sharply. And I waited for his exhale. I didn't notice it; he must have held his breath. "Don't move! Not an inch! I'll get you out of there right now."

Numbed by shock, I was speechless and scrambled for words to ease Dad's bleeding conscience and assure him that I was unharmed. Even though I was completely blanketed by shattered glass, I couldn't find a scrape on my body.

Dad had barely a couple of minutes to take stock of us two girls and check his own bones, when a policeman banged on the window pane on the driver's side. Sir, are you aware that you parked just five steps away from a major intersection? What in the world is going on with you? The young officer who darted Dad with quick and alert eyes and a strong forward chin craned his neck and peered inside the car. Jesus Christ! And you got small children too! Reckless! All I can say damn reckless. He shook his head, knotted his tight brow and took in a breath that sounded as sharp as the sound of his whistle. In an automatic move he pulled out his note pad from his side pocket to scribble down just what he saw.

When confronted like this, Dad never bothered producing any lame excuses. He shrugged and looked straight out front, even though the damage lay mostly behind him. I felt the need to come to his defenses, but didn't know what would salvage Dad's reputation with this young uniformed man who bristled with the indignation of law and order. "I'm alright mister" I said "I'm not even bleeding and showed him the front and back of my hands for proof. The guy flashed me a quick smile. Actually, more of a reassuring nod than a smile. It's a miracle that you are alive, He said in a tart manner. Dad received the officer's ticket in stone silence and without reading any of it, he stuck it into the glove compartment. Then he tipped his felt hat to the police officer and motioned to him that he wanted to get out. The officer stepped back and actually made toward the motorcyclist and the crowd that still gathered around his motionless body. "Will they put you into jail?" I asked Dad, as soon as the officer turned his back and headed for the accident scene behind our Opel. "I've done enough prison time for two lives," Dad said, and his voice was flat as a potato field when he spat it out. I could have pinched myself for asking such a stupid question.

Dad switched from his half daze into action mode. His silent efficient way of getting things accomplished. The way we knew him best. He jumped out of the car. With tender arms he lifted Sister out of her seat and stood her right nest to the car. Then he pulled the passenger seat forward, ducked his head and hunched his shoulders so he could reach me with his arms. His eyes turned into narrow slits and the round apertures at the center turned large and blacker than usual. He inhaled me in with his eyeballs, every bit of me. His gaze was palpable on my skin and I enjoyed the intense sensation. My prince had arrived and he was going to rescue me right now. Unlike Snow White's Prince, he wouldn't kiss me though.

In the rear view mirror I observed the police officer who had turned away from us and strutted his stiff forest-green uniform through the throng of spectators. The truncheon on his side punctuated every step he made. From the talking of the crowd that swelled in numbers, I reconstructed the accident as it happened while I dreamed of the Big Bad Wolf. A motorcyclist, who had taken a right turn off Main Street and into the side road where the Opele was parked within illegal proximity, had bashed into the rear of our car. Wham! His gleaming BMW machine that probably packed as much horsepower as our car keeled over and screeched on the ground. The solid frame now twisted like a corkscrew. Knocked unconscious and with major injuries, the motorcyclist sprawled on the sidewalk. The curious and the sympathetic and those who enjoyed a bit of gore, gathered around him like a cluster of grapes. Some held their palms in front of their mouths. The injuries must have been ghastly to look at.

With that single-minded focus of his, that could shun and send to hell the rest of the world, Dad looked me over. While he picked piece after piece of glass from the top down, I observed Sister standing lost on the sidewalk. Her pinky busy probing her nose, a puzzled look on her face, she gaped at the motorcyclist's pool of blood and shuffled her feet as if the blood was coming her way. Meanwhile, Dad lifted me gently with his arms that looked taut like ropes they use on sailing ships. "Now lower your head, so you don't bump against the door frame. I'm gonna get you out of this mess."

My knees felt a bit wobbly standing out on the sidewalk and bystanders checking out my sudden and pale appearance on the scene. Dad chose to ignore their gaping. He was going to finish up his job and do it properly, like any job he ever did. Inch by inch, he inspected my upright body for any remaining bits and pieces of glass. Sister too got interested in this activity and picked over my cotton dress. "Dad look!" She said for lack of more vocabulary and held a small piece of glass the shape of a dagger up into a sunbeam that got refracted in its jagged edges and made it shine like a diamond spire.

After he had searched me over, Dad hand-picked and swept the glass from the rear seat with unrelenting attention. I continued to be amazed how he managed to completely shut out the curious crowd that thronged the motorcyclist and now made motions to further encroach on the four of us including our automobile.

Leaving Dad in charge of the cleanup, Sister and I made small halting steps toward the bloody scene and also to have a look at the rear of our dear car. We wanted to know the damage the Opele had suffered and at the same time we were also afraid to face it. I found out to my dismay that the trunk of our dear old Opele was smashed in as if a meteorite had hit it. Where there had been a trunk with ample space, the car now had a bowl. The bumper was jagged and the rear lights no longer had any glass around them. The rear fenders splayed away from the rest of the car.

While the damage to the car was real enough, the case of the motorcyclist was much more critical. Inevitably sister and I were sucked into the scene just a stone's throw away from where we stood. We observed with amazement a throng of people that encircled the limp figure on the ground much like a shape shifting amoeba. The bubble of onlookers extended and contracted in tandem with the efforts of the paramedics who did their best to pump life into the chest of the young guy. I admired their nerve.

Despite the blood that trickled from the guy's nose and mouth and alternated in giving mouth to mouth resuscitation. I watched the pool of the cyclist's blood, already separating out into a more watery and clear substance and a blackish gelled and sluggish matter, making a slow snail's trail from the curb to the gutter. Over the din of voices I overheard an older man wisecrack. "These kids today just don't have any sense, driving a heavy bike like this without a helmet. It's plain suicidal."

I did not understand the deeper meaning of the word suicide, but somehow the sound of it reverberated in my mind. The word stuck like a fat mosquito caught in the goo of a fly strip. And for quite a while after this accident a voice rang in my head. It said over and over again "It's plain suicidal."

"You two must have ogled this poor guy enough by now," Dad said, and wedged his body into the narrow space between sister and I. He laid his arms gently around our shoulders. The warmth and slight weight of his firm hand cupped my bare right shoulder in his palm. My tight stomach relaxed into its habitual slump. It felt so indescribably good to be touched exactly in that moment. But all too soon Dad withdrew his touch and darted a quick penetrating glance at the scene in front of us. "Girls, your staring at him doesn't help the guy one bit." The volume of his voice, that had regained its fullness, showed that he had regained composure. "Get back into the car, you two. I've picked every sliver of glass and I'll bet you one whole Deutsche mark or one hundred pfennigs if you find a shred of glass in there. It should be safe now. And we got extra wind blowing from the rear window, so hold on to what you've got! And Anna, you gotta hold down my hat!" He said wryly. To my great relief, Dad had recouped his old understated and dry humored self.

This time I sat in the front next to Dad. "Doesn't it upset you that the Opele has a big... ahem... dent in the back, Dad?" I asked. If he had said yes, it would have satisfied my hunger for feelings to be spoken out loudly. But Dad ignored my question. Instead he pointed his index finger and drew our attention to the mountain. Look at those limestone rocks overhanging where the road coils like a snake. "Some men scale these cliffs with ropes. Now that's courage." Sister and I both stretched our necks and peered intently at the grey-white outcrops of Jurassic limestone that stood like an army of pillars safeguarding the entry way to the Alb range. "Children's Resort, your new temporary home, is just a five minute walk away from those rocks." The moment he said Children's Resort, I slouched back into the fold of my seat.

Dad mentioning the dreaded place, made me aware of my jumbled feelings. I was teeming with them like a can of worms and there was no place to dump the squirming contents. Sister was too small and Dad withdrew himself whenever I made an attempt to approach and show him the alarming color of my dread. Left alone with monstrous sensations, I clenched my fists until the knuckles would turn white. No! I wasn't going to lose control, nor blurt into tears like a crybaby.

Instead, I took inventory of my feelings, tallied them one by one as an accountant does as he moves the beads on his abacus. The most prevailing discomfort was that of a gnawing sensation in my belly. An inside creature was eating away my guts. Such a gnawing sensation carved my belly from the inside out.

There was no way to escape at this point. Not even my fantasies came to rescue me. Undeniably, I was on my way to an institution where Dad would drop me off together with Sister. And leave us behind in the unknown. No telling when he would return to pick us up again. At this very thought, the gnawing became nearly intolerable. I sobbed and swallowed tears. The unknown, a menacing void that gaped open before me and threatened to devour me like the big bad wolf in my nightmares.

Worse than the void of not knowing what lay ahead of us was the certainty that a new baby was waiting in heaven, getting ready to come down and join our foursome family. Would Mom and Dad even want us back if a sweet cuddly thing fell into their lap? Was the one vexing question that threatened to sting me like a scorpion that erected his stinger in alarming color.

This one was a whopper, too big and vague to cross off. So I turned my attention to things more immediate. Our damaged car was a miserable thing to look at after it had been wrecked. I felt a burning sensation of shame in my throat when I first noticed the enormous dent. In fact, I could have puked right then. Hadn't we all been so proud of it when Dad first bought the Opele and showed it to us with a big sweeping gesture, "Voila!" Like a magician who unveils the stunning object that he just created out of air. For once we had a vehicle that was designed to transport people rather than the van and truck Dad drove to haul and deliver flour and oil. Seated like walnuts in their shells, we thought we were travelling in style in this black Opel of ours. Mother told us that it had taken Dad as many years as sister was old to save up for this automobile. For sister and I that was too much time to fathom.

After being rear-ended, our Opele was in bad shape indeed. A lot of Dad's blood sweat and tears ruined in a couple of seconds! And so was the motorcyclist whose eyes I never saw. He had rolled them back into his skull when he blacked out. I prayed silently that God would keep him alive. It all amounted to one hell of a stew of feelings and I kept it churning rapidly, so it wouldn't spill over and disturb my company.

"Opele is holding its own," Dad interrupted my internal accounting and slapped the dashboard. To our surprise, in spite of the severe blow to its rear side, this intrepid car of ours scaled the steep incline like a nimble mountain goat. The engine showed no signs of any strain on the long uphill haul. "The frame's still square," Dad said, "and the brakes are doing their job." I did notice though, that Dad, still under the sway of the accident, engaged hairpin curves much more cautiously than was his habit.

When we came within sight of Children's Resort, I gazed at it with defiance chiseled into my mind. I detest you, I recited to myself, even if you serve me ice cream topped with hot strawberry sauce three times a day. I had to brace myself for all kinds of bribes and brownies, just so I would not falter in my determined rejection of the place. "They have many outdoor activities," Dad interjected, as if he knew my train of thought. "I bet you'll like it. They even dance in circles on the lawn. Now that's something you girls have never done before."

The car swung into the huge driveway lined with ancient looking trees that had canopies so wide they actually rivaled our majestic willows. When Opele came to a sputtering halt, I saw a group of children. And dance they did indeed. On the lawn! It was such a peculiar sight, I got goose bumps all over. For a moment I was tempted to actually like the sight of it. But then I spotted several caretakers who were interspersed in the circle and holding onto the hands of children on either side. The thought of dancing chain-linked to the step-by-step instruction of sturdy looking drill sergeants like these, did not settle well with me.

When Dad had talked about dancing at Children's Resort before, still in the planning stages of our sojourn at the nursery, I imagined myself free and easy like a bird. I would whirl much like my red and blue top when I spun it into a frenzy by applying the toy whip I had. Forward and backward somersaults I would show off. I saw myself doing the pirouette right after jumping jacks. I leaped for distance and height. I outran most anybody my age and chased other kids until they fell exhausted into the welcoming grass. And myself! Yippee...! I would tumble right on top of them. Best of all, I stomped, pawed and bucked like a colt on a lawn as plush and impeccable as Aunt Elma's Chinese silk rug which only on Easter and Christmas I had her guarded permission to walk across; and then I felt like Jesus levitating across water. Those were my fantasies that came to naught as soon as I glimpsed the carefully choreographed circle and watchdog nannies holding tight the pudgy little paws of those entrusted to them.

In all truth I had never seen any live dancing before. Mother and father did not have the lightness of heart to dance together. Dance to me was about as magical a realm as that of the seven dwarfs or the frog king. If the bodies of men and women would intertwine, unforeseen things could happen. Things I still could not fathom. Mother had told me that when she had gone dancing secretly at night her father had come to fetch her off the floor. And he would loudly declare to the audience that dancing was the devil's way to tempt men and women. That had been her last dance in her life. And now sister and I were about to live in a place where the children dance. Boys and girls together...! My fantasies of dance that I cultivated and embellished during sleepless nights were on the raucous side of ballet, more like the witches riding on brooms and dancing around the bonfire on the eve of May Day. However such fantasies made the idea of Children's Resort considerably more palpable. Needless to say, but my fantasy did not contain the trace of an adult authority. Much out of step with reality, I had anticipated that out on that vast lawn I had seen in the Children's Resort brochure, any horseplay would be fair game among a bunch of heedless kids who romped and savored the freedom of distance from their parents' meddling surveillance.

What a crushing blow to my dancing fantasies when I gaped at the tepid circle choreography and watchful nannies everywhere!

We stopped and a lady with a brisk gait made a beeline for our car. She had huge bosoms, that rivaled those melons of Aunt Elma, but not as soft and pliable but tightly squeezed into a corset. In fact this armor-like undergarment firmed up every bulge between her thighs and neck. I knew immediately when a woman wore a corset, for Mother had worn one after Sister's birth and she had showed me the details of its mechanics. About one hundred hooks to fasten the front of it! I had been impressed. But at the same time these belly tighteners would make women's soft bodies look hard and cocooned. I did not like one bit the feel of it. Paired with her imposing height, this lady's body casing made her appear like an armored Amazon. Her air was that of authority and the silver streaks in her hair bun bespoke her position of seniority.

"Mr. Haman we've been expecting your arrival all morning," she said with raised voice. "What happened?" she said with exasperation. Then she stepped back a few yards and held her hand in front of her purse-lipped mouth. "For heaven's sake... your car! Did you have an accident?" Dad nodded. "Someone bashed in the rear of your automobile on the way up here?" Dad nodded again. "Oh Lord! These two girls must be in shock. I've got to take care of them right away!"

Within split seconds and no more words lost between her and Dad, she opened the car door on the passenger side and grabbed Sister and me. Pretty much simultaneously she pulled us out of our seats. And the grizzly lady held two squirming prize fish in either paw. We were wiggling into all kinds of odd shapes to twist ourselves free from her grip, but had no chance against this giant. The fearsome lady whisked us away. We kicked the air to encumber and slow her down. We refrained from screaming though, since we did not want to embarrass Dad. Across the flagstones of the walkway she stepped in her square black leather shoes and hauled her prize catch into the Lysol deodorized interior of the institution.

Before the door slammed shut behind us, I dragged my feet to stall our entry into its bowels. One more glimpse back, but the Opele was no longer visible. So I imagined Dad sitting motionless in the car riddled with regrets. No goodbye hugs, not even a waving hand or smile had passed between him and his two Graces. The three of us had parted as if a tornado had torn us apart. The last view I remembered of Dad was his face unmoved like the stony expressions of Aztec Gods who had always impressed me by the absence of any trait of emotion when they gaped at me from Mother's illustrated books in which I had studied the gods of extinct cultures.

"Put your feet on the ground and walk decently as it behooves a big girl like you!" the grizzly admonished me, for by now I was hanging from her right arm like a ball of lead. She jerked my wrist as if to uncoil a tangle of yarn. In response, I yelped like a puppy. "But our bags...!" I protested, hoping ever so faintly that she'd turn right around and head back to the car. "I'll get them later," she said in a matter-of-fact voice. "And do call me Berta Whitman when you speak to me! I am the head nurse and director of Children's Resort Home." Without letting up a bit, this awesome woman held my little paw so tight within her square hand I could feel my quick pulse against her steady beat.

When we entered deeper and deeper into the bowels of this institution and Berta Whitman cut through oblique shafts of dust whorls, cast like a hurdle course across the hallway by the afternoon sun, I had the sinking feeling of a firsttime offender. Cell keys clanged from the holster at the side of my jailer.

Sister looked miserable to. She dangled like a restive monkey from Berta Whitman's left arm. And tears ran profusely from her eyes over her cheeks, past her chin and down her neck into the V of her t-shirt. Nobody was there to wipe off that salty stream. Although it went largely unnoticed, our arrival at Children's Resort was not a happy sight.

The laughter of the dancing circle that wafted through open windows sounded hollow, a bunch of brats that sent sneers and jeers our way. I let my head hang, for there was nothing else to do at the moment.

Our first dinner at Children's Resort, like all the others that would follow, was in no way memorable. Considering that that our parents had paid dear money way in advance for our stay at this supposed luxury home, I had envisioned waiters taking orders, tantalizing appetizers and deserts that were absolutely buried under avalanches of whipped cream. As with the dance, I was far off the mark. Admittedly the lack of gourmet food was of no big loss to me, since my appetite evaporated the moment I inhaled the institutional smell of bleach in the hallways. Even if they had served us beef mignon with chanterelles and Viennese dumplings plus strawberry shortcakes with said heaps of whipped cream, such sumptuous treats would have made at best a negligible difference to me who suffered from a sinking and gnawing feeling in my stomach, the cause of which was a case of severe homesickness.

I don't recall the specifics of the menu, but then every meal at Children's Resort was in essence a bowl of goo. All that changed was the name they attached to the daily routines of hot cereal for breakfast and dinner. Lunch plates always featured the same dreary scenery. Mounds of mashed potatoes alongside limp vegetables and overcooked morsels of meat all adrift in the blandest gravy that I had ever tasted. If Mother, a spirited and sometimes passionate cook, had sampled our daily fare, undoubtedly she would have yanked us out of there the day we arrived. But Mother actually never set foot in this sanctimonious institution.

Every edible item at Children's Resort had the boring texture of mush. An insult to my strong teeth that liked to tear into tart apples and crack chicken bones. Yes, even drumsticks. Not even the toothless babies savored this mushy diet. On the contrary!

One tragic-comical scene is solidly chiseled into my memory. It was dinner time. Even our butting pet goats Wilma and Derte when lined up at the feeding trough, looked tame by comparison. When I observed the table rites at Children's Resort with the keen eyes of a hawk, I learned that babies have a vigorous sense of humor. Rather than scoop up the bland porridge, they indulged in baby comedy.

"You've got to eat, Anna Louise, or you won't grow any taller," a passing attendant admonished me. I stared into my gruel as if there was something divine in the peaked heaps I had created with my spoon and let her pass without reacting to her comment which I knew was just another adult lie that scares kids and makes grown-ups feel in control.

The porridge sat untouched and I resumed my hawk eyed outlook, for this was crazier than any clown gig that I had witnessed in traveling circus shows together with Sister and Dad. In every nurses' lap there rested a baby to be fed. Those who could hold themselves upright sat in high chairs with attendants at their side. The mission of the evening attendants was to scoop said gruel into the babies' mouths until the bowl was empty. This was a giant mission indeed.

But mothers, like ours, had done it before successfully with much cooing and coaxing and an infinite amount of patience. Virtually every nurse aide I could see appeared oblivious to the feeding habit of the infant in her lap. And wherever I looked, I saw staff members shove grits into baby mouths as if they were tossing sand onto a truck. These so-called nurses were incarnate bulldozers and the babes just helpless receptacles. No surprise then that the babes went on strike. Many of the little ones held their mouths shut as tightly as a grandmother's purse.

The babes' furrowed foreheads and pursed lips not-withstanding, the aides continued to force feed and shove it in by prying at the angles of the mouth. As a last resort, the babes expelled the runny mush through the sides of their mouth. More advanced babies would pucker their lips and expel food like a projectile, which to my delight sometimes landed smack on the nurse's face. Wherever I looked, the scene repeated itself. Adult caretakers shoved and babies and toddlers purged and expelled. The floor was a slippery mess. Here I was at the dinner theatre and the main show was slapstick comedy, so wonderfully repulsive to look at!

I knew from my studies of Mother feeding Sister that there were smoother ways to feed a baby. Eye contact for one! Reassuring smiles and watching the baby breathe, salivate and swallow. These nurses had their heads in the sky though, or more likely were they thinking about the clock advancing toward the magic hour of knock-off when they could join their hubbies and boyfriends who knew how to swallow food properly.

After dinner it was wash up time. The dishes were washed in a gleaming stainless steel industrial size kitchen and the babes got scrubbed in the even shinier pink and light blue tiled bathroom where there were bathtubs of various sizes, but all more impressive than the tin tub that served these purposes at home, filled with strictly organized groups of kids.

It was major detective work on my part to figure out the rationale that lay behind which kids were assigned which bathtub. In the largest oval tub boys and girls between two and four years old stood stark naked and poked at each other's anatomy. Girls touched boys' little dicks and giggled while the boys looked the girls over to find a similar appendage. This group looked like adventure, especially since I had never had the chance to explore the body of a boy. Possibly the head nurse saw me staring with wheel-sized eyes at the goings-on in the oval tub and henceforth decided to install me in the tub with the kids who were still crawling on their fours. Here I was with the pre-toddlers who would actually pee into the tub as soon as the warm water started spouting forth from the faucet and junior sister was in the more graduated tub of toddlers who were able on their two feet and mostly potty trained! I felt humiliated.

One of the greatest tests of my endurance came when head nurse Whitman came to the pre-tots wash with her white apron spic and span over her melon sized boobs and took it upon herself to get four pre-tots and myself spanking clean. Let's start with the ears! The mere announcement freaked me for never had Mother ever cleaned our ears. The utensil that Berta Whitman produced to do the job sent me into a tail spin. Sticks twice as long as matches with cotton wrapped on either end. I observed her inserting these instruments into the pre-tots ears and I cringed at the thought that soon it would be my turn.

I have to explain at this point that no pointed or longish instrument was ever allowed into any of my orifices while I was in a waking state. When mother had tried to stick the thermometer into my butt, I had screamed hell and brimstone and from that episode on she measured my temperature in my arm pit.

It was my turn now and Berta Whitman advised me to angle my head so she could see the opening to my ear. I promptly crouched down in the water. Now on all fours like the pre-tots and stuck my head between my arms. On top of that, I even put my hands over the ear cups to prevent any unlawful entry.

"Now Anna, be reasonable! Are you going back to being a baby like the kids around you?" Whitman inquired with a menacing tone in her voice. I was silent as a rock. My open defiance of the boss nurse created a scene in the washroom. Heads of nurse aids and fellow kids turned and mouths fell open. Meanwhile, I made my hands into tight fists and flexed every muscle of my lean body to resist penetration with the cotton swab.

"Think of the globs of ear wax that are clogging your ear ducts! If you refuse having your ears cleaned, you will turn deaf," Whitman said. Another one of those white adult lies, I thought. Besides I had successfully retrieved the brownish grease from my ears many times before, by sticking my pinky into the hole and probing for matter. In fact I have always enjoyed the sensation of my roving pinky, it was a mixture of tickling and a fizzy feeling that overcame me which was similar to the feeling I experienced when pressing my pubis into the stairway rail while gliding down. Already at that tender age, I knew how to create pleasurable sensations with my body and Berta Whitman looked like she was about to create nothing but pain.

I scored a couple of victories over Berta Whitman who very soon personified my personal nemesis. For one, she never got to clean my ears. I insisted that I be given this swab stick. It had to be my little hand that guided the tool, then I proceeded as she instructed me and to her great satisfaction I retrieved big globs of ear wax which the pre-tots wanted to put into their mouths.

The one victory however that stands out in my mind concerned baby sister. At home baby sister was a reliable as a Swiss watch when it comes to telling family members that she needed to go to the potty. At the nursing chalet, she simply lost control over her bladder and bowels. I suspected it was the state of the toilet that made her pee in her pants rather than the bowl. At Children's Resort the toilets were arranged in one long line of kid-sized toilet bowls. No stalls. So shitting and peeing was the most public affair next to being fed. I could see other kids play with the turds they had just deposited in the bowl while the nurse aide was busy training other kids. In fact I had seen a couple of boys older than Sister who actually ate their own shit and apparently enjoyed it.

Sometimes they would play music that had a watery quality to make us pee rather than just sit on our thrones.

When one child had produced a sizable turd, the nurse aide would praise the kid as if she had produced a nugget of gold. Interestingly, my own bowel movements became smaller every day and in fact, after the third day I ceased to eliminate the brown stuff. I started to clam up in a major way. For sister to do her bowel business in the wide open public where everybody could see her strain and hear her toot was torture, for Margret as small and plump as she was - I used to call her collared herring then - that was insufferable torture.

One morning between breakfast and outdoor games, Sister stood next to me, both of us a bit lost, as we waited for new instructions from the white-aproned authorities. Every turn and every move needed to be authorized if we were to endure our own way and there would be small punishments for our insubordination. We wouldn't get dessert or had to stay indoors when the rest of the gang was out playing Big Bad Wolf and Innocent Sheep one of my favorite running games where you turned into a preying wolf if you got caught by the Big Bad One.

A little clear colored pool of liquid grew in between Sister's shoes as she had a perfectly inscrutable expression on her face. Nurse aides have a sure fire instinct for accidents. Their sixth sense picks up a trickle before it even actually becomes visible. Why didn't you tell me you needed to go to the potty? The nurse descended upon sister like a bird of prey, having a incriminating frown on her face. Her firm hands shaking little sister as if she could pry loose an answer.

Enter my wolfish sense of protection. I must have glared as fiercely as the Big Bad Wolf at the youngish nanny who dared touch my sister as if she were a salt shaker. "She's not even two years old!" I protested vehemtly. The nurse, struck by my surge of rebellion, let go of sister and stepped back to take us both into better view. I was unflapped by her retreat. "There are many older kids here who have accidents," I protested. I was on a run.

Thus early on I gained recognition or to be more exact, I achieved notoriety. The aids' trained their antennas on me more so than any other child, for you never knew when and how I was going to act up.

The greatest coup I landed at Children's Resort was my attempt to escape. The only home visitor we ever got during our stay that lasted an eternity, (my memory will not yield an exact period of time for eternity is immeasurable), was Rachel. Now Rachel was our teen-age baby sitter at home. She had two long brown braids as thick as the largest part of a Swabian Brezel. Her eyes had a happy glint when she took us into her arms and whispered news from home into our ears. Dad had bought her a railroad pass so she could make the twelve mile trip up the mountain on the steam engine train. Because of us, she had a major adventure happen to her that day. Oh how I would have loved to be in her shoes!

"Why is Dad not visiting us?" I asked her as soon as she stepped over the threshold into the play room where sister and I built ramparts out of wooden blocks. She gave us both a big bear hug and then she gave us the classified news in the lowest voice, so I strained to understand it. Rachel knew full well that Berta Whitman and her charges were on the lookout and would not tolerate any incendiary news that would turn Margy and I even more recalcitrant.

Your Dad was here the day after he had dropped you off, She said in whispering tones. "But I didn't see him anywhere" I protested into her ear. That's because he wasn't allowed to come in. Berta

Whitman told him to observe the two of you from outside, through the window. I was stunned, near speechless. "But Why?" is all I could muster in response. Rachel took us both by the hand and went into the hallway where aides were busy getting to their chores and didn't watch us as closely. Berta Whitman told your Dad she couldn't allow him in because the two of you suffered from separation anxiety. She thinks if he was allowed to visit, you would hang on to him like vines and not let go of him. My mouth fell open. How could Berta Whitman know exactly what I had been cooking in my mind?

It was on that day, spurred on by Rachel's account, that I devised the grand rescue scheme. As I had hatched the genius plan rather quickly in my head, time seemed to stand still. And the moment of dinner, when the adventure was to unfold appeared infinitely remote.

It was a golden afternoon in August, that memorable day. Berta Whitman had scheduled lawn activities until sunset. I was in the dancing circle where we sang songs like that of the Washerwomen who show different parts of their body. So I stretched out my arms, when the song called for that activity. I turned my palm upside down, as much in sync with everybody else as I could possibly manage having to hold at the same time the grand plan and its imminent execution in mind. The song called for washing dirty laundry on the washing board. So that's what I did, even though the ditty seemed so mundane and childish compared to the real dangers that come when people go out on a limb. "Put forth your shoes, and point your toes...!" We sang along with the nurse aides and Berta Whitman who sang the ditty as if she were the lead soprano in church choir in a huge gothic church. And then because we had done it so well, she granted us the greatest pleasure - freedom, those two notions I have found since my earliest days to be inseparable, ever since Sister and I arrived at Children's Resort. Now, you all get to take off your shoes and socks. And feel the cool grass. And we'll do the Washerwomen one more time barefooted.

During our second round, I looked over to Sister's group of toddlers playing in the sandbox under the shade of a tilted umbrella. They enjoyed the greatest pleasure of all, skinny-dipping in the mud. For the first time this summer, a garden hose spurted forth water to fill the moats of their sand castles. The kids over there were delirious with joy as they were allowed to actually get into the wet sand, sit in it, roll in it, pee into it and get covered with muck. The piglets were promptly hosed down by the nurse aides who barked and bellowed with laughter. It was a day of exhilarating freedom for everyone and I almost let go of my resolve to finish this day off with our grand escape.

The suns hot rays fell in a sharper slant and turned into a deep orange. Soon it would be roll call and hooking up by linking hands with a partner, in goose-march style, as Berta Whitman called it, we'd all trot back to the chalet to be scrubbed down for dinner time. I chose to link up with a boy, because nobody else among all the kids would do that. Carl, the kid whom I chose to link up with, was my age, but much less versed in matters of rebellious behavior, so he blushed the color of a watermelon, when I, without any verbal invitation or even a smile, took his hand in mine and virtually pulled him to the Children's Home.

The cleanup was not worthy of memory retention. However, I did graduate to the round bathtub, where my age peers explored each other's anatomy with unceasing curiosity as soon as the nurse looked the other way. We also had rubber ducklings and fish as toys and little pails to throw water over each other's head. I had to admit, these water follies were pleasurable and the grand escape came close to falling by the wayside.

With the chimes of the clock, which I couldn't read yet, dinner feeding time rolled around. I had let Sister in on my escape plan, but deemed it best to keep the details to myself, for her capacity for intricacies was that of a fish net. I didn't tell anything to Rachel though, despite the fact that she was, unknown to herself, the flagship of the whole operation. When the feeding of the babes started, she would get ready to depart to catch the last train that would take her down to the valley and home again.

Until then Rachel sat with us and even tasted the dinner menu, which consisted of mashed potatoes, carrots and peas all smothered with gravy. The babes were fed their usual gruel slop, which they expelled from the sides of their mouth. By now, it was a familiar scene. The scene was still distressing to my tender stomach nerves though.

As soon as Rachel put away her spoon and bowl and reached for her wool cardigan to depart, my eyes, ears and all the other senses perked up. We didn't have anytime to lose once Rachel slipped out of the doorway. For early on we had to catch up with her on the way to the railroad station, otherwise we wouldn't find the station nor would we be able to catch the train back home. In my plan I had taken it for granted that it would be alright with Rachel, if Sister and I caught up with her and made her take us home.

Rachel had always been a true buddy, always acquiescing in whatever I suggested. Although, she did tone down some of my more outrageous ideas. Like when I suggested that we hitch our German Shepherd and part wolf dog Prince to Sister's tricycle, so that Sister could experience the thrills of speed without having to pedal so hard. Rachel mildly shook her head and indicated that it would be a far better idea if she hitched a rope to Sister's tricycle and pulled it down Lauer Street. I gave in because Rachel had such a persuasive way about her, in the way that she used just a few words that she spoke so mildly and embedded in the biggest smile. Nobody could ever take offense with Rachel. She was our sweetheart babysitter and surrogate mother at times.

Rachel hugged us goodbye and Sister had tears well up, as she did every evening when Rachel bade us farewell. I usually swallowed my tears and tonight I had none to spare, since this was going to be our last day here anyway. My mind was already ahead of my body, on the platform of the Longstein train station where Rachel would buy two tickets for minors. The thought of holding that train ticket in my hand was sweeter than a whole bouquet of candy bars.

The very moment Rachel slipped out of our site. I surveyed the whole scenario like an eagle ready to swoop down to catch the rabbit. First I had to ascertain Berta Whitman's whereabouts. It was quintessential for the success of this plan that she have her back toward us or better yet that she would be called out of the dining room because of some emergency happening down the hallway. When I spotted her square frame hovering over an aide with a infant in her arms, I prayed to God that He intervene and present a small emergency. Presently I clenched my fists, for I thought that would intensify my prayer.

And indeed, the miracle happened. Carl, the guy who I liked to embarrass by escorting him during goose march and at whose nipples I picked when we bathed together, was throwing a temper tantrum down the hallway of such severity that the whole feeding agenda got thrown off balance and babies had ample time to eject every bit of carrot and mashed potato slop and to sully the aprons of the nurses' aides with remarkable stains.

I grabbed sister by the hand, as soon as Berta Whitman hurried down the hallway, "Act normal!" I whispered to Sister, even though I did not have the vaguest idea myself what normalcy was like when you're about to do something outrageous. However, instinctively, I knew to avoid any eye contact with nurses and peers. Rather than straight as an arrow, we meandered leisurely past small stations of high chairs and round table settings with kids seated in kid-size chairs with bibs around their necks and carrot muck in their faces. The meandering also came instinctively; or rather I had remembered how our cats and dog behaved when they were ready to steal a treat from the table. They slinked around as if they were trying to catch their own tail, barely lifting their gaze from the ground and then, after a good deal of inconspicuous wandering, they struck. In one incredibly swift swoop, they seized the forbidden tidbit and virtually evaporated from the scene of crime.

Yes, evaporate, that was the idea, but how to do that in a room with more orderlies than I had fingers on one hand? The din of the dining room was now behind us, as we had made it past the threshold and entered the sacred hallway that leads to the exit into freedom. I dropped my head looking intently at the linoleum tile that would lead us to the heavy entrance door, or rather, the gate to freedom. Sister tagged along like a well trained puppy, mimicking every gesture and step that I took. I dared take a deep inhale when the brass handle of the entrance door was gleaming in front of me.

I studied the handle with great intent, for I knew this main door would have some other lock that needed to be activated at the same time with the handle. Yes there was a dead bolt above the gleaming handle, and it was a major stretch to reach that far. On another inhale I jumped up and stretched my lean body several inches beyond its regular length. The latch bolt went click and clunk as it pulled back, and the sound of it was magic in my ears.

But just when I depressed the handle and opened the heavy oak door as far as to let a slither of the outdoor breeze enter in, a leather leash plunged over my head and was pulled tight around my chest and upper arms. I was roped like an animal, like I had seen cowboys do with out of control broncos in western movies. Sister was caught with the same device. Just as my splendid escape maneuver was about to come off, there came Berta Whitman with her child catcher smack down on us. I barely dared to look up and check, but for sure it had to be Berta Whitman. No one else would have the panache to execute this roundup with such total efficiency and cold blood.

"Got ya," She tooted ecstatically. All she needed was a horn at this moment to sound her victory for she had reeled in a prize catch indeed. Still entangled in the dreaded leash that she would harness to toddlers and pre-tots who crawled into forbidden corners and would eat grass and discarded paper napkins from the trash bin, she jerked us into the dining hall. Now the true gauntlet was waiting for us. Sister and I hung our heads and if we had owned tails we would have tucked them tightly between our hind legs.

"This what happens to you when you do no obey the rules of Children's Resort," Berta Whitman exclaimed and pointed with her open faced right hand at the two of us. She underlined her statement with a vigorous nod and as I gazed around from under my eyelids I saw peers, tots and pre-tots alike staring at us in the greatest silence that dining room had ever experienced. Even the babes held the carrot and potato mush in their puffed out mouths. The feeding frenzy was suspended, disembodied as if caught in a snapshot photograph. Even though I was humbled and the embarrassment was real as I felt my heart beat fluttering and a series of blushes engulf my face, there still was a sense of glory and vindication.

The impact of my grand escape scheme couldn't have been more profound, I held every head at Children's Resort in my spell and that gave me a twisted but tangible sense of satisfaction. I was an instant celebrity at this moment and while I didn't get any applause, I knew that many of my peers rooted for me, for they too yearned to shake up the buttressed system themselves but didn't have the gumption nor the wits to do so. I may have been vanquished for the time being. I may have looked foolhardy, but at the same time that spotlight Berta Whitman directed onto my lithe figure felt like the nimbus of holy martyrdom and secretly I savored every bit of it.

Chapter 7

Little Brother

Bruederle, *our little brother*, had a great giggly and contagious laugh big and loud and radiant for this child just six months old. When we tossed the ball over his small body in the crib, he stretched out his small arms in utter delight. Just two ounces of more mature coordination and he would have joined us, Dad, Sister and me in our ballgame triangle. He laughed so deeply all of his body jiggled and wobbled. He kicked away his blanket so as to expose the length of his body, his slightly plump belly, chubby legs and arms and hands and feet that wiggled in the direction of the ball that passed overhead like a glider plane.

In moments like this, I forgot that something terrible was eating away at Bruederle. The medical professor who specialized in pediatrics had given his official verdict to Mother and Father who listened with wobbly knees and a tightening wrench in their guts. The university doctor that our parents consulted, was far and wide the most reputed specialist in childhood cancer, diagnosed leukemia. This word took on more and more a life of its own as it unfolded its parasitic existence in Bruederle's body and spread into every cell of this most beautiful child.

I noticed the tendrils of leukemia working their way into Bruederle's brownish curly hair. Once his hair had been as perky as his deep brown eyes. The little quirky spirals turned and wiggled with his laughter. Now they lay sullen, as if pasted to his skull. When, without pause he hit his head against the wall of his crib, *bang*, there was nothing I could do to stop him. Even more painful to stand by and watch helplessly, I did not stir from his crib but stayed with him from morning until evening as if I sensed that our moments together were on a merciless countdown.

I was just four years old, too young to take on this wagonload of a babysitter's responsibility but nothing could pull me away from his crib. And nobody made the slightest attempt to coax me away into the make-believe world of sandcastles, and the rough and tumble of wrestling our shepherd dog Prince. It was as if the Fates had assigned me this place in the corner of Bruederle's nursery where the lacy curtains were drawn shut to keep out the glare of the springtime sun that would show up the pallid color of his skin, the sunken cheeks that once were as full and feisty as those of a well-fed squirrel. We shut out the stark sunlight that would dig into the hollows of his eye sockets and reveal the purplish cast that made his eyelids look heavy. This was a twilight nursery, for no one in the family was ready to face openly the state of decay in which Bramwele had fallen. *Bang! He did it again!* With full force of his weak body he bashed his head against the crib wall.

I put my fist into my mouth and bit into the flesh. Maybe to muffle a scream or more likely to feel the pangs of physical pain myself, sharing a communion of pain with my entrusted Brother.

Fredrich Wilhelm was his proper German name. And I never understood why my parents would give him so many syllables to tackle with in later life. On top of that, this name bore the likeness to Prussian kings, one of whom was a flutist. I would have given Bruederle a strong and contemporary name: Thomas, Matthias, or Wolfgang perhaps. In, Mother's books of European royal families, I saw nothing but boredom and vacant looks in the portraits of those with royal blood. Royalty to me meant as much as the lazy lives of those who have servants wipe their ass, who stuffed their stomachs until they were ready to throw up, and slept in beds with tons of cushions and canopies, and devoted lap dogs at their feet. My little brother had none of that. When he was still a healthy child, his body was alive and buoyant as that of a butterfly. His eyes would marvel at you like obsidian set into cherry-wood. These eyes glowed with love and their radiance would make you feel beautiful no matter if in actuality you looked like a slob.

Wham! He hit his head again and the whole crib shakes. The reverberations of his pain ripple through my small body that sits helpless on a chair at the side of his crib. My Bruederle is on a relentless self-destructive bent. Without thinking, I grab his right hand. So soft and relaxed, it lays plump in mine. It has the weightlessness of trust and I'm overcome to cut into that trust, wake little brother up from his head-banging metronome. I bring down my mouth to his rosy hand, with fingers curled and pudgy, not yet ravaged by the invasion of leukemia. My front teeth and canines dig into the softness of Bruederle's hand, his fingers curl with pain inside my mouth. He gasps in agony, I dig in further. Then I let go. His hand withdraws from the trap of my mouth. I cannot stand to look at this face. So I stare straight ahead at the window where a gentle April breeze fills the lace curtain, billows its folds and creates manifold shapes that I used to fill in with the life of fairy tale creatures. Right now my concentration was singular. I waited silently for the next head-banging to take place. It didn't happen. Instead Bruederle sobbed and whimpered and when I glanced at him I noticed that his left hand cupped over his right hand to comfort the pain that my teeth had inflicted on him. I avoided his eyes. I wouldn't be able to bear their expression of betrayed love, the question that he couldn't utter yet but that hung over us like a sack of lead. *"Why did you do this to me?"*

I don't know why. But I had to do it to break the monotony of your self-destructive habit. I didn't say this out-loud but I thought it and hoped that he would get the gist of my intent.

What happened after is lost to my memory. How long Bruederle whimpered and comforted his hand, I do not recall. The next day though, Mother, came up to me, in the most direct motion I'd not seen her in, in a long time, she positioned herself squarely in front of me. *"Why did you do it?"* Was all she asked me. *"Do what?"* I said back because I truly did not know what she was referring to. The incident from the day before was like erased from my mind. "There's no use denying it. The teeth marks on Bruederle's hand are still clearly visible. It's you who bit him? Who else could have done it anyway?" Her eyes lay on me like that of the judge spelling out the terms of the sentence to the accused. I didn't move, nor blink, nor breathe. I was frozen in guilt and shame. I could not find any words to expunge my offense. The intent that propelled my deed, my desperate wish to yank Bruederle out of his head-banging habit, all of that was inaccessible to me in that moment of cross-examination. Mother's eyes bore into me and I felt like the most despicable vermin that ever crawled on the face of the earth. It seemed for the longest time Mother and I were locked, she in outrage and contempt and I in utter self-hatred.

When she finally stepped back, I started to breathe again and my frozen limbs loosened enough for me to go into retreat. I hid in the garden under a cherry tree where I would usually listen to blackbirds sing in the dusk. On this dark day, I did not hear a sound other than roaring guilt in my ear drums and the ceaseless sobbing in my throat. Tears ran down my hot cheeks and fell onto spring flowers like one of those April showers that appear out of nowhere.

Chapter 8

Snowman

I remember the time of picture book winter seasons. The snow was white, deep and bore heavily on the bent tree limbs. The snowy winter coat muffled the hubbub of the major highway, the artery that fed all the commuters of the Alp Mountains to their factory and clerical jobs in Reutingen the largest and most industrious town within a 25 mile radius. This thoroughfare was within earshot of our home, and from the orchard garden adjacent to our home we could look down to the seamless string of bumper to bumper traffic during rush hour at about 7 am and 6 pm. However, once the landscape was snowcapped and a wintery sky hung over the valley, the business of the highway retreated into more distant dreamy realms.

This was the time when Dad was up when it was still night outside lighting a fire in the woodstove in the living room. So when Sister and I would emerge from our adjacent room, we were cozy and warm. In these wee hours of the day Dad would also light a fire in the huge cannon stove in the mill, so his workplace would be comfortably warm and the water pipes wouldn't freeze. Dad called it the cannon stove because it had the color of a cannon and the stove pipe projected out like one long barrel radiating heat like no other furnace in town.

The bitter cold of five years prison camp in Siberia, where Dad had to withstand -30 degrees below zero and trudge through knee-deep snow or otherwise be bitten and chewed to death by starved and vicious dogs trained to kill prisoners of war who were faltering from exhaustion. This experience had left an indelible imprint in Dad's mind, so every year when winter rolled around, he became like a professional stoker tending to several fires at the same time and never letting the family experience an inhospitable home.

The art of laying a fire, Dad had it down to a science. When to use small round coke and when to put in brick-sized briquettes, just how much kindling, how much air flow to feed the fire, when to choke the fire through various regulators so it wouldn't burn up so fast and when to make it searing hot so the stove pipe would turn a reddish glow as flames leapt through every leaky seam and crevice of the stove.

In those days frost would paint the most wondrous designs on our window panes. While warmth radiated from the stove I studied the fern woods and other lush foliage that frost had layered upon our windows. I found myself transported into the fairyland of fronds that beckoned me to imagine these frosty scenes as magic woods where winter-spirits played hide and seek.

We also had a couple of modern windows which had an insulating gas wedged between two layers of glass. Not a trace of frosty leafage appeared on them. This was ample proof to me that modern inventions were inimical to the magic of the seasons and the elements.

Eager to brave the cold and test the new snow that had fallen silently over night, Sister and I bundled up in woolen leggings, caps and mittens all knit by Mother in the late night hours on her knitting machine.

Prince our part wolf, part German Shepherd dog greeted us with glee, licking our noses and telling us with short happy yelps that this was his kind of weather. To both our amazement he ploughed through the snow and belly whopped into snow embankments so only his wagging tail was visible, telling us like a pennon that, yes indeed, Prince had found the perfect playground for his thick winter coat.

Sister and I were just as ecstatic as the dog. We scooped up snow with our mittened hands and smashed it into the dog's muzzle. This he enjoyed thoroughly; I could tell by the sparkle in his eyes. I would marvel at the fluffy texture of the new fallen snow and then scoop up one mouthful with my tongue. Every snowfall tasted different, so I found out. Just like every year wine has a different aroma. This particular one had captured sunshine in its taste; the sun had truly ripened it, as it was a bright and sunny day turning the snowy land into one shimmering and glittering ice palace. Under the radiant sun each crumb of snow turned into a multi-faceted prism, and Sister and I called it sparkle land.

This snow was the perfect building material for the snow man that was already standing in his full glory smiling with carrot nose in our imagination. Dad joined us in our exploration of the perfect snowman site, visible to all our neighbors. Indeed, we intended to make it something of a monument so even all the automobile travelers coming and going to the Alp Mountains or the city would be able to see our rounded white man with the benign look on his face.

Dad showed us a trick-how to scoop a whole lot of snow onto the spot that we decided was going to be the snow man's base. He supplied us with shovels so we could be more efficient in our building project. Making the snow stick so it would glue together and grow into one big ball was no small enterprise. It took much patting with our hands and the flat side of the hand trowels. The bottom of our snowman was as wide as my arm span. Sister and I were ready to have a sandwich with butter and blackberry jam and a glass of milk to replenish us with new energy for there were still the trunk and the head that needed to be built before sundown. Centering the middle part on top of the bottom came close to being an engineering project. One of us had to take several steps back and tilt the head either way to gauge how well the trunk was placed right above that solid foundation. After trial and error, it occurred to us that flattening the top of the snow man's bottom so we would have a flat platform was the way to build our construction up in height.

Dad came by, but we were working so furiously we hardly noticed his presence. He mustered the half-finished project and told us that we were great builders; he sounded truly proud of us. Once we had finished the trunk part, we barely could wait to set the head on this man and get to the fine-tuning. Because of our impatience our snowman turned out to have a small head, though we made up for it by placing a conspicuous wide-brimmed black hat on top of his head. Sister and I had paid a visit to Aunt Elma, pulled at either of her arms and moved her plump body up to the kitchen window and proudly presented to her our man that stood now full grown and rotund but just a bit naked. "We need to dress him up Aunt Elma." "You sure do," She said nodding with that broad smile of hers. Then she led us to various treasure troves. Sister and I had our eyeballs grow bigger and bigger when she opened the closet and pointed to all the various clothes her deceased husband and two stepsons had left her. Overalls and knickers, black woolen suits they wore on

Sunday morning to church, jackets with lamb lining, fur hats, hats with high and low crowns, wide and narrow brims. She reached for the largest hat on the rack and handed it to us ceremoniously. "Here, put this hat on your snow man and he will look more respectable than any snow man ever built in this neighborhood." Sister and I were both ecstatic, both of us holding on to this precious garment.

"I'll give you some coke so your snow man shows big black buttons," She said. We couldn't believe what a great expert Aunt Elma was with dressing up snowmen. Loaded with hat and coal the size of large eggs wrapped in newspaper we stormed down several flights of stairs. Somewhere on our downward rush, Dad held out his arms and held us up, "Wait a minute, you guys and don't you think you're missing something?" We were so happy with what we got we hadn't thought any further. "Look at this hat Dad," Sister said and placed it on her head which promptly was covered all the way down to her nose. "Splendid," Dad said and again we could feel the warm tone of affection shine through his words. Dad lifted his arms and let us pass by, for we were like colts bucking and butting, having no minute to spare in conversation.

Once the hat was in place, snow man looked like a Mafia Godfather. Two coals functioned as eyes, but the hat's wide brim partially obscured his eyes, thus making him a mean old dude. We buttoned him up and down with the rest of the coal and found that something was missing. Sister stepped back and craned her neck and so did I, but the missing object wouldn't release its name right away. Dad came by once again now appraising the almost finished piece of art. "Could this guy be alive?" He asked and Sister and I looked at him in puzzlement. "It's just a snowman Dad," Sister reassured him. "Ah so! But don't you think he'd appreciate a nose and a mouth perhaps, just so he can breathe in and out?" Sister and I looked at each other dumbfounded that's exactly what we had been missing, but couldn't really name it.

So we went upstairs again bursting into Aunt Elma's kitchen where we smelled the rich aroma of lentil soup with bacon and home made noodles that she had tossed into a skillet with butter. This made us almost forget our urgent purpose. "We need a nose and a mouth, Aunt Elma," Sister said, and poked her nose into the steaming pot with the lentils and bacon. "You think a carrot will do for a nose?" She asked. We both agreed strongly by nodding our heads at the same time. With her small but quick steps she went to the pantry where she kept produce in wicker baskets. After she pulled off the greens, she handed me the largest carrot and asked with a wide grin "Satisfied?" Of course we were satisfied and again we bolted downstairs giving our Mafia man the nose to breathe with. We put the nose in crooked which further accentuated his image of being a crook. Once more we stepped back and found him perfect. "Except for the... what was it, Dad said he still needed?" I asked. "Oh, he needs a broom," Sister said with excitement, and up we stormed toward the house again. Appearances had turned gray as the twilight of dusk was settling in. We looked around in the shop near the table saw where Dad would keep his countless tools: leather belts for the elevators and transmission wheels, screws as big as twice the size of my index finger, nuts wider than my open mouth, and bolts so fat and long, you could knock a full-grown man unconscious with one. Here, Dad also kept brooms of all sizes and shapes, brooms to push the dirt and brooms to collect dirt from the corners and niches. Sister and I opted for a scrawny one that had lost much of the broomcorn straw.

Once we stuck that broom into the snow man's side he looked truly happy. Sister exhausted by our day's work, with much contentment and great pride walked back up to the mill where Mom and Dad were expecting us to join the table for dinner.

Chapter 9

Wallpaper

A naked kitchen is a sad place. It can bring about extreme limitations, far beyond a child's imagination. I spent the seventh Easter Holiday of my life within denuded kitchen walls, which held the memory of past generations and threatened to undo the fabric of my own family.

Mother and her spade-like hands scrubbed down the kitchen walls. She clutched the wire brush with both hands, her big chest moving up and down in sync with the arm motion. Up and down. It reminded me of the job the guy did on the billboard at the intersection where our Valley Street crossed the Burgerstrasse Street, a road that dated back to Caesar and Roman soldiers marching through Teutonic lands. That guy in blue overalls would scrape down the Marlboro Man, cigarette, horse, and canyonlands and paste up a cheerful looking Mother. "Ah Rama," the word bubble dribbled from her smiling lips. Her boy and girl stood by, eager anticipation on their faces, while she slathered slices of dark bread with margarine. I liked this advertisement because the word 'Rama' had a nice roll to it, thereby it was easy to remember almost as easy as 'Mama'. Similar to that guy on the ladder, Mother had discovered that our kitchen walls were billboards too. Mom's spade-shaped hands unearthed layers of past generations' wall decor. Overnight, she had become a kitchen archeologist. "Mom, the walls peel like my back after a sunburn," I said, and Mother chuckled.

"You come up with the funniest notions. But you've got a point there. Wallpaper and paint are like the skins of a wall. And I'm going to peel it all off until I get down to the marrow." She straightened her back and turned her head quickly to the left and right and let out a deep sigh when her neck cracked as if she had just stepped on a walnut. "Ah, now that I got this kink out of my spine, I can go right back to work and dig deeper."

Up and down, and not a sound she would make, although beads of exertion formed on her forehead. I watched her intently. Her muscular body spread into the seams of her hand-sewn jumper, the color of the willow leaves when they burst from their buds. But spring was still on hold and so were the willow buds. It was snowing on this dreary Good Friday and the clouds hung gray and low. What else was there for me to do but watch Mother go up and down and skin the kitchen walls down to the bare wood. At first it had looked amusing to see Mom working full throttle. She looked as intent as our physical education instructor during morning calisthenics and just as relentless. Indeed, I had found the spectacle entertaining, but now that she had been at it for the second straight day, the project had the cold and soggy feeling of the snow that banked against the kitchen window.

"Mother has the strength of a horse and grace of a deer. That's a rare find," Dad had said, and flashed a big grin. "She can lift me up and swing me around and next thing she sits in my lap," He'd say, and I could tell he was proud to have such a strong-horse-deer-woman as a wife. I had seen Mom's extraordinary muscle power in action myself. Once she pushed the biggest closet from one corner in the bedroom into the other. "I just transplanted an oak tree," Mother had said, her face filled with pride. For this was an heirloom piece, solid oak through and through and stacked inside with three generations of bed linen.

The calendar on the kitchen floor said it was Good Friday, the day that Jesus our Lord was crowned with thorns and nailed to a cross. The solemn harmonies of the Jesus' Passion drifted into the kitchen from the radio in the living room. Mother had set the dial on the station that broadcasted the Good Friday Mass live from the cathedral in Stauffenberg where the bishop held service. You could have had an impression that Mom was a Catholic for Mother adhered to the rules, only fish on Fridays, or pancakes with compote made of gooseberries and currants. Our family went along with her Catholic habits because everything that Mom prepared was made with love as Dad would say and most tasty. Except this Friday she had gone beyond the rule. There was nothing to eat at all but scraps of cold leftovers in the pantry of our kitchen, and strains of Jesus' passion came from the radio in the living room. As I looked around, I found the coziest place in the entire grist mill gaping empty and cold. Mother, the dynamo, behind this kitchen remodeling project, had thrust her body and soul into this project and labored on layers of ancient wall paper and coats of oil-based paint. "What you're looking at?" She asked noticing my presence behind her without even turning her head.

"Aw, just watching Ma," I said and shuffled backward retreating a couple of steps, so she wouldn't feel like I was looking over her shoulder. I would have liked to join the wall scouring operation, but Mother rarely recruited me for work other than drying the dishes and sweeping the kitchen floor. *"Kids learn mainly by watching adults and by copying adults in their own games,"* She'd say if I volunteered to help. "Kids learn by doing some simple work things. Nothing teaches you like work itself." This was Dad's idea, and he put it often to practice calling Sister and myself from the midst of our games to do some simple work project for him. "It's just 500 paper bags that I have here for you to put two things on," and he'd hand us the rubber stamps that said Type 405 which meant the flour in the bags was whiter than tooth paste. And another rubber stamp that had the address and phone number of our gristmill.

But the kitchen being turned inside out wasn't Dad's project. In fact he hated what Mother had done. I could tell by his conspicuous absence. He was hiding out in the gristmill two floors below our kitchen, watching wheels churn. "I'm letting time spin round and round," Dad had told me when I had come down to visit. "Aren't you gonna come up and join Mom?" I had asked because he looked waxen and his cheeks were drawn down.

"I'm no demolition man. Let your Mother tear the kitchen down and then let her count the casualties," Dad had said. I didn't know what a casualty was, but it sounded gloomy just by the tone of his voice. So I left him watching the wheels go round and returned to Mother's construction site.

I observed her busy body standing on the threshold between living room and kitchen. She'd rise up on her toes on her way up, and then crouch down deeply as she pulled down. "Dad's so gloomy. All he's doing is staring into those milling wheels churning," Mother glanced in my direction and with her arm sleeve she wiped sweat from her forehead. "He abhors remodeling. It reminds him of war times when his entire family got thrown out of their estate in Russia and were homeless wandering across Eastern Europe. It's part of his war memories that give him those night terrors when he screams and awakes dripping wet from his sweat."

I scratched behind my ear trying to make sense of that which she had just explained to me, and the fact that she had reduced our most favorite living space into something like a grotto. "If Dad gets so upset over changing things around in the house, why then are you re-doing the kitchen?"

"Now-now, aren't we getting a bit testy here?" Mother pleated her forehead into a number of folds. "Let's get this straight. I'm beautifying the kitchen for all of us. This place needs a makeover so badly it's not even funny. Last time I gave it a facelift was four years ago. I was pregnant with your Sister then and you were crawling on the floor getting your fingers into the paint. With the wood stove and the smoke the walls get dirty-looking in no time. I believe in white sheets and white walls." She nodded her head to underline what she just said.

"Now, back to work!" she said and her big hips grew in all directions as she hunkered down and dug into the face of the wall. "Come here and look at this," She motioned me, waving her arm as at traffic cop does. "Would you believe it, Albert and Hans, those two shrewd brothers, the cleverest millers in the whole Ortzan valley, actually used the kitchen walls to do their accounting! It is hard to believe that two grown-up men would behave like this using the walls of their kitchen to do business graffiti." I looked closer to make out the writing but the script was foreign to me. "That's gothic writing, the older people were schooled to write like that. I had to learn it when I was a child but they switched the style on me in second grade. I traced the numbers with my fingers, up and down the crooked columns. Numbers that were added and subtracted were underlined and made strong by exclamation marks on either side. "These are names of neighbors long since gone," Mother said. "Herta Klein owed the millers money. You know his daughter down the road with her upper teeth missing. And Frieda Schienhal, who is now in her nineties, owed them milling money for her chicken feed". I knew Frieda Schienhal well. Sister and I regularly visited the blackberry bushes along her picket fence.

I noticed that *Frau Kummel,* the *five Marks,* the date, and exclamation marks on either side were all boxed in as in a coffin. The outlines made fat and black with coal. "What do you think this box is all about? I'm curious." "It's hard to say, but these two penny pinchers would get their money, even if they had to go to your funeral and collect it from the bereaved." Mother nudged the coffin of Frau Kummel with a razor blade. "It's such an oddity, I just have to keep this and show it to Dad." She carefully lifted Frau Kummel's account, a paint swatch as big as my palm, off the wall.

Mother shook her head for a while. "You look at all these numbers and they get to you. It's as if they swim around in my head," She said, and resumed the up-and down project with renewed zest. "There is no time to let up for I've got to get at the bottom of this. So I can start all fresh and make us a virgin kitchen. *Just imagine!* Here we've lived all these years in our kitchen and unbeknownst to us we were exposed to the aggregate greed of these old hoarders." Her jumper strained in the seams as she straightened, arched back and cracked her spine. "That feels good," She said, and back to work she went.

"I'll make us a cup of mint tea," Mother suggested and sent me to fetch some dried peppermint that hung from the rafters in the attic. "And get some rosemary to. I'm starting to feel my days coming on. While I didn't know what exactly Mother meant when she announced the onset of her monthly days, I knew from experience that she could be like a weather vane during her days. She'd be talkative and cheerful one moment and sooner than I could blink she'd change into something akin of a deaf and mute rock. To put it mildly, I found her days bewildering.

"Oh dear, you brought down an entire rosemary bush! I only need a twig as big as this." She held up her forefinger. "Go back up and tie the rest of the rosemary back to where you got it!"

The tea kettle was hissing and Dad opened the kitchen door just wide enough to stick his head through the opening. His gray-blue eyes searched the naked walls and the tile floor buried under debris, brushes, buckets, and the salvaged chunks of wall covering. His gaze lingered on the center of the kitchen where he found an empty space, the large kitchen table, the wooden wall bench where Sister usually sat, Mom's chair where she'd sit across from Sister and his chair opposite of mine, the hub of our family was missing. His eyes narrowed and withdrew from the empty spot. In my guts I knew how he must have felt. I too missed the largeness of our kitchen table, always cheery looking with mid-morning and mid-afternoon, he'd be installed at the table and take a break from milling, enjoying a small glass of red wine and a slice of Mother's home baked bread piled with butter and salami and horseradish as red as the wine. He liked his horseradish that way. When Dad and

Mom started their household together, he had his sister instruct Mother in Russian cooking, the way he liked his food to be prepared. And horseradish had to be marinated in the juices of beets that were cooked and spiced with cloves, bay leaves, cardamom, pepper, balsamic vinegar, and the best of oil. "Red wine and red foods build blood," Dad would say, "and relish, melons and beets, tomatoes and raspberries and most of all horseradish the color of burgundy."

"No place for me," Dad said and his voice cracked on *for me*. It was a sound similar to that of Mother snapping chunks of old paint off the wall. Dad shut the door without a sound; and Mother continued her scraping. Had she not noticed that Dad had come and gone?

I had installed myself to the right of her and was leaning against the gas range, a piece of heavy equipment that even Mother wasn't able to move. Mom said, "the wives of Albert and Hans used to cook on that stove. During the cold season they had a fire going day and night in that old wood stove next to it; so the millers could have hot mulled wine and toasted rolls in the middle of a winter's night when they couldn't go to sleep because of outstanding debts that needed to be collected."

I braced myself closer against the range. The smell of paint thinner made me dizzy. My stomach started rumbling as if it was tumbling dice. Mother looked across her right shoulder and studied me from top to bottom. "Good God, you look as transparent as a ghost! Go open the window before you pass out on me! These fumes are hard on the old body, especially with kids." She reached and got a hold of the can of paint and in a hurry she replaced the lid knocking it down with a hammer. "That'll take care of that."

Mother got up and put the can in the far corner away from me. When she resumed her spot, she gave me a long hard look. "It's strange to see you lean against that gas range. Really peculiar…! It reminds me of Aunt Margret, the sister of my father, your Great Aunt. With your pale cheeks you look just as forlorn as she did. Bless her heart. I remember visiting the mill when I was about your age and Aunt Margret would lean against this kitchen stove and stare holes into the wall. It looked to me as if she was looking at some movie that was being projected on that empty wall. She was oblivious to the rest of the world when she was in one of her staring states. Milk could boil over behind her, but she wouldn't bother to turn around until I would yell, "*Aunt Margret* look, the milk for my hot chocolate is running down the sides of the stove!" Only then would she wake up and be startled like a wild animal that finds itself discovered. I had to get a dish rag and clean up the mess myself, because she'd still be in a state of shock from me yelling at her." Mother sighed deeply. "Yes, yes, indeed, your Great Aunt Margret was different altogether."

I peeled my back away from the gas range. "I'm not in a staring state," I protested.

"No need to get upset. It's just a vivid memory. That's all." She picked up the scraper and whittled away at a blotch of faded oil paint the color of old snow. "Bless her heart, Aunt Margret was pregnant then with a child that never saw the light of day. I clearly recall those gloomy days in February when I came to visit and she was leaning over the pots of big meals. Those millers could devour a wagon load of food. And you know what...?" Mother paused and layed down the scraper, next to her right knee. "I bet you anything, during those black moods of hers, when she leaned against that gas range and let the meal get burnt to charcoal, that's when she hatched her final plan."

"What plan?" I asked. Mother had me hooked.

"It's just a thought, I couldn't know for sure. Whatever she was thinking, Aunt Margret wouldn't tell a soul. She was as glum as those trout down in the stream. But, by the way she stared at the walls, I could tell a wild storm was brewing behind those hazel eyes of hers." Mom paused and sighed once again. "It's a gruesome, cruel thing she did. And it's not the kind of story a child your age will comprehend. Maybe I'll tell you the whole thing when you're older."

It occurred to me right then that Mother and Sister and this Great Aunt - I had only known from yellowed sepia photographs, *standing next to her husband Leopold, a willow sapling next to a gnarled oak tree* - that all three of them shared the same first name. And, Mother always said there is great meaning in a name.

The Passion of Jesus set to music by Johann Sebastian Bach streamed into the kitchen. As I gazed out the window, a pale late-March sun fell below the western horizon leaving the kitchen even darker. For most of the afternoon Mother had worked the wall scraper in one hand and wire brush in the other.

"Ouff, I'm ready to take a break. My back feels like I've been tied to the rack." She pulled a pile of newspapers close to her and shoved it under her rear.

"Turn on the light and then come over here, I've got something else to show you!" She waved her right arm like a tired traffic cop. "Look closely now and tell me what you see!" "It looks like puke stuck to the wall."

Mother wiped her sweat-beaded forehead. "I'll go with that. But can you actually imagine that someone would paint these walls using a paint the color of horse manure?" "Maybe it's decomposed?" I ventured as a guess. "And maybe it looked halfway decent when it was still fresh?"

"Maybe so, but most likely not." Mother straightened and had a lecturing expression on her face. "From that accounting the millers did on these kitchen walls you could see for yourself that any old penny meant serious business to them. They cut corners where regular people wouldn't see any. Now I believe these two geniuses poured all the leftover paints they could find into one bucket and for good measure they added flax seed oil which they had in large amounts since they were operating a oil mill on the side. So they concocted this paint soup and applied it straight to these walls. The color scheme was of no importance to them. What counted is they had enough of this stuff to coat these four walls three times over. Now, can you imagine Albert, Hans, their wives Elma and Margret and Albert's two sons all sitting together around the table eating lentil soup and looking at walls the same color as the soup in their bowls?"

The taste and smell of lentil soup came up for me. And I could see it clearly along with a steaming slap of pork belly and a plate of home-made noodles - it was my favorite dish.

"These gloomy walls are the honest to God proof that there's been something wrong with this gristmill, something crazy-making, something dark indeed," She said and her voice trailed behind the syllables and dropped so low I could barely make out the words.

"Mother, look at this black snake!" I said and traced the outline of a swarthy black wave that intertwined with the shades of olive, and brown, and turned into a solid black stain above the wood stove. I tilted my head sideways and made my eyes into narrow slits. From the window that was still open a chilling gust blew straight into our kitchen and made memories come alive for me. The shades of brown and black and green turned into *Fastnacht Witches and Warlocks*. On Shrove Tuesday, just a few weeks ago, they had danced down the cobbled alleys heading to the bonfire in the market square of Joseph's Platz our neighboring Catholic town. The vision made me shudder.

"Mother it looks to me as if the place once burned. That's why the paint is so blotched and murky." "That wind chills me to the bones. Shut that window! We're all going to catch pneumonia or worse," Mother said. "So you think there was a fire. I'm not sure. Nothing in the town chronicles tell anything of the mill burning in recent history. The last time it was consumed by flames was during the Seven Years' War. Surely dear old Elma would have told me if there had been a fire in her living quarters. But I can dig deeper and we'll find out for ourselves what happened."

Mother took up the scraper again and started digging under the puke paint, this time while standing up.

An achy feeling made my stomach churn, I was hungry. Since mother hadn't cooked all day, I'd have to go to the pantry and find any leftovers there. Just when I was about to walk out I noticed the handle of the door to the hallway lift slowly. Someone was about to enter the kitchen; it was Sister. As if too shy to make a full entrance, she poked her head through a narrow opening. Sister had bangs down to her lower eyelids. We all wondered how she could see through this curtain. "Aw, you're still scraping Mom?" Her voice sounded flat as if she was holding down a strong feeling. "I'm finishing up. Your sister thinks there was a fire in this place and I'm trying to find more evidence for that. But why don't you come in and show the rest of yourself!"

Sister wandered into the kitchen as if by accident. She was dragging her raggedy doll Elizabeth behind her. One of Elizabeth's floppy arms was coming undone, with the cotton batting spilling out. Mother had recently mended the other arm, which was still holding up.

Sister installed herself at the center of the archeological site that once had been our cozy kitchen. She peered intently at the stripped-down walls. "There's smoke on the walls," She said loudly. "Look, look up there!" She pointed Elizabeth's still functional arm at the spot where the pipe coming up from the wood stove bends into an elbow and then juts up through the ceiling. "There's a cross on the wall!"

Mother and I stepped closer. "Get me a chair, I've got to look at this from up close!" Out in the dark hallway I groped among the huddled kitchen furniture and found a chair. Mother stepped on top of the chair and, for balance's sake, she hugged the stove pipe. "What do you see?" I asked. I was hungry and curious and most of all I wanted to get at the bottom of this puzzle real quick.

"Like, Sister said, it's a cross alright. And letters are written beneath it. Too bad! I must have scraped off most of the writing when I attacked the walls with much enthusiasm this morning." "You mean you erased the inscription?" I asked.

"Let's not give up right. There's still some writing left. I see a lower case 'a' and an 'r' to the right of it. The word ends with a 't'."

Sister shook Elizabeth as if the doll could spit out the missing letters. I too got agitated. As if the wall was a horse that could be prodded, I stubbed my toes against it while Mother searched beneath the sooty ring around the stove pipe for other traces of writing.

"Wait girls, there's some numbers here too," Mother yelled down from above. Soot fell onto Sister and Elizabeth. "There's a 3 and a space and a 2 and then there's 1 and 9 close together."

Unimpressed by details like numbers and letters she hadn't learned yet, Sister asked, "What does a cross mean?" "It can mark the site of a treasure and some people who don't know how to write use it as their signature. It's also on graves, and there's a cross in every church." I said. "Jesus died on a cross," Sister said. "That's it," I yelled. "Someone died and someone else marked the name and date of that person's death."

"You're both right," Mother said. She took off her glasses and stepped down. Then she stood towering before us fixing us with a firm and also pained look. "You know who is being commemorated here?" She asked in a tone that told me she already knew the answer. We both shook our heads at the same time. "The cross, letters, and numbers were put there to mark your Great Aunt's death." "You mean Aunt Margret?" I said, for there were a number of other great aunts.

"Yes, there's no doubt in my mind it's her." Mother said. "The only thing that puzzles me is that she did not die on the third of February, like it says. I clearly remember the inscription on her gravestone and the obituary in the newspaper; they said that she took her life in March, the Ides of March to be exact." "What do you mean by 'the Ides of March'?" I inquired. "It's the 15th of March when Caesar was killed by his former friend Brutus."

Sister let the doll and banana hang from either arm, the particulars of dates and other bits of knowledge invariably bored her, and it looked as if all interest had dropped from her body.

"Maybe Aunt Margret tried to kill herself by setting the kitchen on fire?" This was a bold speculation on my part. But the grimy paint scheme of brown and dirty olive, and the swirls and blotches of black, made sense that way. "You're a persistent detective," Mother said, and gave me a smile. She got down from the chair and looked around her. "Now that I am standing up and can see all of the walls at once, I have to admit the walls look like they had been touched by fire," Mother said.

"And like you said, it very well may be all connected to your Great Aunt Margret. People say she was a crazed woman. And as a child I was scared to get near to her. At times she was fierce, behaving like a rabid cat, and at other times she was fragile, like a hurt doe," Mother said. And I remembered her expression, as of a hunted animal that I had seen in one of the sepia photographs of her. There's a good possibility that she might have tried to put an end to her life by setting this kitchen on fire. But she didn't succeed.

"Because one of the old millers came running upstairs and put out the fire," Sister said, clutching Elizabeth and the banana close to her chest. "Yes," Mother agreed, "but that still leaves the question as to who put the cross there?"

Sister stirred, new interest in the matter had entered into her body. "I've got it!" She said proudly, "Aunt Margret drawed the cross there herself. She do it before she put the fire, because once she is dead she cannot draw the cross and her name anymore."

Mother and I both looked baffled. What a feat of logic for someone who was just three and one half year old! While the gravity of Sister's discovery took a hold of us; the three of us stood speechless looking at the cross above our heads.

Slowly as if her joints had turned into lead, Mother returned to the place where her tools lay on the floor and resumed her labor excavating our kitchen wall. Not knowing what else to say, Sister and I left in single file. Elizabeth's feet dragged on the floor. And Sister shut the door behind her so quietly it made me think that we had just stepped out of a morgue. In the hallway, I let out a deep sigh and Sister whimpered, as if she was crying. "I am hungry and I am cold, and there is no warm place to be."

Most of Good Friday had passed. Father was nowhere to be seen. Sister and I had played who-can-build-the-tallest-tower-out-of-wooden - blocks - and - then-knock-the-whole-structure-over. It had been chilly in the hallway and the light had flickered since the bulbs were lit by direct current generated by our waterwheels. At the time I thought it flickered because their was an interval of time between the troughs filling and emptying the water as they revolved. Our playing was punctuated by strains of the Easter Oratory and Mother's loud singing accompaniment coming from our kitchen - a forbidding site that she had successfully turned into an archeological dig.

"Come see what I found!" Mother hollered down the hallway. When we filed into the kitchen, she waved her arm like a magician who had just produced a rabbit from the inside of his hat. "Step closer, and see for yourselves!" She said, and her excitement made her voice compelling. "This tops it all!" She dropped her scraper and started using a screwdriver and hammer to chisel away stubborn blotches of army fatigue paint which underneath revealed a much more elegant past.

"Now how's that for a dramatic change of colors! Have a look at this girls," She said. I stepped up next to her right side and squinted to see the details. "Looks to me like the cover of Grandma's velvet sofa," I said, and thought I sounded quite the expert. "Close, but not quite as contemporary as Grandma's time," Mom said, and slid her spade-shaped hand across the treasure she had just found. "This is brocade," She said, and her voice sounded important like the tour guide at the *Rothenburg castle - the closest castle to my home. "B-R-O-C-A-D-E," She repeated as if she needed to hammer the spelling of the word into my brain. "Textile wall coverings like this were all the rage in Queen Victoria's time; you would find them in castles, and noble houses, maybe in a fine parsonage, or in doctors' homes too."

Mother took a long sharp breath and her big chest inflated her jumper. "Girls, this is a rare find indeed. Maybe I should call the newspaper?" She said, placing her forefinger to the tip of her nose. There was a long moment of silence then we heard flies buzzing above the sink. "Come to think of it," Mother said, and scratched her head which she had wrapped in a hand-sewn kerchief; "It's the day of our Lord's self-sacrifice and people are not supposed to work on such a holy day, much less do home improvements like this. It'll be foolish to go public with my discovery. We'll keep this as our secret. No telling what kind of story some reporter would come up with. They are so sensational and blow everything out of proportion anyways."

Agreeing that we would keep it to ourselves, the three of us drew close into a huddle. Sister settled into Mother's lap, I stood to her side and together we gazed at the intricacies of a patch of fabric: that still had a faint glint of glamour and nobility. Golden threads ran through the design of grape leaves and ostriches. The colors of the design were still rich and reminded me of the egg yolk of soft boiled eggs, the green of ivy, and a scintillating blue that must have vibrated when they had put up the brocade. "Aw," Sister said, taking a bite off the banana and burped. Then she freed herself from Mother's hold and asked the one thing she'd always asked, "Can I touch it?"

Mother pushed her closer with one precise shove in the space between Sister's shoulder blades and then her nose pointed right at the center of the ostrich's fanned tail. Sister gathered up skinny Elizabeth and drew her doll's limp arms along the golden threads in the peacock's tail. "It moves," Sister exclaimed. I couldn't stand by any longer and just watch this, I had to see for myself. Shoving Sister to the side, I put both hands flat upon the patch of fabric and noticed nothing more but the brittle texture of fabric that was older than anybody I knew. "It's so crumbly and frail," I said. "Now I know why the tour guide tells us not to touch anything at the Rothenburg Castle," I said.

"That is so true," Mother said. "What we've got here is the relic of a gilded era in the history of this gristmill. In the past millers, bakers, and butchers thrived when there were hard times. Possibly they put up this expensive piece of wall covering when a crop had failed and they could drive up the price of flour sky-high. Peasants and townspeople would trade in their china and golden wedding rings for a kilo of flour," Mother said, and pushed the kerchief off of her forehead. "Girls what you are seeing here in our kitchen is what archeologists and those artists who restore ancient sites do for a living," She said. Now her voice dropped an octave lower, "there is method and precision in such work," She said, and cut a swatch of the brocade using a razor blade, kitchen knife and then more successfully her thumb nail. Then she placed it on the kitchen floor, next to a large sample of the pukey olive wall paint an entry from the millers' record keeping.

"All this information I just lifted off these four walls," Mother said. "If the newspaper were to write about it they would call these finds artifacts, material testimonials of times past." Mother straightened out her arched back, let out a deeply-felt sigh and looked at the two of us with greater solemnity than the minister during Sunday service. "You are the only witnesses of this important find," She said. "We might call it a moment of scientific adventure. And don't you forget that every moment lived in this kitchen, no matter how long ago, left a trace on the walls and remained there for us to find out its meaning." Sister and I looked back at her in silent awe.

After a pause, I asked, "What about our lives, Mom? What kind of traces are we going to leave behind?" The question remained hanging in the air of paint thinner. There was no answer forthcoming.

Mother resumed her labors with greater zest than before. Since she had uncovered the brocade which told us of a gilded era, her sanity and common sense had fallen by the wayside. She now worked the kitchen walls as if a chest of treasure lay embedded there. She talked loudly to herself, "There's got to be more!" And so she dug deeper and deeper to find out what other mysteries might be hidden below the mill's aged brocaded peacocks.

It was the Saturday before Easter. Still half asleep, I trotted to the toilet at the end of our long hallway. The neighbor's rooster hadn't crowed yet and I was surprised, a light was still burning in the kitchen. I entered and found Mother in the center of a pool of light seated on the cold kitchen tile floor still taking off pieces of brocade. By now she had changed her technique and was using a different arsenal of tools: tweezers, pincers, a spatula on which she usually served pieces of cake, and Dad's meat carving knife. In some places she had holes in the walls, gaping like open sores, the red of brick showing through, and where mortar had crumbled pine and oak studs sneered at her in defiant mockery.

At this wee hour I was a lone witness to her frenzy. I clutched my nightgown close to my body and stood in the far corner, the furthest I could retreat from her feverish activity and just watch. Although I didn't say a word, I was deeply concerned. Mother was going to tear down the kitchen, the only place where the four of us would sit and experience that we belonged together. "Please let her come to her senses," I prayed to Jesus, but quit halfway into my prayer, for my problem was no match compared to his suffering on the cross.

It was now Saturday, around noon, before Easter and the kitchen looked less inviting than a mole's hole. I vaguely remembered Mother's grand plan earlier this week. She had a dream of a brand-new kitchen and now she was going to implement it. She had persuaded Dad, who had looked skeptical throughout the entire account of her dream, to drive us all to the paint store.

"You think two large cans of paint will do the job?" She had asked the store clerk. "Let's make it three," She said before he could answer. Then Mother said "I want eggshell white paint, something neutral but not cold."

"Don't forget the paint thinner!" The store clerk said, and pushed his glasses up his ruddy nose. "You want to save those brushes, they're real horse hair and expensive," he said, and glided one brush across the back of his pawish hand.

"Now let's look at your wallpaper," Mother had suggested, and we gathered around a huge book of samples. Dad quickly lost lost interest because remodeling upset his sense of safety and belonging. Unlike Mother, he preferred to keep things as they are, as long as the millworks hummed twenty-four hours a day, he was content, even if the wall paint looked faded.

He loaded the paint into the van and waited there for Mother to finish her shopping. Meanwhile Mother was completely engrossed. She thumbed through the book forward and backward. "This is it!" Mother exclaimed, and put both hands flat down on a sample of silver thistles growing into a wreath against a background of a light blue sky. "We'll put wallpaper on the wall around the hallway door." "But they are nasty and sticky flowers," Sister had protested. "These ones won't hurt you," Mother said, and told the clerk she wanted him to cut twelve meters of this wallpaper. "It's a good number," She said, "and we always can get more if it's not enough."

Dad raised his eyebrows when Mother showed him our final choice.

"Thistles?", He said, and it sounded like ouch. But as usual he was a man of few words and so we bought the thistle wreaths in an ocean of blue and looked forward to spending Easter in a cheery flowery new kitchen. I envisioned that on Easter Sunday we would sit around the kitchen table and paint large eggs, laid by our fat brown chicken. The smell of vinegar that we used to fix the paint for the eggs would mingle with the aroma of the lamb roast broiling in the oven Dad would check in every once in a while and see whether dinner was ready. At some point he'd sit down with us and have a small glass of red wine, a piece of Mother's bread with liverwurst and horseradish, and then he would examine the freshly painted Easter eggs and not say a word. This had been my memory of past Easter Holidays. And memories have an inner need to rehearse themselves.

These images of the warmth and culinary comfort of past Easter holidays made my stomach churn and squeak like a rusty door.

We hadn't had a proper meal for two days. Sister and I had scurried like hungry mice into the pantry to steal a handful of cold rice and a snippet of chicken meat. In the evenings we nibbled at slices of rye bread and wedges of Swiss cheese. We ate on the run or standing alone in the pantry or the hallway watching the steam of our mouth fog up the window panes, where wet snow was banking against the sill from the outside.

It was Easter Sunday morning, and the church bells of *Saint Joesph rocked us out of bed. Snow flurries blew in dense sheets against the window pane and frost flowers on the glass dimmed the morning light. On my way to the lavatory I met Mother scurrying through the hallway, dragging a ladder behind her. She must have forgotten this is Easter I told myself and trolled back to bed to curl up under my warm down-bedding. By the time I finally rose the falling snow had bent the tree branches severely. Winter had come to re-visit on the rear end of March.

For Easter Sunday breakfast, Sister and I took the kitchen chairs from the hallway and installed them in the pantry. Even though there was nothing warm to eat in sight. At least we were going to sit down. "Let's treat ourselves," I suggested. So I buttered sandwiches for the two of us and piled them so high with raspberry and blackberry jam that Mother would have protested sharply had she been around. Once we had downed the sandwiches we both had mustaches of red and black. "I'm cold," Sister said, trying to take a swig from the jug of milk where a disk of ice prevented the flow at the neck of the bottle. "Why didn't Dad make a fire in the living room?" Sister asked, and blew into her cupped hands. It occurred to me that as far as I could remember Dad had always made a fire in the living room when it was cold outside. Something was terribly amiss here.

Sister started to sniff, and it wasn't just from the cold. I tried to comfort her, thinking of an excuse for Dad's neglect. "To get to the living room, he'd have to step through Mother's piles of taken-down wall. You know how much he dislikes when things are moved around, it reminds him of war times when he and his family were thrown out of their homes," I said, remembering what Mother had told me the day before. We burped and wiped each other's mouths.

"Let's see if Mother is done by now," Sister suggested.

We opened the kitchen door like thieves. Mother sat in her chair in the middle of her kitchen that looked like Lepers from Calcutta. I had seen them in Mother's book of people of different races, their bodies shrunken brown bags and they had holes on top of their bones.

"I'm done excavating," her shoulders sagged, arms hanged to her sides, with her tools at her feet. No more artifacts, the show's over kids."

"Aren't we going to have Easter eggs?" Sister asked.

"Is there going to be any cooked dinner today?" I added. Mother straightened up and wiped her hands on her jumper.

"This is one mess of a construction site, kids! How am I going to paint Easter eggs and cook a lamb roast when the walls are down? You tell me? Have you seen Dad, by any chance? I haven't seen his face since I got up early this morning. I am worried. He always gets up before me and starts a fire."

"But you took away his kitchen so he couldn't make his coffee and toast," Sister said. "And we froze our teeth eating in the pantry," she added, as her tone was plaintive, trembling, and close to crying.

Mother pulled down her kerchief and threw it to the floor. "First things first," Mother said. "This has gotten out of hand. We've got to find Dad. The mess won't run away, but Dad could disappear. This is serious," She said, and wrung her hands. *Dad's got a gun and....,* " her voice failed her and she started to sob.

Mother crying on Easter Sunday, that was about the worst thing I could imagine. As for Dad, I was less concerned. He was probably still watching the wheels turn around. Mother bent over and picked up her kerchief. She shook the dirt out and draped it around her matted hair. "Would you tighten this in the back?" She said. I made a double knot and Sister came up to her and shoved some stray wisps of hair back under her tight head cover. Mother wiped her wet eyes with her shirt sleeve.

"Forget history, archeology and the rest of that, my family is all I got. You are priority, especially today," She said. "I'm going to straighten this place out, as best as I can. I promise. We'll have some kind of Easter celebration later on. But not without Dad, we've got to find him first."

"Where shall we start looking Mom?" I asked. I felt the need to jump into action, do something, anything, just to rescue Mother from her tears and Dad from his lonely sentry post.

"Better pair up with your sister," Mother said. "She's your Dad's heart beetle, as he calls her. If she cries out for him, he won't be able to resist. He'll come out from wherever he's hiding."

I was feeling less important if our mission was to hinge on Sister, Dad's supposed heart beetle. If she was his darling, whose darling was I?

"You better hurry up or it might be too late." Mother sounded close to panic. "I didn't tell you girls, but I already have looked for your Dad this morning long before you got up. I yelled his name Willy, Willy, Willy! But wherever he is hiding he would not come out for me."

"Only you and Margret have a chance to change his mind. Maybe if the two of you...," Mother's voice cracked a tear streamed down her cheek. "His own children... still so small... If you would, *yell Daddy,* with all your might, louder than you've ever done before... and if you'd pray in your heart to Jesus that he might pluck Dad out of his darkness and...." Her voice broke again and she wept into her lap. Mother's whole body bent sharply like the branches of the poplar trees under masses of snow.

"Don't worry Ma," Sister said, "I'll bring him back to you. He listens to my voice. I am his heart beetle. No else can do it like I." Mother barely looked up, but she did not move her head that was still buried in her hands. Sister wheeled and ran out of the kitchen leaving the door wide ajar. The cold from the dark hallway flooded in, and Mother gathered her arms around her chest. "I'm cold to the bones," she said, then, she started to shiver.

"I'm going with sister," I said and I was out the door. Sister must have been flying, because, I only heard her slam the door about three stair flights ahead of me. I heard her screaming at the top of her voice. "Daddy, Daddy, Daddy it's me. I'm coming, wait. Don't do anything bad to yourself. Please, Daddy, pleas... Mom's gonna paint Easter eggs and cook a lamb and we'll have Easter in the kitchen.

Dad...Dad we need you. It's so cold without you, we're freezing our teeth and the milk is frozen too."

I finally caught up with her. "Wait, wait for me!" I grabbed her by the shoulders from behind. It was strangely dark in the mill. The snow falling outside kept the daylight at a dim setting. "You can't save him all by yourself, you're just four years old, too small for a big job like that."

Sister turned around and I saw the dark pupils of her eyes, bigger than hazelnuts. "But Mother said...," She was about to protest and remind me of her heart beetle status. "I know what Mother said," I interrupted her whining, "And now I'm telling you, *it's you and I, we're in this together*." I took her by the hand and started to lead. "It's so dark here," She said. "Turn on a light, or I'll fall down the stairs."

"We don't have time for that," I said, and led her down the stairway. My taking the lead piqued her defiant spirit. Dad would call her the stubborn one, and this was the way she was going to behave with every fiber of her chubbiness. "I'm going to turn on the light. Let go of me!" She said, and resisted me going any further. Finally she succeeded in pulling away from me. With both hands, she groped the wall to find a light switch. "Yuck, this is cold and wet," She said, and drew away from the wall. "Sure it's wet," I said, have you forgotten that the Ortzan flows right outside the wall. Water seeps through everything even walls as thick as you are. There, I had it out, a little barb in about Sister's flesh just to remind her that she was a plump little rollmops. Usually it would infuriate her if I'd make remarks like that, but this time she just bit her lips and started crying again.

"Where's Daddy?" She sobbed, "Without the lights we'll never find him." "We will," I said, and took her cold hand in mine.

"Daddy, Daddy we're coming. *Please don't play hide and seek any more*. I'm tired of playing this game." Sister'voice sounded like the sirens in war movies - up and down - and so shrill it could make even frozen milk curdle. *"Daddy come out, so we can paint Easter eggs!"* I had to laugh to myself. It never ceased to amaze me how Sister could string together matters of emergency with those of a far smaller importance.

Suddenly she jerked, freed herself of me, jumped about four stairs at a time, and was out of reach. "I know wher's he is," She yelled and took off like a bullet.

Now I was looking for the light switch. Without her pudgy hand in mine, I felt anxious. Descending the steep and narrow stairway in the dark was too dangerous a thing to do all by myself. Finally I found the switch and the light came on just in time for me to see Sister disappear behind the door to the coal cellar.

I didn't dare cry out for Dad like sister had. What would I say that she hadn't already put out. Other than the whirring drone of the machinery and the ever-present rushing sounds of the river behind the wall, there was nothing to tell me whether Sister had found Dad. But wait - the door to the coal cellar opened again and two shadowy figures emerged.

At the same time, I heard the heavy footfall of someone who was hesitant to come down the stairs. My head swiveled around, and I saw Mother blotting out the light behind her. She had followed us.

Mother approached me and took my hand. "Maggi must have found him," She said. We both stood on the middle of the steps, not going further either way. We just stood there and waited for those two figures to come closer. Mother's hand squeezed mine tighter.

Just then the light behind us went out. "Wait for us, we're coming up," Sister yelled. "I don't see you," I yelled back.

"You don't need to see us, you know what we look like," Sister hollered back. Even though she was contrary, I liked the tone of her voice. It had volume and confidence.

Within seconds the light came on again. Dad held his hand in front of his eyes to shade out the glare. They were both approaching us at a slow pace. Sister had him in tow, dragging him toward us like they drag boats to shore.

Without his perennial cap on his bald head, Dad kept shielding his eyes. Had he cried like the rest of us, so I wondered and searched his body for other signs of grief. Shuffling slowly behind Sister, he looked limp, even hurt. "Did you fall Dad?" I called out to him. There was no answer. Mother put her other hand on top of my head and shushed me. "Leave him alone. When there's hurt it's best not to probe any deeper."

Mother and I waited in the kitchen for the rest of the family to join us. We left the door wide open and gazed out into the dimly lit hallway expecting them to emerge any moment. Mother held a broom close to her bosom but didn't sweep. Next to her, I stood holding the dust pan.

Finally Sister and Dad stepped into the kitchen. Dad wore his woolen winter coat. His hands were in leather gloves. "Were you going to leave us Dad?" I asked since he looked dressed for outside winter weather.

"Mother, would you find my hat!" He said and his voice sounded mechanical, not a sign of feeling. "I'm taking the girls to the movies. They deserve some holiday treat." He took off his gloves and put them in his right pocket. I followed every motion of his, as if I hadn't seen him for ages. Something stuck out of the other coat pocket. It wasn't his kerchief, nor his cap. I looked more closely. It was the shiny handle of a gun.

"What d'you say? Would you like to see a movie?" Dad asked, and turned toward me. I averted my glance from the shiny object in his pocket and looked back at him shrugging my shoulders. "Go get the paper and we'll see what they're showing," He said, and I went to the living room, cold as a freezer, to get the holiday edition of the Ortzan Messenger from there. "What about if I take you girls to the movies? Anna Louise, get the paper and we'll check what kind of kid shows they have." Grateful that the frozen stillness of our family together broke into simple steps, I leaped to the stack of papers Mother had left in the kitchen so she could use them to clean brushes, and to cover the tiled floor. The weekend edition was still intact and I handed it to Dad in a shy way, eyes cast downward. We still didn't look at each other but the handing over of the paper was a contact of sorts and I felt reassured by it. With Dad unfolding the paper, Sister slid from his lap, thumb in mouth. Still, she leaned against his side in easy comfort.

"What about Snow White and the Seven Dwarfs?" He suggested, and sounded like he had already made up his mind. "You two used to listen to that story on the record player over and over again. Now you've got a chance to see it on the big screen. Come on now, get yourself ready! The show starts in about an hour."

Mother dressed us up quickly, mittens, and hand knitted wool caps with pompons. We slid into our winter coats. "And don't forget to wrap the scarves around your neck; its blustery cold out there!" Mother said.

She was proud that our winter outfits, which were made during countless hours during the night when everybody was asleep. They were color-coordinated and our identical clothes made Sister and I look like twins, except that I was thin like a stick, and Sister was chubby like a cherub. So when people saw us they were quizzical in their guesses. "You aren't twins, are you?" They asked, and I got to explain then that I was fully 18 months older and two inches taller than sister.

At the movies, Dad sat between us. And I looked at him from the side when the movie started. After our rescue mission and Dad's hiding in the recesses of the mill, he appeared now as unreal as the pictures on the big screen. Here he sat, slouched in the cushioned velvet chair next to me with movie glimmer flickering past his face. He didn't seem to notice me peering at him. He seemed vacant, not inhabiting his body, still in his hideout, holding the revolver in his lap, then lifting it up to his temple and dropping his hand slowly back into his lap. That is how I envisioned him in the dark room where transmission belts waited to be greased and repaired. Some were worn thin and shiny by abrasion, like Dad's nerves after placing his gun at his forehead, and the thought of the explosion bursting his brain. The ugly mess of it. He must have thought of it and shaken all over.

What if his children found him, spattered with blood, sprawled across the floor? Surely, he had thought of Sister and I, still so young, and he couldn't bring his hesitating heart to break the connection yet. He must have seen Sister and I doing acrobatics on the bars he had attached on either side of an old pear tree. The one higher than the other was my territory. Sister had the lower bar, as she was smaller and altogether plumper. We would both hang from the crook of our knees, dangling freely, looking at his Leica camera, heads upside down. We'd smile big toothy smiles while our white underwear gleamed in the morning sun. The canopy of our cotton dresses draped over our shoulders like a parachute upon landing. He had captured those moments on film many times, enlarged and framed them, and put us right over his head in the bedroom. So we'd smile at him, upside down and all, and make that morning in May forever lasting.

I knew that picture must have saved his life. I settled further into the upholstery and was resigned to Dad being somewhere else, as long as he was breathing. And his wrist was still warm to my tentative touch. In fact his palm turned around as if to invite my small palm to nestle, but then I didn't know for sure, so I let the opportunity slide by.

Chapter 10

Aunt Elma

Aunt Elma had a good-natured look about her. Her face was as full as the fullest harvest moon. Her two eyes twinkling, happy, but shrewd beads set in this roundness. A reddish-blueish whirl of veins ran through her cheeks, giving her a ruddy complexion. Her short nose poked toward heaven at the tip. This I read as a sign of optimism. However anyone who ever met Aunt Elma was mightily impressed by her rotund body which she carried with as much grace as a big sized-cat. The soft and substantial layer of blubber that upholstered her bones cushioned her whole personality. In my positively biased view of my great benefactor during the first ten years of my life, Aunt Elma, because of her soft flesh, rosy complexion, and sweet disposition, was one big, juicy, and ripe peach.

More impressive yet were Aunt Elma's boobs. Like two pillows that have been much rested on, these boobs padded her chest substantially despite their sagging nature. All the daily nuisances with their minor shock waves, that tend to shake up most grown-ups, bounced right off Aunt Elma's well cushioned chest. She survived it all with a broad smile.

In one of my coziest childhood fantasies, I'd crawl between her melon sized boobs and take refuge there. I imagined myself nestled like a newly-fledged sparrow between these two giant soft pears of hers that had turned longer and flatter with the passage of more than sixty years of wear and tear. With one of her pink nipples dangling on either side of me, I'd get memories of the hung-up flesh, so deeply pink and tender, of slaughtered rabbit. Tucked into the warm folds of her stomach, I saw myself lying back and waiting for that ultimate dream come true - her reaching with her pudgy hand into her low neckline, parting those two benign boobs and handing me a sugar cone with scoops of spiraled whipped cream.

Now these were my dreams of Cockaigne, the fabled land of flying roasted ducks and chocolate cakes flying through the air into the gaping wide mouths of all those lazy folks getting suntanned in lounge chairs. Aunt Elma's boobs were the perfect backdrop for such easy gluttonous living.

Twice every week, I came within reach of this dream of mine. It was Aunt Elma's habit to walk by foot the length and width of our small town and stop by the highest quality grocers for gossip, with her one arm-long shopping list of delectable foods.

However, her visit to the dairy was the focal point of my urgently expecting her back home in the mill. I knew her shopping routine from accompanying her on various trips to the town's merchants. At the creamery, she would get milk fresh on draft. Aunt Elma routinely brought her metal milk can on her shopping spree to be filled up with two liters of milk to feed her black and white tom-cat and to serve me an occasional cup of milk, accompanied with a butter sandwich with blackberry jam. For herself, she liked to pour milk into her strong morning coffee brew. I loved to watch the lady behind the shiny counter push down the chrome lever and dispense that most wondrous liquid *milk* which spilled forth from a gleaming clean chrome spigot. Cleanliness was the number one commandment of this place.

Other items on her dairy list included stinky Limburger, which, when cooking a simple dinner at home, she would blend together with butter and spread it over steaming boiled potatoes. This typical peasant dish together with buttermilk frequently comprised her frugal meal. The potatoes were special indeed, small golden balls, newly harvested by her brother's family of weathered and hardy Heideners, an especially frugal breed of peasants indigenous to the mountain range that divides my homeland Swabia from the rough Bavarians.

Since Aunt Elma loved the rich flavor of fresh butter and nearly every food item she put in her mouth, she would also request one half pound of sweet cream butter and one dozen eggs. A biblical number, that she, being a devout Catholic, liked to apply that to the mundane business of shopping. Also medium-thin slices of Emmentaler with more air holes than matter.

The absolute whopper on her dairy list, as far as I'm concerned, consisted of an occasional order of one sugar cone of whipped cream. The whip also was dispensed out of a shiny chrome spigot. At times, when I held an important seat in her ample heart, Aunt Elma would expand into greater than usual generosity and motion the store clerk to pump not just one but two artfully spiraled dollops of white creamy fluff into the sugar cone and then carefully wrap it in wax paper.

In the late afternoon, having canvassed the town's latest news far and wide and having made arrangements which funerals to attend and which to avoid, she finally became weary of carrying the heavy shopping net and basket brimful with goodies. So she'd come home and holler my name down the hallway with a sweet intonation.

When I came rushing into her wood fire warmed kitchen, I'd find her there relaxing in a rustic peasant chair, knees falling wide apart, unconcerned with feminine crotch protocol, free and open like usually only men sit.

It was time for what I called the "food parade," one of several highly idiosyncratic rituals that punctuated Aunt Elma's life, and made it magical in my experience.

With a festive glimmer in her eyes, she'd lay out her groceries on the big oak wood table and exhibit her food riches with Taurean sensuality.

As far as I can think back, she arranged the lineup of cheeses, cold cuts, sausages, choice cuts of meat, rye bread, and crisp rolls from the bakery in the very same order week after week. However, she played one wild card, the folded little package of wax paper. Its size (single or double ecstasy) as well as its strategic position within the layout would change, and this was Aunt Elma's trump which she held over my rising excitement. Regardless of the smell of fresh baked poppy and the sting of Limburger in my nose, like an eagle would transfix a bunny rabbit, I had my eyes glued on that odd-shaped wax paper with delicious grease spots bleeding through.

Patience was Aunt Elma's strongest suit and she expected even more from her contemporaries. So in due and steady course she would unwrap each and every packaged food item and hold it up beneath my nose for me to get a whiff of its goodliness. Everything passed my nostrils in slow motion. I saluted every passing edible by nodding with my most genuine approval for this was part of the ceremony, which in turn made Aunt Elma happy. Once she had proven herself a wise and discriminating shopper, even a six year old girl like Anna could appreciate that.

The solemn pace of the food revue made me think of all the solemnity and soul elevation I had experienced when visiting Sunday's Mass. Baptized a Protestant, but I had the opportunity to attend an occasional Mass by accompanying Catholic friends who had entranced me with stories of seeing Jesus bleed on the cross, and Mother Mary wink at them from the altar.

I found out that the Catholics truly knew how to do ritual and ceremony; they even perfumed the air with myrrh, which made me slightly dizzy and lightheaded. I fully comprehended that many gestures and solemn pacing were needed in any ritual that promised to actually wash away all of your sins. The consecrated food that the priest placed in the sinner's mouth was Spartan though, one small gulp of wine and a bite of bread. And in my Protestant community it was even sparser than that.

However, Aunt Elma's food ceremony culminated in her ministering to me one sumptuous and luscious treat, which immediately removed any and all misgivings I may have held against any of the neighbors' kids, Sister, parents and other bothersome people.

I always held my breath, when she finally reached out ceremoniously and grabbed that one remaining food item that waited urgently for me on the table. Like the best of any Catholic priest I had ever observed ministering any sacrament, Aunt Elma passed that cone with whipped cream, still wrapped in translucent paper, into my perfectly still and spellbound hands, cupped like a bowl to receive the holiest host of all communion.

Once, I got to unfold the paper and assessed the size of the scoop, whether double or single generosity, the ceremoniously placed food parade changed into one rapid-forward food orgy. My eager fingers drove in to the white creamy mess like burrowing rodents. Fingertips punctured and hollowed the mounds of white softness, picking up globs of whipped ecstasy. My mouth was an unceasingly garden gate, wide open until all the whiteness filled it with a velvety taste of utter bliss.

I never got to lounge in Aunt Elma's lap though. And the true color of her nipples remains a secret to any mortal, except her long deceased husband Albert. I never ever nestled between her two giant pears though, because I did not have wish fulfillment in this. My yearning for the ultimate embrace, the vision of it, loomed large in my fantasies.

I don't know how to measure Aunt Elma's intelligence because unlike her voluminous chest and forearms, as big as full grown trunks of walnut trees, her intelligence did not show up conspicuously. However, I always suspected that she was playing a shrewd camouflage game with her mind power, making sure that things were done exactly as she had envisioned. This power of persuasion was flowing from her body in unmistakable signals. The way she raised her eyebrow when someone would suggest something that did not sit right with her. Or the manner she crossed her powerful arms in front of her boobs proved to be as formidable an obstacle as a German built tank in the Third Reich days. Nobody dared to disregard her silently displayed iron will once locked into that posture.

With no children of her own blood, she held close and dear the memory of her two stepsons who died barely into their twenties, on a *World War Two* battleground. Aunt Emma held their memory as close to her bosom as that ivory clasp which graced her big cleavage, with the profile of an Austrian Empress who had mothered a dozen or so offspring, and had launched them into marriage all over Europe's royal families. Now, that was one whopper of achievement on Aunt Elma's list of achievements.

Upon entering her cold living room, heated only on holy Sundays, I could immediately spot Albert and Heinrich, centrally positioned up there on the marble mantle above the fireplace. Here they stayed youthfully preserved in brass frames in their early twenties, right before they were sent off sent with kids as young as sixteen years old, to shore up the crumbling German battle lines deep within freezing and starving Russia. All Aunt Elma knew about their fate was that they ended up two anonymous frozen casualties sprawled on the body-littered battlefield of Stalingrad. 150,000 German mothers lost their life's blood and everything they had prayed for.

The more I gazed at Albert and Heinrich, the more I became aware that their strained camera smile was falling away from their lips, or so I've been told by Aunt Elma. "That photographer took *so damn long* to get the shot. Here they were already getting mentally prepared to shore up the deadliest battle line in all of Europe, and that damn flash wouldn't come off! A bad omen indeed."

While the smile is waning, the mischievous look in their eyes still has a scorpunlike sting to it. For inscrutable reasons, both of these two lads, tightly buttoned-up in the German Reich's uniform, had their eyeballs screwed heavenward showing a crescent of conspicuous white underneath.

Now, these white crescents never ceased to intrigue me in people. Sometimes at the dinner table, Dad would roll back his eyes all the way into the skull, and there was nothing but scary whiteness in his eyes for me to behold.

Mother told me once that habitually screwed up eyeballs meant the person was a notorious liar. The same was true for people licking their lips in between bits of talking. Mother was an expert on reading bodies and finding clues to otherwise hidden personality traits.

The love between Aunt Elma, Albert and Heinrich was spun over time in her memory into one continuous thread of pranks and practical jokes, featuring herself as centerpiece. The most gullible mother ever to be suckered into any slapstick comedy.

Heinrich and Albert's all time classic prank was so bawdy that I curled my nose in disgust when I first heard Aunt Elma relate it to me, in her most animated gestures and facial expressions.

In those good old days, as Aunt Elma loved to say, comedy time started when evening fell over the mill. The busy pace had slowed down, teams of horses and oxen were homeward bound after the peasants had emptied their wagons of wheat to be milled between stones. At this cozy time Albert and Heinrich would gather around Aunt Elma. She sitting with knees falling open in relaxed comfort at her sewing station near the woodstove where she used to darn the clothes of her three men folk; and darn it so neatly it was hard to spot the former tear once she was finished with her mending.

Now close your eyes, Mother! They'd tell her while prancing like tomcats in heat. She never failed them. Gladly, Aunt Elma feigned to be as innocent and unsuspecting as a newborn lamb, and she'd close her eyes so tightly not even a flicker of the boys' wicked conspiracy entered her sight.

Meanwhile, Heinrich and Albert slipped off woolen socks and approached Aunt Elma from the front and the back, both of them hiding their three days' old harvest of accumulated foot odors behind their backs. Now keep your eyes shut and *guess* what's right under your nose! Playing her part to perfection, Aunt Elma would take a deep breather and then, lo and behold, she'd erupt like a volcano. At first she'd gasp in violent spasms, having her nose filled with the odors of four socks, all crumpled into one ball of stench flush up to her flared nostrils. She'd cough and laugh at the same time, hardly getting any air in between.

The laughing cough visibly reverberated through Aunt Elma, and pulsed into the outer layers of her blubber making it jiggle and wiggle. The folded mounds of her belly were one sight to behold, as they heaved up and down from the billowing of her laughter. For a couple of minutes, Aunt Elma's body went into earthquake tremors.

Wide eyed and mouths open, Heinrich and Albert watched speechless and utterly puzzled how such a simple trick, even though they had repeated it countless times before, admittedly with slight variations, could throw their mother into tribulations that looked from afar as if she was being submitted to an act of exorcism.

At special times, so Aunt Elma told me with glee in her eyes, these rascals had a particularly naughty trick up their sleeves. While she held her eyes tightly closed shut in strict obedience to the rather simple rules of the game, Heinrich and Albert would strip down to bare bottoms, and proceed to impress Aunt Elma with the rich aroma of their underpants. They would hold up to her nose those choicest parts of their undergarments, the brown spots as they called them. In these good old days of no flush, primitive toilets, and news print to wipe one's ass, such brown spots were especially dark and pungent smelling.

No matter, whether stinky socks, brown spotted underwear, or the rancid smell of sweaty undershirts, any and all of these odorous affairs, offensive to any regular citizen of my town, sent Aunt Elma into paroxysms of laughter and darn near into suffocation. However, at the end, she always emerged like a newborn babe, light as a lark, and truly purged from any heavy feelings she might have harbored against one or another of the male triangle that she comfortably inhabited at its very epicenter.

When, I first heard this story and noticed the excited twinkle in her eyes, and her saying aaahs and ooohs, as if these two pranksters had just presented her with a double scoop of whipped cream rather than smelly socks, I wondered how Aunt Elma could get so excited over plain offensive body stink. I pondered her potential reaction if I were to pull this trick on her. After all, my feet and socks weren't half as smelly as the boys, since I washed up frequently and changed my socks every day. Besides, I knew that boys by nature were so much more of a mess than girls when it comes to basic cleanliness.

I never had the gumption to play a smelly trick on dear Aunt Elma, as I had an inner shy voice tell me that *being just a girl* I wouldn't fare too well instigating such bawdy comedy. Aunt Elma, had a chemistry with Albert and Heinrich that she couldn't replicate with any girl, like me. Girls, (so I had learned from overhearing my grief stricken Dad talk with my Mother,) when my baby brother had died of leukemia, will never measure up to boys.

This particular loving earthly body chemistry between her and the boys, the like I have never experienced first-hand in my own sweet life, made Aunt Elma sit unabashedly with her legs wide apart, it made her jiggle and giggle, and it so much piqued the guys that they would go beyond common decency and actually drop their pants right in front of her.

Perhaps, so I speculated, it was the muskier smell of males, their voices that register about half an octave lower, and one kilo graver than mine, their sprouting facial hair, the bristling strength in their biceps, the wienerwurst that dangles between their legs…the possibility of them going off into combat and never making it back…?

At times, Aunt Elma's gleeful reminiscing of those naughty good old days together with the boys made me a bit sad and envious, for I had seen nobody delight in my smelly socks. As deemed proper for girls, I would discreetly dispose of my underwear in the laundry basket and hide my panties under more neutral garments if any brown spots soiled the crotch. In my wildest imagination, I positively could not conceive that anybody would ever love me so much as to thrive on past memories of my dirty underwear once I was dead and gone.

Except for a large emerald stone embedded in gold around her pudgy little finger, there was little in Aunt Elma's appearance and demeanor that would tell the world that in all likelihood she was the wealthiest widow in town. I was one of the few she initiated into the secrets of her riches. Riches that were scattered on the Alb plateau in the form of tillable acreage and fruit orchards handed down over centuries by her stout Alb peasant lineage. She held riches in the form of jewelry that she kept in chests rather than on her wrist or neck. For in her estimate, ostentatiousness counted as a cardinal sin, or rather a major mistake, for it would make people envious and jealous of her. If they saw her all decked out in her riches, she reckoned her kin would get all itchy and impatient counting the days toward her final departure. Having a sizable inheritance on her own, she potentiated these gifts by marrying a widowed miller. Even in the Dark Ages, millers and bakers had plenty of bacon hanging from their rafters in the pantry and gold coins stashed away in odd places. Unlike other common folk, their craft made them indispensable to all those who wanted to eat bread and that was just about everybody.

Aunt Elma had told me stories of her husband's wheeling and dealing with poor Alb peasants who journeyed down the long steep mountain road with a team of oxen pulling newly thrashed wheat, barley, and rye to be milled into various flours and feedstuff for chickens and hogs. Hans and his brother and business partner Albert were the premier millers in town having the largest and most modern milling machines engineered, and put into place in the mid-nineteenth century by men who came all the way from the British Isles.

Unsophisticated and barren of cash, as most peasants on the rough Alb Mountains were, they carted their grain harvest into the large garage paved with wooden cobbles; several wooden carts could park there in a cluster with Albert and Hans inspecting the haul of grain. They'd fetch a fistful of wheat grain and smell it, rub it between their fingers, and let it sift to the ground. This stuff is awfully wet, we'll have to elevate it up to the granaries and fry it for several weeks, they'd comment to the simple peasant standing next to his teem of oxen. That means we have to invest our precious space, man power and time. As most peasants dealt with the millers on a non-cash barter basis, meaning they'd receive flour and animal feed for their grain, the millers had much latitude as to how much flour they would receive in return for a cart load of grain. If the peasant needed more flour than the millers would offer him in exchange, then family heirlooms, gold brooches, wedding china, and silverware were thrown in to make up the balance.

Aunt Elma told me of an underground cache of peasant heirlooms, all co-mingled in one big heap taking up the basement of one of the bigger storage sheds. If I were to dig in this heap of forgotten treasures, so she told me, I'd find bracelets with embedded gems, blue and gray Bavarian stoneware, pots for aging sauerkraut next to eggshell-thin teacups made of the finest porcelain with golden and silver rims. But, alas, most of it was broken to pieces, due to the carelessness of the milling brothers who had little esteem for fragile beauty and antiquity. However, these brothers both were driven with the hunger for more and more things, even though once acquired they'd end up in that burial site of trade-in treasures. Their greed would drive them to bizarre extremes I was told by a neighbor rather than Aunt Elma.

During hard times, when after and during war and depression, famine stalked the farmhouses, Albert and Hans and their wily predecessors in earlier times conspired with the owners of the sawmill, who were upstream neighbors of the flour mill. In their shrewdness they devised this scheme; they would increase the bulk of flour by mixing in ample amounts of sawdust. And by this deceitful route more heirlooms piled up in the depths of her nautilus shells arranged on the fireplace mantel. The emerald green of this ring of hers spoke to me of the color of the ocean and its inscrutable mystery.

In my awe and wonder vis-à-vis this mysterious gem, I would touch with a tiny caress the multiple facets of the stone, and stroke its perimeter with the delicate touch of my finger tips. And while doing so, I pondered who had worn this heirloom before it banded Aunt Elma's left pinky. She vaguely remembered, like most of her treasure, it was a barter item, dating back to inflation times in the twenties when once again the cyclical hunger dance visited those who had no land to provide pasture for cows and grain for bread.

Evony, the wife of the president of the bank couldn't bear the sight of her children gnawing at bacon rinds and the crust of dark rye bread for supper. At this juncture of time, the value of the Reich Mark had bottomed out and people went grocery shopping with wheelbarrow loads of bills. Still, these mounds of paper money had only negligible buying power which eroded on a daily basis.

Sometimes a whole cart loaded with money didn't buy the food to have a decent supper. Baker, butchers and dairy grocers all wanted valuables like gold jewelry and crystal dishes rather than currency that would lose its value overnight. Only those frugal Alb peasants plying their rocky and unyielding acreage had the wherewithal to fill their stomachs and spare some of the food staples to barter for other necessities like woolen clothing and fuel for heat and lighting. However, city folks like Evony had to raid their jewelry boxes and part with the most delicious of their gems, just so the family would not starve.

I have rings studded with rubies, diamonds, fire opals, sapphires... you name it, Aunt Elma told me, *in* one of her most extroverted moments. She had loosened her notorious secrecy surrounding the riches which slept in dark places and hardly ever would see the light of the day, for fear of arousing people's greed. The emerald ring in its oceanic glory was her favorite though, and it had become an appendage of her voluminous body, just as that brooch that managed to bridge that enormous cleft between her right and left bosom.

Chapter 11

Fox in the Hen House

The curtain is about to rise and the kitchen circus show will be on in a minute! Sister and I stood next to each other, we anticipated Dad to enter any moment now.

Maggi and I much enjoyed his rendition of Punch and Judy, the flea circus gig. Alternating between awe and giggles, we would watch Dad chase the lice that had jumped on him in the early morning when he had collected fresh eggs in the chicken house.

The door flung open and there he was, with a sly and at the same time tortured smile on his face. Seeing that smile, we instantly knew Dad was ready to go into slapstick combat with his tormentors. Dad took pride in having us cheer him on as his loyal audience when he went after these itchy parasites.

He flashed a smile and acknowledged our presence with a wink to Maggi and me. Then he got started right away. First he set his left foot on a kitchen chair and rolled up his white long johns past his knees. Sister and I drew closer to see the action.

With sighs of relief, Dad first scratched the area where the lice had dug in. Then he got more serious about the chase and combed and plowed with his fingers every inch from his knees to his ankles. As he did this, he left red streaks running down in parallel like the furrows in a field.

By the minute now, he would turn up the intensity of his wild chase of the elusive lice. He slapped, and pinched, moaned, and cussed.

When he was hunting for lice, Dad's facial expression changed rapidly like the weather in April. First anger would wrinkle his brows and ruffle his forehead into a knotted frown. Next, we gawked at Dad's expression of complete elation, as the frown uncurled into a broad smile, and a mischievous glint flickered in his eyes. I knew from experience, that in those moments when his face lit up like a Christmas tree, Dad had snagged one of his tormentors!

"There, I've got the rascal!" Dad yelled with glee and held something smaller than a pinhead up in the air. He examined it as if it were a shining trophy.

Without much ceremony, he squeezed the sucker between his fingers into louse pulp and rubbed his hands on the side of his denim work pants. It all proceeded as seen one hundred times before. Still, it never failed to intrigue us. Since this species of parasites specialize in pestering fowl, scientists call them bird lice. As one inspects them up close, they look like flat bodied spiders.

While they chew and nibble at the chickens' feathers and skin, these pests debilitate their hosts and make them susceptible to further disease. Once they got infested with this pest, our chickens would lose weight and no longer produce eggs. It was as if the lice sucked the life out of them.

Although bird lice prefer poultry, they are also prone to jump on people, for a change of scenery. As soon as they have landed on an unsuspecting host, they dig in their mandibles and bite off tiny chunks of skin. These bites cause a terrific itching sensation. Dad told us, he couldn't think straight until he would catch and kill the beast.

For some unknown reason, the lice in the hen house didn't jump on me or Sister. Possibly our body odor, which at the time was all peaches anyway, didn't appeal to them. Dad, however, smelled of garlic, and bitter almonds, with a sprinkling of cheap cologne. This scent walked with him wherever he went. It was his second shadow.

The way Dad smelled would make my nose twitch. His scent was too musky and male for my taste. Pets, like our dog, would come close to Dad, take a sniff, and then retreat with a puzzled look. Like me and Sister, our pets also must have questioned the way Dad smelled. Bird lice however, had taken a liking to Dad's body odor, for they delighted to jump on him and gnaw at his body.

Now that he had squeezed the louse out of existence, Dad sighed a huge sigh of relief. He could think straight again.

To Sister's and my surprise, on this particular day, Dad was in a more sociable and chatty mood. "You two ladies, the show's over. But there's something I'd like to tell you, so sit down right next to Daddy."

"You want to hear a scary story?" Dad asked, and gave us a somber look with an intermittent mischievous twinkle in his eyes. He loved to make us sit at the edge of our seats.

"You caught the wild animal that kills our chickens!" Sister and I spurted out at once.

Our whole family had been on red alert for an entire week now, because some wild animal had pillaged the hen house twice within less than a week. So far, the thief had stolen only chicken soup material, as Dad and Mother would call senior chickens who had retired from the egg laying business. Soon, however, he could be ravaging our premier egg laying hens.

"What kind of animal killed our chickens?" I asked, swinging my feet rapidly in and out from under my chair. "Let's start at the beginning." Dad made a blocking motion with his hands to signal that he was going to ward off our avalanche of questions.

For days now, my imagination had been out of control. Before curling up in bed, I'd see ferocious animals prowling our hen house. At first, I imagined predators native to our woods. A weasel perhaps or a marten? But decided they were too mundane and unexciting. Just to keep my fantasy working at high pitch, I decided that the intruder had to be a truly wild animal, *one that could kill people*, hopefully a wolf. Although officially extinct in central Europe, driven by hunger wolves could have quite possibly migrated west from their native woods in Russia.

Or better yet. Bears roamed the woods at the edge of my home town. They had migrated all the way from Siberia, and also driven by starvation, would invade people's premises, including our chicken house.

I got a tingly sensation just thinking of bears and wolves roving in the neighborhood. Blood rushed to my head at the thought that I might come face to face with one of these great predators in our backyard. These fantasies, *to my own surprise*, made me sleep more soundly, feeling secure and safe in my warm and cozy bed next to sister who cultivated similar fantasies.

"Let me start at the beginning, O.K.? I'm going to tell you bit by bit what I saw this morning when you girls were still fast asleep under your covers."

Not in keeping with his storytelling plan, possibly by accident, Dad dropped a bomb, right in the middle of the kitchen.

"By the way did you hear me shoot my shotgun around 5 A.M.? Twice!"

Margret's mouth fell open and I think mine did too. "Did you kill him?" We asked at the same time. But Dad wouldn't bat an eye. Born a Taurus astrologically, he was going to tell his story in a slow and sensual way, like going up a sinuous mountain pass and enjoying the panorama at every bend. So Dad prolonged his account with detail and chronological correctness, and thus made us draw up our behinds to the very edge of our seats.

Dad had heard much commotion in the chicken house and when he checked he found a bloody trail leading from one of the chicken cubbies to the center of the chicken house. There the chicken thief had left a bloody mess of brown feathers. Dad counted and indeed one chicken was missing.

I remember how Dad was so upset that day, he actually skipped the louse hunt and scratching himself all over, he reported on the chicken house incident instead; all the while squirming and wincing as lice pestered his legs. "I'll blast that bastard's head off with one blow, next time he dares come close to our chickens!" Dad had said and positioned his arms like he was holding his shotgun. Since Dad was a great marksman, we knew this was serious business.

A couple of days passed without anything exciting happening. Our anticipation and alertness started to flag. On the third morning after the first chicken raid, Dad was busy oiling the gears of the mill works. Sister and I woke up in a startle as the first sun rays flooded into our bedroom. Prince, our watchdog, barked louder and fiercer than usual and he wouldn't let up.

When Dad came to the kitchen that morning, he merely went through the motions of his routine louse chase, without his usual expression of elation once he squashed them. "He got away a second time!" Dad admitted in a grumbly voice. It was hard for him to say this, because he deemed himself an expert hunter, having shot more wild doves in flight than any of his hunting buddies in his native Romania. "That makes it two big old chickens in four days. He must have supported a whole family clan on chicken meat or put it away in his cache." He said like a detective, Dad was starting to figure out the lifestyle of the chicken thief. Dad scratched his bald head. This gesture made me wonder whether a bird louse had actually nestled in some small crevice on his shiny head.

"And Prince, this lazy bum of a watchdog, is not around when something major like this happens. I bet he's been prowling the neighborhood, hanging out at the butchers. If he had been here on either of these days, that rascal would have never dared trespass on our land."

In his rotten mood, Dad piled all the blame on Prince, even though the dog had gone to the butchers for years now with our parents' silent approval. For thus the dog had supplemented his diet with fresh meat, mostly guts, that the butcher would routinely toss out to him. In fact, my parents had been proud of Prince, pointing out to friends that this dog was smart and independent, whereby he could make it on his own if push came to shove. "Or maybe he went around screwing one of the bitches in the neighborhood!" Dad was visibly upset, by what he perceived as major betrayal - *Prince's failure to do his assigned job.*

I straightened up in my chair and braced my arms defiantly. Morally, I just had to intervene on Prince's behalf. "He did bark like mad this morning, Dad, didn't you hear?"

"Sure he barked, but the damage was done by that time. The damn dog came home from his pleasure trip when that rogue was already off with the chicken in his muzzle." Dad had made up his mind; Prince was going to be the scapegoat one way or another.

I felt terribly outraged seeing that Prince, my longtime baby-sitter and most loyal companion was held responsible for the chicken theft. "Prince hasn't betrayed us, Dad! It's just a freaky accident." Dad gave me a slightly puzzled look.

Prince was a bold and fiercely independent dog. This I had always known. He wasn't going to live the conventional life of a watchdog. He lived by his own law and determined himself who and what he would protect. Our chickens just didn't hold his interest. As far back as I can remember, his calling in life was to be bodyguard to Sister and me.

Dad smiled at me, as a story teller, he liked to see me burn with curiosity. He drew in a long breath and sighed with contentment, he had us spellbound. This was going to be an epic suspense story, not a short story, as we had hoped.

We were fully aware that during the nighttime most of our chickens roosted on top of their perches, those parallel bars arranged in ascending order. There our chickens would retract their necks into the recesses of their feather gowns and go to sleep, feeling assured that they were perched high enough to be safe, and out of reach from any marauding predator.

And indeed the chickens perched up high were spared by the thief. "Instead he went after the old and debilitated hens that couldn't make it up there any more." Dad told us. Sister and I agreed by nodding. Every crime had its own logic, so did chicken theft.

"Even if he stood on his hind legs and jumped, a fox still wouldn't be able to seize any hens roosting up high."

"You shot a fox!" Margret and I exclaimed. Though at the same time I felt a sensation of sorrow, for I had a special liking for foxes.

Foxes are so wonderfully mischievous. In Aesop's Fables they even outwit such smart animals as crow, lion, and wolf. In school and through my own reading I had learned that foxes are playful, fierce, and mysterious. By doing tricks like somersaults and chasing their own tails, foxes were reputed to charm rodents or frogs out of their wits. Beguiled and transported into a trance-like state, as they watched the fox display its antics, these simple-minded suckers made easy prey for the fox.

Even though foxes belonged to the dog family, they looked elegant and smooth like felines. Especially their elliptical pupils gave them an air of superior intelligence. I simply admired foxes for their flaming red coats.

Unfazed, by our urgent request that Dad should deliver the fox to the kitchen right away, Dad proceeded with his story. We wanted, show and tell, instead Dad chose to give us the documentary version.

"Like a spy, this fox had made a thorough inspection of the chicken house and its inhabitants. Its instincts told the fox that it was best to strike in the wee hours before daybreak, when creature and man is the least suspecting of any danger. So the fox made its entry when the sun was still below the horizon, and before the rooster would wake up and crow."

"At this threshold time, chickens still dwelled in their drowsy state. Warm and cozy in their fluffed out feather coats, they dreamed of earthworms and fish meal. When the fox first peeked into the chicken house, it was all peaceful and cozy. Just seeing this idyll, made the fox's hungry mouth salivate for the taste of fresh warm chicken meat."

"As it surveyed its hunting ground, the fox stood on its hind legs on the top of a pile of scrap wood outside of the chicken house. Its claws on its front paws dug into the loose plaster of the window ledge."

"In the twilight of dawn, the fox appeared like a gray shadow."

"Did you really see him at this point?" Sister inquired.

Dad flagged down her question. Such interruptions, so Dad felt, would only detract from the flow of his story.

"So, for the longest time it stood there on its hind legs, its body length stretched out to the max. All the while, this clever thing memorized a mental map of the inside of our chicken house."

Sister sighed, having resigned to hearing the long version, and Dad continued with glee.

"The musty odor emanating from our chickens tickled the fox's nostrils and made its snout curl and sniff in every whiff of chicken smell. Its yellow-greenish eyes glowed with eager anticipation. In fact, its eyes and sharply pointed muzzle were so eager, it appeared like he had left the rest of its body behind the barred window, and had already successfully entered the chicken house. This fox could barely wait to sink its teeth into warm, sweet chicken flesh."

"You couldn't imagine how thin a fox can be, if it needs to squeeze through a narrow entry."

Dad was amazed to see this animal taper its sleek body into one long red stripe, narrow enough to barely pass through a small opening in the window. A corner of the barred window where plaster and cinder block had chipped away provided the fox with a chance to make its entry.

"Once on the inside, the fox dove to the ground, its body taut like a flaming lance. In one big swoop it lunged toward the chicken cubbyholes."

"While surveying the scene earlier from the outside, the fox had decided exactly which of the hens it was going to tackle. Without hesitation, it made a pass for the fat brown hen, snoozing in the lower left cubby, next to the outside wall."

"This poor hen was weak on its legs and a little mangy. Other chickens had pecked sores into its neck."

"I know which chicken you're talking about," I said, for I could picture it clearly in my mind, looking scared as it waddled behind the rest of the chickens. Dad looked at me, and continued his tale.

"As if it had sensed that something was going to happen, that particular chicken opened its eyes and looked at the fox standing right in front of it. It stirred in its nest and let out a series of muted crackles. The fox tilted its head both ways, visibly amused by the chicken's futile attempt to withdraw further back into its cubbyhole."

"Why didn't you shoot him right then?" Sister asked. "I'll tell you later," Dad said.

"It appeared that the fox was sending silent messages to the chicken by the way it tilted its head and leered at it with mischievous eyes. It was animal hypnosis. The message the fox sent to the chicken was a death sentence. It held the promise of swift execution. The fox's bemused mien suggested I'll finish you off quickly if you don't give me any trouble!"

"The chicken understood and stopped squirming and flinching. It had been pecked down to the lowest rung and now it was time to disappear altogether."

"Like a flash of lightning, the fox's head darted into the cubby hole and yanked out the fat old chicken whose body jerked, and heaved. Once, after some mawing, the fox gripped it securely between its jaws, the chicken's neck dangled to one side of the muzzle, and its feet jerked. However, one prolonged gurgling shriek escaped the moment the fox clenched down with finality and severed the chicken's neck."

"The shriek of their dying fellow chicken awoke hens on the upper perches from their drowsy state. The moment they rolled up their eyelids and peered at the fox with prey in its mouth, they startled and went into a frenzy."

"The whole flock exploded into a deafening cacophony. Whatever little composure they naturally have, the poor chicken wretches lost it all in that moment. In senseless disarray they hurled themselves to the ground. Other fat and senior chickens scurried out of their cubby holes, and, to their own amazement, made it all the way to the perches. It was down and up, up and down in utter confusion. The specter of wings flapping around it, and the rooster, who started to crow its heart out, alerted the fox to leave this place in a hurry."

"It wouldn't let go of its prey though. This fox held on to that chicken as if it were the only source of food available. Its incisors had dug deep into the chicken breast, and dripping blood punctuated every inch it stepped. The fox was determined not to let go of it, regardless of what would happen next."

"Besides the alarming raucous all around it, the escape route proved much trickier than anticipated. Turning its head sideways the fox looked at the door which was closed. It turned its head into an oblique angle again, as if to charm the door, like it tended to charm toads and field mice."

"Unsuccessful with its attempt at enchanting the shut door, the fox turned to the window. However, dragged down by the weight of its heavy front load, the fox found it impossible to hoist itself up onto the window-ledge. It wouldn't give up though. With fierce exertion it clawed the crumbling plaster and pulled itself into a chin-up position. Would it be able to hoist itself up onto the ledge and pull its bulky supper through the tiny exit way?"

"I suppose this problem greatly puzzled the fox, but I supplied it with a quick and dirty answer. I blasted its brains out with my shotgun. There you go, I said, when he slid down the wall." Dad looked at us with an air of achievement.

"How did he get away with the other two chickens though?" I inquired. Dad agreed this question needed to be clarified.

The first time the fox had stolen a chicken, it must have entered and exited the chicken house through the door, because Dad had found it slightly ajar that morning. The second time the fox pillaged our chicken house; it dashed out the moment Dad had flung open the door to enter the scene. It practically brushed by Dad's knees on its way out. No wonder, Dad was so embarrassed to admit that it had gotten away that morning and piled the blame on Prince!

I couldn't keep the most obvious question down any longer. "But why didn't you shoot it before it got the chicken?"

Dad paused for a moment, then he said looking at both of us with a broad smile and a twinkle in his eyes, "because of the two of you I wanted to save the pelt for my two princesses." Sister and I were flattered and felt ambivalent at the same time, since a dashing fox had to die for it.

The third time the fox struck, Dad had stood by, peering through a small opening in the door. His fingers itching on the trigger, Dad had patiently watched the fox's entry and attack while waiting for the exact right moment to shoot. His intent was to shoot straight, so he would hit the fox dead center on the back of its skull. This would damage only a minimum of the fox's fur. It paid to wait for the exact right moment. Dad managed to limit the area ruined by charring and pellet holes to less than the size of a tablespoon.

"Show us the fox!" Sister insisted, like a small empress, she was speaking for me too.

"Sorry kids, the fox is already at the furrier. No time to fool around, it's best to have the fur stripped off right away." We were dumbfounded in our disappointment.

Weeks later, Mom showed us a fox's pelt. "This is not the same fox that your Dad shot," she said with a defeated shrug.

Since the day of the shooting, Mom had raved about the beauty of the fox dad had killed. Supposedly it was one magnificent specimen with a luxuriant, flaming rusty-red pelt.

The fur that Mother held in her hands and showed to us was far less impressive, than the original. "It is more scrawny looking," Mom said, and sadness came over her face. "We got cheated kids," she said. I noticed a resigned finality to this statement. To my disappointment, neither, Mom or Dad were willing to champion their cause and go into the ring and slug it out with those who took advantage of them.

During the night, Mom got busy sewing the pelt caps she had designed earlier. They looked like the hats Russian peasant girls wear in winter. One morning she had finished her nighttime sewing project and proudly placed the fur caps on our heads.

At grade school, kids would congregate behind our backs, snicker, sneer, and talk about us. No other children in the whole school, not even in the whole town or county for that matter, would wear anything resembling a fur cap, or other item of clothing made of fur. Sister and I stuck out with our fox hats, literally like red sores, so we thought.

Since Mom had a habit of watching us go to school from the window, we would leave the caps on until we turned the corner. The moment we were out of her sight, however, Sister and I would grab our caps and pull them off. During our school day we kept them stuffed in our boxes. Only when we turned that corner on our way home, would we place the fur caps on our heads again.

The sly camouflage ways of the fox had rubbed off on us. I don't remember how long we kept the camouflage going, but luckily by late spring mother didn't make us wear the caps any longer.

When next winter came around, the fur hats remained buried in the closet smelling of moth balls. Buried under layers of winter clothing, the fur caps lay forsaken in this cavernous closet until the death of my parents.

Stricken by the untimely and violent death of our parents, Sister and I decided to give away most all of the personal belongings that reminded us of our parents. Among those who came to take what we were discarding was one elegant, red-haired, young woman. She spotted the caps and immediately cried out, *Oh God, these are adorable!* Sister and I handed the fur caps over to her and assured her she could keep them for good.

Chapter 12

Wareneke

Once, every three months, or when Mother was otherwise in an exceptional mood, she'd get the table-size flour board out at nine in the morning and start organizing the array of ingredients that go into making *wareneke.* One of my all-time favorite dishes, that Dad had insisted Mom had to learn once she was his wife. So Mom duly took cooking classes from Dad's sisters who initiated her into the secrets of Russian cooking as done near Odessa, Russia on the Black Sea.

Wareneke is the Russian counterpart to Italy's Ravioli, except this dish, when prepared by Mom and adapted to her Swabian way of preparing dishes, was so much better.

Because of her exceptional mood this day or by calendar's count, it was time to make wareneke again. This I didn't know yet. Mother got her crispest white apron out of the fresh dish towel and apron cupboard. She crossed the straps behind her back and asked me to button them into the waistband. In this outfit she looked like the boss of the kitchen, more so than when she wore her flower patterned cotton dresses that made her look like a country girl dressed for the city. In the same crisp white cotton as her apron, Mom wore a scarf tied around her head in peasant women's fashion, so no hair would garnish the wareneke.

I was functioning in the role of aide-de-camp without apron and headgear, just in my knit pants-and-sweater outfit, bangs hanging deep within reach of my eyelashes and the length of my hair near and around my ear lobe - a cute mophead. At the time, I had just entered first grade and suffered much confusion because I had to switch from my natural left-handed script, which I just mastered with much pride, and go through the torture of acquiring that same writing skill with my right hand. Needless to say, the whole switch-over caused confusion in my brain circuitry and damaged my handwriting into perpetual illegibility. In anything requiring dexterity I managed to become dumbfounded. My first grade teacher, and Mom as well, were on my back constantly, and as soon as my left impulses came through in writing or otherwise they told me to do it over in the *right way*. So left and right became a way of looking at life for me. I felt sore for the good old left ways that were now being reprimanded, and rejected, and the right way seemed alien and artificial to me. More than any other kid on the block, I had to think hard when doing simple things with my hands. Knitting and sewing classes, even more so than learning how to write *a and o's,* turned into a nightmare; for my natural response was to hold yarn and needle in exactly the opposite way as the teacher was demonstrating us to do, and I had to switch to the *right* way. I was forever lost in making loops and generally making every conceivable mistake that one can possibly knit into a sock. In fact once finished, with the help of Grandmother who saw me struggling with knitting gear and forever-entangled yarn, my socks managed to look more like oversized mittens. And I earned my first *D* grade on my report card. My needlework teacher would have flunked me, but then politically she couldn't make me repeat the first grade just because my first (and last) knitted pair of socks looked like a pair of mittens.

So, on this exceptional wareneke day, I was in the midst of my left-right haze, but nonetheless I wanted to be Mom's aide-de-camp and see the procedure through from the starting point of setting down the ingredients in one line, to the finishing point of serving steaming wareneke for lunch.

My first assignment was to spread flour on the kneading board. Now, this immediately threw me into a left versus right dilemma. Should I use my right hand and be official and accepted, or should I use my left hand and be comfortable but sneaky? Actually Mom didn't pay attention to what hand I was using, it was the manner of me creating heaps of flour here and there and leaving other parts of the board bare. She poured some flour into her hand and showed me the flowing motion, in which she flicked her wrists, and sifted the flour through her fingers, while sweeping with her right hand across the board in elegant loops thus creating an even flour dusting, much like late November's first snow. The task was more than a left versus right affair, so I noticed, one needed to be nimble, quick, and steady, and, most of all, it helped not to have one's thoughts all knotted up in the left versus right way of doing this thing.

After my first assignment had needed Mother's mending, I stepped more to the sidelines, a little sobered about my ingenuity as cooking assistant. With keen interest, I watched Mom's square hands shape a heap of flour into pastry dough. The flour she had shaped into a cone like sculpture with a crater in the top, much like the cold volcano Aukenberg which I could see from the kitchen window. Into this crater Mother would pour egg yolks. Today she looked at me with encouraging eyes. "Have a crack at this," She said, and handed me one of the brown eggs laid by our chickens. "Just crack it on the rim of this mug, like this…" Mother tapped one large egg and it cracked apart exactly in the middle. She used half of the egg to separate out the egg white, by cupping the egg yolk back and forth while the egg white was dripping into the mug. When the egg yolk was nicely separated, one golden blob, she emptied it into the crater and added some tepid water. "Now you do the same."

This time I wasn't going to let left nor right deter me from doing my best. With a tiny bit of trepidation, I held the raw egg over the cup. How to tap it softly, and yet hard enough so it will spring open right through the center? *Bing,* here it went egg white and yolk intermingled and inseparable like twins dropping into the mug. I winced like our shepherd dog, when he gets wet, sending one big question mark toward Mother's face that held a quizzical, slightly annoyed expression. "There goes my egg white for an omelet tomorrow morning." Again I had missed an opportunity to be of genuine help. I was starting to feel uneasy in my role as kitchen help and told Mom that for now I'd rather be watching from the sidelines than actively participating.

You always work from the center, Mom explained as she dropped more egg yolks into the crater and mashed them into the flour with ample sprinklings of water. Her hands were like busy gophers burrowing, and poking, squeezing lumps, and turning the whole mess upside down and inside out. Under her busy fingers the mound of flour transformed into this yellow, smooth, and moist mass of pastry dough. But this is when the work really started.

Mother rolled up the sleeves of her cotton dress, and made her hands into fists. "You've got to work it hard," She said, and punched the dough left and right, the more she punched the more it sprung back into shape like a resilient animal. Every time she turned it over, she sprinkled top and bottom with flour so it wouldn't stick to the board or her hands. "Here you punch!" She said. I made a tight fist and released all the frustrations over my former mishaps into that piece of dough. To my surprise it took it willingly, even cheerfully, and leapt right back to where it was before I banged into it. The smoothness of the texture felt soothing to my fiery fist. It talked to me and said, "Don't worry," and "you can punch me as many times as you feel like. I'll always jump right back."

"See how it doesn't stick to your skin, and bounces right back into shape!" Mom said, with a chef's authority. "It's ready to be rolled out now." She took the rolling pin which was one of the many cooking utensils she had lined up for this project. Dusted flour the length of the roller and bore down with the full strength of her upper body stretching the dough ball this way and that way like a formless amoeba. "Here you do it!" She said, and handed me the rolling pin. I dusted it like she had showed me, and then applied all of my arm strength into this rolling piece, more squeezing the dough than actually flattening it out into all four directions. "See this fat lump? Roll it out so it's as thin as a washcloth. You need to have a mental picture how you want to shape this beast." I took another run at the fat corner and envisioned it way out near the end of the table, so strong was my zeal. I even stood on my tiptoes to further bear into this operation. While I steamrolled the dough into wafer thinness and sent that fat corner as far away as it would stretch without tearing; Mom came up from behind me and gently pushed me aside. She picked up the lopsided sheet of dough with her hands and formed another smooth ball. "It takes a while to get the knack of it," She said, then dusted the rolling pin and let her weight roll out the ball in even distances from the center. The dough being as thick as one of my composition books in school. She gave me yet a second chance handing me the pin and turning the dough over, so it would get a whack from the other side.

This time I took a deep breath and went at it more slowly with greater awareness of where I was going to shove and pull the dough, working evenly from the center. It felt good to feel the slight resistance of the resilient piece of dough, and I nudging it still another inch toward its final shape. "You're doing a great job," Mom said, and gave me an approving wink.

Chapter 13

Haman Family Name

"You can find yourself in the bible, first and last name," Mother said. "Not many people can. Now with your last name there's a bit of a problem. Jewish people may take issue with it."

"Why that?" I asked.

"Because they think of Haman, as a wicked vizier who was out to kill the Jews in Persia."

"You can read it for yourself in the Book of Esther. He cast lots, to see on which day he should start his plan, and for that reason the festival that commemorates this event is called Purim which means *lots*. The beautiful Jewish Queen Esther and Mordechai, who was at her court, prevented the massacre. The Jewish people, all around the world, celebrate the fact that Haman didn't get to them during Purim, which is much like our carnival. Jewish kids are confused about the true nature of Haman. Some even believe he's a hero because they are encouraged to stomp their feet, pound the pews, jeer, and whistle in the synagogue whenever the name *Haman* comes up in the story of Esther."

"Like our carnival, Purim falls at the end of the winter, and is really a sweeping out of the grim and cold season. Just like we do during carnival, the Jewish people drink plenty then, so there's the saying *he's so drunk he doesn't know Mordechai from Haman*. During Purim they have masquerades just like the Catholics do, and men dress like women and women dress like men. We eat doughnuts filled with jam during carnival and the Jews eat *haman tashen* or *oznei haman* (Haman's ears) which are triangular poppy-seed cakes."

Chapter 14

Rabbits and Wolf Dog

Sister and I had been given twelve rabbits, as an Easter present. Dad had wanted us to have some small and snuggly pets other than our big old dog, who was more for rough play and protecting us.

Starting the day that the rabbits moved into the old chicken house, Prince fell into a depression. Even dogs are subject to the blues. His fortune had turned sour. After years of our undivided attention, the idea of having competition by twelve dimwit fluffs gnawed at him. In fact, we had to lock him up in the cow stable when we let the bunnies run free. As soon as he heard us play outside, he started to whine and whimper behind the locked door. Jealousy had turned him into a puddle of misery.

At Whitsuntide the sun shone fiercely from the sky making us scramble for shade. Sister and I had found a new hideaway: the old chicken house. This brick stone structure was a cool and dark place, and now home to our rabbit family. Sprawling our legs apart and making them into fences, for our two favorite rabbits, Sister and I sat in the hay bedding, and cuddled and teased Max and Moritz. The rest of the rabbits were romping in the courtyard. Nobody had thought of locking up the dog.

Rabbits do not scream when they are killed, they are too dumb for their own good. It was the total absence of sound, even the constant rustling of the giant willows had ceased, which made Sister and me suspicious. We stepped from the dank cool of the chicken house into the glaring sun. At first we had to squint to adjust to the piercing luminosity. Once my eyes could discern distinct shapes and colors around the courtyard that which I could perceive felt like a dull thud, a hammer whopping me over the head.

The still life, Prince had arranged for us, was ghastly beyond belief. In a straight line he had laid ten rabbits, spacing his prey at even intervals, strung them like beads along a bloody string. At the very same moment, Sister and I erupted into a scream the likes of which has not been heard in this courtyard ever since the slaughtering of livestock was legally and expertly done by those who were butchers by trade.

As, if I had been there in the courtyard all along, I could see before my mind's eye Prince's deadly rabbit rampage from start to finish. Prince had kept a low profile all morning. I imagined he hedged the plan while hiding under the dense elderberry bushes. There, in the cool shade he bided his time, waiting for the perfect moment to mount his attack. I figured that the raid on the rabbits must have come like a blitz; it was Prince's style to strike swiftly once he had made up his mind. He was an expert in stealth attack. Like no other dog that I knew, he could sneak up on the most elusive animal and jump it when it was oblivious to anything but the clouds in the sky. I remembered one of his stellar stealth attacks, when close to All Saints' Day, he had caught a weasel, and presented it to Dad, his tail wagging with such pride he could have swept the courtyard clean. Dad had greatly appreciated Prince's exploit. He had worried at night that the weasel would find its way into the chicken house and cause mayhem there. Compared to the weasel and its razor sharp teeth and claws, the rabbits were a piece of cake to Prince.

I imagined that the dog's predatory presence and his shadowing the bunnies' activity must have loomed like a large and dark cloud over the courtyard, but went unnoticed by the trusting rabbits. His keen eyes would survey the scene, observing each and every pet rabbit that frolicked in the courtyard. He would hate it for its cuteness, for having successfully displaced him from his rightful position - the center of our family. Camouflaged by the shade along the base of the western wall, he would sneak along the edge of the courtyard across from the chicken house where Sister and I discussed which of our doll dresses would make the most comical bunny outfit.

Observing every hop and leap among the bunny bunch, he would focus on the ones he would wrestle first. Saliva frothing in the corner of his mouth, he would glue his eyes on his first unheeding victim.

Finally, his predatory brain could stand the waiting game no longer; he would shoot forth from his ambush, explode like a time bomb, and dive into the midst of the playful rabbit scene. No longer was he a shepherding dog, but Prince, the Big Bad Wolf. He snatched the rabbit closest to his muzzle off the ground. His gruesome incisors dug in as if the rodent was nothing more than a stick of softened butter. He gripped the furry skin folds of its tender neck, and shook it furiously only to drop it lifeless as a rag.

Even though I was not present at the scene of the rabbit rampage, the agony of that which had happened to our pets pressed upon me. It was as if the still air held the unscreamed screams of the rabbits, their unexpressed anguish, and their torment; held it suspended and hushed, and I was tapping into it by means of my susceptible imagination.

The warmth and heartbeat of my favorite rabbit, its delicate bones, and fragile aliveness entrusted to me, hauled my wayward imagination right back to the here and now. All of a sudden, I became acutely aware of the real danger that our dog posed to the two remaining bunnies.

Prince had not anticipated our arrival on the scene. He stood obliquely to us. Like a thief caught in the act, he avoided any eye contact. But I could tell by the bristling of his hair, the tail held up high, and the jumpy nerviness in his hind legs that the nightmare wasn't over yet.

Instinctively Sister and I braced our arms tight around the two pet rabbits that were left in our care. We virtually suffocated these two darlings by pressing them flat against our chests, their fluttering hearts beating twice as fast as ours. This show of affection only further incensed Prince's raging jealousy. He fixed his gaze on us. It was the look of an assassin. Gone was the love and care he had cultivated for us, his allegiance, his mission to protect us from any harm. Before our very eyes he had transformed into a mad monster.

Nothing could stop this feral beast. Not even Sister's and my yelling, "No Prince don't you dare! Stay down! Be good! No Prince! No! No!" He ignored every word of it, deaf to our entreating, unwilling to stop the carnage now that he was only two counts away from successful completion.

Between Sister and me, Prince chose me as his next target. He approached me obliquely. For a moment I thought he'd pass by me and go on, relinquishing his lethal plan, but not so. Faster than I could count to three, he turned toward me making a beeline for my arms crossed over the bunny flesh which he desired and detested at the same time. He leaped up on his powerful hind legs and snatched the trembling black and white Moritz out of my desperate hold. I wasn't going to stand by and see him maul my favorite pet. Faster than in dodge ball, I gathered up my courage and grabbed Prince by the tail. Nothing happened; he merely turned his head looking back at me, his eyes mocking my foolish attempt. He wouldn't let go of Moritz whom he held fiercely between his two rows of deadly teeth. I didn't get discouraged yet and flung myself over his back, straddling his rump. I threw my arms around his thick neck and tried to choke him, so he would disgorge Moritz. I sensed a ferocious vigor ripple through his entire body. Despite my choke hold, he shook me off like water after a dive into the Ortzan stream.

Prince didn't even bother to look around and see me fall to the ground. My elbows hit the hard cobble stones, and screaming pain shot up the length of my arms and rang inside my ears. Prince was all action again - a lethal weapon on the loose. In large bounds he leaped toward the center of the courtyard. There he stood on the other side of the blood track and looked at us darkly, daring us to come near. He held my rabbit securely by its nape. Moritz was still alive and wiggled and pawed the air using all four legs and his tail.

The bunny was kicking for his life, and I felt shame for not being able to rescue him from his sure fate. Prince gazed at us intently, he wanted to make sure we would catch every bit of the lesson he was about to teach us. In plain view of Sister and me, he shook the bunny fiendishly and crunched down on it, smashing its tender neck. The bones of its tiny vertebrae being ground to bone meal registered in my ears as if a bee had stung me. Sister's knees turned soft like jelly. No longer could she hold her own weight but had to crouch close to the ground folding her chest over her endangered rabbit. Fresh blood dripped from the gaping mouth of Moritz. As he had done ten times before, Prince deposited the eleventh casualty - evenly spaced at the end of the straight line.

Sister panicked when she saw Prince turn around and head in her direction. In the hope that Max would manage to escape, she let her rabbit run free. The frightened animal scurried toward the woodpile where it could have hidden safely, but Prince wasn't going to let this last one get away. Prince bounded across the blood track and landed right over the rabbit that froze in fright. He grabbed it expertly by the skin fold of its velveteen fur, and tossed it up in the air. For a moment it appeared like he was going to play catch the ball. He jumped high and caught Max in mid-air. When he was back on the ground, Prince looked at Sister and myself, his eyes as cold as steel. As the grand finale, he wrung Sister's pet more fiercely than mine. We both heard the cracking and crunching noises of his jaws grinding the bunny's backbone to bone meal. He had twisted every spark of life out of the bunny's neck.

The lower half of Max dangled from the dog's jaws. Where was his chest and head? Had Prince actually swallowed half of Max? The very thought of Max being eaten by Prince was more repulsive than looking at ten dead rabbits. Prince bade his time finishing up business. Almost leisurely, he sauntered down the blood trail of dead rabbits stopping at the very end. There he disgorged the contents of his mouth. Max emerged in three separate pieces, first its mangled rump, then the front legs, and part of its tiny chest. And finally Prince divulged the bunny's head. It was mashed flat by Prince's molars. Sister gasped - it was like the hissing of wind down a dark and forbidden alley. She stared at the three-piece remnants of Max. Gone was the luster of his black fur which Sister had groomed every day with her old tooth brush. Then she broke into uncontrollable sobbing, shaking like the willow leaves.

I had to squat down like Sister. My stomach started to churn. My chest started to heave, I gagged and gulped. Finally I couldn't hold it down any longer and let myself throw up, what I vomited was a greenish looking brew - just as repulsive as the picture of Max and Moritz torn apart.

Sister's screaming and my own had brought Dad on the scene, albeit too late to do much of any good. A man of few words and quick action, he counted the casualties. "Twelve down," that meant Prince had killed them all. "You son of a bitch," that's all Dad said. He whipped his belt from his pants, and flattened Prince to the ground under a torrent of lashings. Dad unleashed his anger like I had never seen him do before. The bludgeoned dog crawled in submission, his belly scraping the cobble stones. Prince yipped and yapped, pleading for mercy. He squealed in a high and piercing pitch, more alarming than the sirens of an ambulance.

Sister and I hunkered low like wilted potted plants. There was nothing we could do. We were the unwilling front-seat audience to Dad's rage. It gushed violent and mean like the Ortzan stream after a summer rain storm.

Twelve lifeless bodies lay in one row on the blood smeared cobble stones. And yet the terror continued. The stakes had been raised. Dad was about to kill the one creature that had loved me most when I was a forsaken infant. Deep inside my sore and cramped guts I knew that there was no word in the German language, no gesture in my body, no amount of tears in my tear glands that could stop Dad. Besides, my vocal chords, muscles, and joints had all seized up on me. I was as dumb and frozen as Max the bunny when Prince's muzzle picked him off his legs.

I stood by motionless, speechless, and devoid of any other sign of protest watching how my childhood companion was being clobbered to death. Seeing the dog writhe and squirm in pain, his proud muscular body flat as a doormat, it was too much for me to stand, so I shielded my eyes using both hands to screen out the terror. Still, glimpses of horror seeped through the slants in my fingers. They were horrid enough to stay with me for a lifetime.

The way Dad bore down on the squirming dog; there was a real chance that Prince would not make it through the ordeal. Soon, so I feared, Prince would sprawl there as mangled and limp as the dozen rabbits he had savaged earlier. Even though Prince had destroyed my most cherished toys, he was still close to my heart. Six years of his companionship had carved a big space in my heart. And from the way he was beaten flat into the ground, less than a doormat, I anticipated that this space in my heart occupied by Prince would very soon be a vacant lot.

Dad's arms appeared to get weary; the furious vigor had fallen away from his body. He looked exhausted. In a weary motion, he slung the belt over his shoulder and pulled a white handkerchief from his blue denim work-pants, wiped the sweat from his brow, and the drooling spit from the angle of his mouth. To let off the heat he lifted his cap from his bald spate, and then he bent over and grabbed Prince by his collar and dragged the lifeless looking dog into the cow pen, a dungeon-like place where no cow had lived for a long time. Here the spent dog could die or survive. One way or another, it didn't matter to Dad.

Dad emerged from the cow stable, his face as sullen and gray as a granite grave stone. He put his belt back on, buckled it, and arranged his cap. Before he went back to tend to business inside the gristmill, he looked at Sister and me. It was a look that spoke volumes of mute words. As so often before during crisis, Dad had no actual words to say. He believed in action and action only, and this we had seen plenty of. In an abrupt movement, pulling harder at the handle than necessary, he flung the door to the mill wide open. The hum of the machines that ran nonstop all day and night spilled across the battle zone.

For what seemed like an eternity, Sister and I remained motionless with no words spoken between us. We were two forlorn figures squatting under the lengthening shadow of a gray wall; no one there besides us, but the company of twelve dead rabbits.

On that day I had learned a central lesson in my life. I had experienced the murderous reverse of love, and understood that it could flip from one to the other within a blink. I had peered into the savage eyes of jealousy. It was a mighty dangerous force. For it could turn a loyal dog into a rabid brute; and this made me wonder what jealousy could do if it took root in a human heart.

Sister departed from the scene. Her face was waxen, white as the candles during church on Whitsuntide Sunday. I knew she would fly up all of the six flights of stairs it took to get to our living quarters; she'd grab Mother by her apron and spill her guts, tell her every bit of the story, and thus find a measure of relief.

Like Dad, I am not of the talking type. I digest feelings like cows digest grass, chewing the cud in silence. All alone among twelve dead rabbits and no sound coming from the cow stable, I had an urgent desire to hole up some place where nobody would find me, and no family member would pry into my pain or try to fix it. Unnoticed by Dad who was busy lifting sacks of wheat onto the elevator, I crawled into the darkest and least accessible corner of the entire gristmill, a place where I could re-assemble my dismembered parts and feelings. The drone of transmission wheels and belts that whirred above my head at a breakneck speed drowned out much of my crying and sobbing. The monotony of the machines felt reassuring, it nicely camouflaged my presence. I felt free to let loose and bawl like a running faucet.

My sadness pulled me into its black undertow. It was a place of oblivion to the rest of my surroundings. So, when I thought I heard Mother's voice it was like hearing sound when you're underwater, every word drawn out like toffee, and muffled as if spoken behind surgical masks. Finally she must have been quite close, for I heard her yell my name loud and clear. She chimed it in a high and urgent pitch that told me she was scared.

Mother was looking for me I thought, and I relished the idea of my importance, the fact that she had missed me. At first I remained silent, but eventually I couldn't bear it any longer. "I am right here," I yelled, my voice choked by tears.

"I cannot see you. Tell me, where are you?"

"Here under the wheels and belts."

She followed the trail of my voice to the cramped place where it came from. After what seemed a long time she finally found me, a whimpering and sobbing mess, huddled into a tight ball. I was rocking back and forth because it gave me a notion of comfort. Mother approached me deliberately slow like she would approach an exotic wild mushroom during our regular fall foraging in the woods.

I could make out the white parts of her body in the dim light of my hideout. The gentle curves and valleys of her bare arms reminded me of a Greek statue was it Aphrodite, the goddess of love or Artemis, the huntress? I had studied Greek statuary in Mother's art magazines that featured sculptures, temples and other relics of the past.

The late afternoon sunbeams filtered through a small bared window above my head casting upon Mother's finely-chiseled face. She looked at me as if a spider web hung in front of her face. When she came close to the machinery, she ducked low, pulling her head into her ample chest. We all heeded Dad's incessant warnings about the dangers of the transmission works. And Mother too knew full well that if she made one wrong move, the churning wheels and roving belts would rip her head off faster than Prince had maimed the rabbits' necks.

A shaft of slanted light, whirling with dust motes, sliced past her strong body like the blade of an ancient sword. Her breasts rose and fell rapidly. The ugliness of this Monday's history must have churned her insides like it had lacerated and whipped mine. She squatted close by but couldn't come any nearer than within the reach of her outstretched arm. She didn't say a word, but reached out to touch my cheek with her fingertips. "You must be cold," She said, when in fact I was freezing. Her large dark eyes, gentle as those of a doe, looked at me steadily. I sensed that she was searching for the right words, trying to find a soothing gesture that would stay the stream of my tears.

"I have experienced in my life hot and cold rage - they are twins. One's as destructive as the other. They generally have a long history. It takes time for them to kick into action. But eventually they become forceful like the steam in my pressure cooker." That

Mom would relate something out of her personal life, took me by surprise. I had expected a story from her stock of favorite parables, like the testing of Jobe, the Fall of Eve, or the trials of Odysseus. She always liked to fall back on bible stories or Greek mythology when things got out of hand in the family.

Often I have asked myself. "Where does rage begin, and what does it do during the time it stays hidden?" She stirred in her big boned frame as if she was looking at this very moment for the hidden place of her own rage. I would ask myself, "How come that rage and anger remain invisible for so long, accumulating silently as snowflakes do overnight. And then, when you least expect it, an avalanche comes down and buries a whole village?" She wiped the flour and dust off the wooden floor boards and sat down. From where she sat only her fingertips could touch me.

I saw her think deeply. Her forehead furled into three well-worn pleats, a crease marked the center between her brows. "At other times I've seen rage start like a slow fire, more smoke than flame. Yet, when I was the least prepared, some gust would blow and turn the glowing embers into a hellish inferno." My sobbing started back up again. Her words made me think of Dad's fiery rage and Prince's cold-blooded and callous attack. Or maybe it was the other way around, and Dad had been cold-blooded while Prince had burnt up with rage?

Mother's finger tips touched my hand which I kept tightly clenched and pressed into my belly. "I know it was a grisly massacre," Mother said, and tried to loosen my fingers, but I resisted. "Your Sister told me everything that happened. And she finds comfort by blaming Dad for each of the dead rabbits and Prince's ruin too. I can only pray that in time you and your Sister will find the courage to trust Dad again."

"The fact that Prince took it upon himself to kill your dear little bunnies was more than just a gust blowing over hot cinders, it was an electric storm. Something, that happens as rarely as the ice castle. Dad simply came undone, when he walked into this carnage. He got unhinged, simply lost it. His mind and body were no longer acting together." The tides of crying and sobbing started to subside again as Mother kept on talking to me in her slow and measured rhythm.

"You've got to understand where Dad is coming from," She said, and stretched way to her left to push aside my bangs that were soaking wet from my crying. I too felt like cleaning up and I wiped off a long and slimy string of snot that hung from my nose. "You probably thought that Dad was cruel beyond reason when he whipped your dog. But in reality, deep down inside, he was more like one of those battered bunny rabbits."

"How so," I asked. The proposition sounded absurd.

Mother scooted her bottom up closer to mine and rested her chin on her knees. "I never told you, but Dad's father, your Grandfather, was a cruel man indeed. Everybody feared Manfred. In his family he ruled like the Czar. A no for an answer was unheard of. Your Dad was born right into the middle of twelve children, that's worse than being the runt of the litter." The black disks in her eyes searched mine.

"So often when one of his eight brothers did something wrong, your Dad ended up being blamed. When your Dad was even younger than you are now, your grandfather Manfred would beat your Dad savagely. Most of the time, he was just being scapegoated, taking the brunt off his Father's rage, while the older brothers, who were in the wrong, went unpunished. It all happened in the same manner as you witnessed today in the courtyard."

"His formidable Father would walk into the scene of sibling squabbling, "Who did it?" he would ask. Then fingers would point at your Dad, he being younger and weaker and always short of words to speak. In every gesture Manfred would radiate his severe authority. He acted as if he were a judge, headmaster, and police officer, all wrapped in one. Really, if you ask me for my honest opinion, your Granddad was a pompous ass."

"Without any more questions asked, Manfred would make Willy step forward and pull down his pants. Just like your Dad did today, Manfred would pull his buckled belt from his pants and whip this small boy's bare bottom so bad, that this terrified child would lose control of his bladder and piss all over himself. This would infuriate Grandfather even more, and he would give your Dad another set of lickings."

I looked up at Mother, astounded that she had used bad language twice in a row. Normally she would keep her language as clean as her linen closet. In many ways this day had disrupted the normalcy of our family discourse.

I studied her lips, the angles of her mouth quivering as she recalled Dad's angst-filled childhood. I could neither believe nor imagine what she had just said. I only knew Dad to be tough, unemotional, and always hair-trigger tempered. The thought of him bent over, lashes across his ass, and pee dripping down his bare legs, this very image of humiliation, did not register as believable in my mind.

Mother continued, oblivious to my startled reaction and the disbelief that must have shown. "Just imagine the constant fear in which Dad lived throughout his childhood, never knowing when Manfred would enter and pull his belt and make him bend over in plain view of his brothers. This is where it all started, that cold and hot rage that you witnessed today." She squeezed my hand, and I noticed that my tight fists had relaxed.

"What you've just gone through is a harrowing experience. And there's no way that I could erase it from your memory. All that blood and guts must have been a wrenching site, and in the next instant watching your dog being beaten into the ground and you not knowing whether your longtime companion will come out alive. You barely had time to breathe between these two disasters! My God, that is way too much to bear for such a young soul. But maybe you have an ancient soul inhabiting your childlike body. I've often wondered about your wise old eyes when you were just a newborn."

I turned my head toward Mother, *our gaze level as water*. Throughout this ordeal I had never even thought that I might have a soul. Whether it was young or old didn't matter to me. However, I knew that on this Whitsuntide Monday it had to be a bleeding soul, just like my heart.

Warmth radiated through Mother's finger tips while she kept hers on top of mine. "I'll grant you that something irreparable has happened today, and at the same time it has been a great release for your Dad. The rabbit killing has been a strange opportunity for Dad to let his rage come out, cold and hot at the same time that was held back over so many years. It gave him a chance to purge demons that have tormented him since he was your age and even younger."

"Prince who broke all the rules of permissible dog behavior created an opening, a justified situation for Dad's anger to enter center stage. Aren't you glad that this avalanche of lashings didn't come down on you, or Sister, or even myself? Maybe, Prince stepped in and did this to take the charge out of Dad's penned up rage, he diffused it by sacrificing himself. If I think more about it, I even find it possible that Prince acted as the ultimate watchdog, saving us all from Dad's lethal rage." The full weight of her hand bore down on mine. The warmth radiating from her palms increased and I sopped it up. "We have such a narrow vision of the weavings of destiny. Our logical thinking cannot possibly grasp the vast scope of the invisible world that surrounds us."

"Dad has never used any force against us women folk and possibly because of what happened today he will never put a hand on any of us in the future," Mother said, as thought she had finally found the right words to soothe me, but quite to the contrary, I was infuriated. Why was there need for sacrifice to stop a man from raging? Why twelve rabbits dead and a proud dog beaten into a wretched pile of misery? Why Sister and I deprived of our playmates and longtime companion? Why? Why? Why? I crawled out of my hiding place and squeezed by Mother who remained sitting.

"If Dad ever lays a hand on Sister or you, *I'll kill him,*" I said, standing there next to her and the transmission wheels whirring less than an inch from my scalp. During the silence that ensued between Mother and me, I re-considered the enormity of what I had just said. The words had come from deep within my guts, as if an old person was sitting there, and already had a master plan in case this eventuality should become real.

In the days following the rabbit killing, the image of Dad raging over Prince, whipping him into the shape of a rolled-up rug ready to be ditched in the dump, superseded the loss of the rabbits. In a real way Prince's spirit, the proud expression on his face, the happy twinkle in his eyes, was broken that day. From then on, my relationship to Dad was never the same. My direct line to God had been disconnected. Now that I had seen rage pour through Dad, as if he had been the extended arm of a wrathful god, I had made up my mind that Our Father in Heaven must be evil to condone such blatant injustice and brutality in the world at large, and more specifically in our own home. This made him the most unfeeling Father of all. It was in the wake of the rabbit slaughter that I ceased to say my prayers at bedtime or before meals.

Chapter 15

A Stream Called the Ortzan

The constant murmuring of the Ortzan stream as it tumbled day and night, seamlessly and ceaselessly, over the huge waterwheels, is the most steady backdrop to my childhood memories. The swift Ortzan waters fell into the troughs of the waterwheels, and spun them twenty-four hours a day. They supplied the power that turned the mill stones, hoisted heavy grain loads up to the granaries and illuminated the mill, one of the largest buildings in town. The upper mill, Jrosse Muehle was my home's name, and presently was a grain mill. In earlier times a gun powder mill, and also a paper mill centuries ago. This place was the hub of many people's lives; it had a history more eventful than most any opera I know.

I remember the shivers that ran the course of my spine, when I stood so close to the inside belly of those tireless draft horses. Possibly because of the chilling spray, but more so because I was utterly enthralled, and my small and lean body trembled. Goosebumps popped up all over my bare arms. This was more exciting than the rides at the amusement park, or the daring moves of circus acrobats I had seen hang by their teeth, hair, or toes high up on the trapeze.

I was so completely dwarfed by the waterwheels that churned right there in front of me, bigger than mammoths, the largest mammals that once roamed this land. Like most children, I respected bigness above beauty and smarts. Next to dinosaurs, saber-toothed tigers, and woolly mammoths, our waterwheels gulped down the Ortzan stream much like real life monsters, they intrigued me more than any other creature in my childhood days. This tireless work team had been around long before me, when carts drawn by horses and oxen made up much of the traffic in our town.

And they churned away while *two World Wars* ravaged the face of Europe.

Today was one of the rare occasions when Dad would give me the inside tour of the waterwheels. We both stood on the wooden plank landing inside the waterworks. The stream rushed and gurgled above us. Just one arm length away, water fell in dense sheets from the disgorging troughs. It was chilly standing on the wooden landing that gave access to the man-sized hubs of the water wheels. And even in mid-summer a misty spray engulfed me like a November's fog shroud. Unlike standing waters like ponds and lakes, the temperature of the Ortzan remained fairly constant throughout the year. In summer I would jump into the stream and splash the water on my body to the rapid count of five, but then I had to get out quickly for otherwise I'd catch pneumonia. In winter the stream would steam like a wash house during cold days. Compared to the frigid temperature of the air, the water was still comparatively warm.

In spite of water seeping through every crevice and crack, Dad and I remained dry enough. Luckily, the top of the water works held the Ortzan stream in safe abeyance. We were in fact under the stream bed, a slightly disquieting thought. But the wooden construction that kept us safe was made of the best hardwood around, and Dad told me it would withstand possibly another fifty years of the stream's erosive effect.

Watching with amazement how water, wood, and gravity worked hand in hand as if they had always been intended to be a team of workhorses, I was an immediate witness to the laws of mother earth's gravity. I marveled at man's ingenious application of these laws for the sake of saving blood, sweat, and tears making production a smooth-going elegant process. At a gut level, I appreciated the simple beauty of physics, converting the stream's wayward flow into useful horsepower.

The men who drew up the plans for the flour mill were English engineers in the 19th Century, who still embodied the splendid reputation of British industrial genius. They were hired to squeeze the most power possible out of this stream. Especially since these technical wizards were commissioned to come all the way across the North Sea, and make the long trip down to the Southwest of Germany for the sole purpose to make this mill a profitable proposition, more so than the existing competition up and down the

Ortzan Valley these men scrupulously measured the stream's volume, and calculated how many gallons of water it carried per second. Their blueprints of the mill required overshot water wheels, which means that the millstream hit and thus engaged the wheels at the top of their circumference.

The water level of the Ortzan was substantial, and yet they needed more to build a highly competitive flour mill. The thrust of the Ortzan waters needed to be increased, so they engineered a precipice, in this case, about 18 feet of artificial waterfall. The simplified calculation according to Newton went like this; the higher the water fall, the greater the impact, and more blessings to the water wheels.

In my child's eyes the mechanics of the water wheels was obvious enough. As the stream fell, the water wheels with their troughs would lap up the tumbling waters like thirsty animals do. Trough after trough would fill up and then empty itself much like a circular conveyer belt arrangement. Ultimately it was the weight of the falling Ortzan that spun these monsters. Unlike factory machines, these beasts had their peculiarities. For example, their turning speed varied depending on the swiftness of the current and the amount of water available through the seasons.

The stream's flow fluctuated even during the day. Whenever the town's pumps engaged, to replenish the community's drinking water reservoir, I could detect a visible drop in the water level. The water level also changed when men who proudly held water rights to their names, opened or shut irrigation gates and diversion channels. Much to Dad's chagrin, these men would leave the gates open even when they didn't need the water, so we had so much less power available because of their thoughtlessness. Or was it deliberate mischief on their part?

Knowing full well his tenuous position in the community, Dad assumed it was the latter. Many times, when the water level dropped and the milling operation slowed down, Dad would put on his rubber boots that came up to his crotch and wander out into the wet meadows. There the irrigation water reached up to his knees, far beyond any reasonable level, so it definitely was high time for Dad to close the floodgates. Taking thus the law into his own hands, he made even more enemies among neighbors who already were wary of this Russian fugitive who had the nerve to meddle with their sacred water rights.

Dad was a man of quick action. The art of negotiating, the dance of give and take, were not skills he had deemed necessary to learn. To him social intercourse was like dancing on ice. Especially in this country, *in Germany*. It had become his default homeland, because of Hitler's invasion of his true and much beloved homeland, Russia. He plain didn't know how to confer successfully and assert his rights with men whose tongues would only loosen up if they could speak in the Swabian dialect. A *strong dialect - akin to Swiss German*, which Dad did not speak. And the quaint subtleties of its idioms escaped Dad's grasp. He was bound to be dumbfounded as soon as things turned Swabian.

Conversely, Dad spoke German with an accent that still bore the imprint of his ancestors' way of talking. To the townsmen, Dad's speech sounded strange and archaic, the way they talked at the time of Frederick the Great, of Prussia and Catherine the Great, the Russian empress.

It was at this historical juncture, when the two majesties had power-brokered a deal to let land-starved, but efficient German peasants colonize parts of Russia and educate the natives about more effective ways to work the soil. This is when Dad's ancestors followed the call to adventure, and said goodbye to their native Swabia. They left behind the medieval looking town Schwaebisch Hall, where the great German poet Schiller was born, and embarked on rafts to journey down the Danube to its very delta. Once they arrived in Russia, their way of speaking became preserved like pickles or jam. And that is how Dad grew up learning a tongue that was in many ways outlandish.

Interestingly, I wasn't aware at all that Dad was speaking in a manner different from other people around me. It came to my awareness through friends at school who, after visiting my home and meeting my father, would make snide remarks about Dad's peculiar way of talking. It is around this time when I lost my innocent belief that Dad was great and unbeatable. And, *unfortunately,* I began to see him through the eyes of those who made judgmental comments about him and described him as being *quite an old Dad* and *really different* on top of that. I became highly sensitive, and even embarrassed about Dad's behavior and mannerisms. Nothing was worse when I was in grade school and needed to belong than being regarded as "different" by virtue of having a misfit father.

Dad was an intensely private man, and so it was ironic that the Ortzan, a truly public resource, constituted the lifeline to our family income. We therefore depended on the good will of people who also had legal entitlements to this stream. They had little sympathy for outsiders like Dad. At times, it seemed that neighbors conspired to divert the Ortzan anywhere else rather than letting it take its course in the direction of Willy Haman, that hot-tempered misfit miller who ignored the good old boys way of settling business.

Since the Ortzan water was being diverted for numerous reasons, our water wheels were irregular machines. The power they provided had an erratic quality not recommended to operate sensitive machinery. The power that the wheels supplied was perfectly suited to drive sturdy milling machines, and three elevators that hoisted heavy sacks of newly harvested grain up to the granaries to dry there.

At maximum capacity, the Ortzan imparted so much power to the water wheels so when they were going full steam they were able to turn a dozen millstones. Each one of these granite stones was so incredibly heavy, it took four strong men to budge just one specimen as much as an inch. However, the raw muscle of the water wheels had to be translated by multiple belts, wheels, and gears. Driving axles, *transformers,* as Dad would call them, with a sense of pride in his blue eyes. Aligned and staggered in their sizes, these wheels, shafts, and belts were Dad's toy shop. He would keep his power machines lubricated with the dedication of a priest keeping the altar dignified and beautiful.

Particularly with the leather driving belts, Dad was supremely scrupulous in his maintenance. He always made sure they were in immaculate shape. These driving belts that transmitted power to the milling machines and elevators were substantial in size. About four times as wide as Dad's widest leather belt that held his blue cotton workman's pants closely fit to his trim waist.

Dad's diligent maintenance care was critical indeed. Just a rip in one of the belts that drove the elevators could result in a fatal accident. A deadly plunge from the height of the fourth floor, where we lived, to the rock bottom of the mill. One accident already had happened. It was Dad and Herbert Stalzer, Mother's father, and a third adult, a friend of Grandfather, who were ready for a ride, standing in a close clump on the elevator which Dad operated on the way up. Suddenly, about one floor above the ground floor, a violent jolt tossed the three bodies into one confused and fearful huddle. The belt had ripped, and the elevator plunged downward smashing into the ground with one big wham.

Dad's memory must have gone blank, for he only remembered that the elevator dropped downward like a rock. The moment they came to their crash landing, Dad thought his spine was going to push right through his skull. When they took stock of the casualties, Grandfather was groaning about his shoulder which turned out to be dislocated. The third person had fallen first upon crashing and involuntarily had cushioned the fall of Grandfather and Dad, in that order. This poor guy had blacked out and the doctor found out later that his left arm was broken in two places. Dad, being wiry, limber, and light had survived with the least damage.

However, Grandfather would never forget the incident, and at one point told Mother that this accident had been Dad's attempt at getting back at him for being such an autocratic father-in-law. Indeed, Grandpa Stalzer, the proprietor of the mill, ruled like a feudal lord over his manor. It gave Dad, who was an expert miller, no chance of being heard when he proposed changing outmoded ways of doing business. Conflict between them was smoldering like cinders. I felt almost sick, to my stomach, by the suppressed anger that floated in the air when Dad and Grandpa met. I often wished that this ball of anger would flare up into one big explosion, and thus be cleared once and for all.

Regardless of that one-time accident, everybody in the family was fond of using the elevator rather than making the arduous trip by foot. It was an arduous climb from the ground floor up to where we lived. We had to scale half a dozen steep and worn stairways having one hundred and eleven stairs, one of my first counting projects, that were slanting downward, and worn shiny from a century of foot traffic.

Always desirous to speed up locomotion, I learned to operate the elevator before I knew how to read. Like with the automatic ease of pedaling my bicycle, I was able to lift myself, and Sister, plus a fully grown person next to me, simply by pulling at a rope with a determined and steady grip. This pull would activate the elevator gears greatly assisting me in hoisting myself and my party off the ground floor, and up to the living quarters.

Mainly for the safety of his family, and to keep the mill machinery running as smoothly as the famous Swiss clockworks, Dad made it a habit to replace weekly, belts that showed slight marks of wear and tear. Whenever he was occupied with the belts though, Dad's concentration was as impenetrable as a bulwark In those moments when he shimmied the new belt into position, he wouldn't answer any question, no matter who approached him.

Dad was a perfectionist when it came to the execution of his milling trade. Machines were his best friends. Many times I saw Dad stand in front of a transmission wheel, on his face a meditative gaze, much like Tibetan monks I had seen in Mother's educational magazines. His next best friends were those people who serviced, tooled, or manufactured parts that would go into his flour mill. "You always want to be friendly with the people who supply you with the tools of your trade," Dad instructed me once. One of these friendly relations was the local leather craftsman who fashioned transmission belts exactly according to Dad's specifications.

Curiously enough, Dad would not practice the art of friendliness with the hardy peasants who made up the backbone of his business. In dealings with these weathered men, Dad was about as terse as he could get by with without plain insulting their simple minds. He strictly talked state of the crops and milling terms, sometimes he'd go the extra mile and discuss the weather. Since he didn't bother indulging them with any conversational niceties, such as inquiring about the wife's health and the children's progress in school, these men remained as unyielding in their dealings with Dad as the soil they cultivated with so much toil.

Dad's reputation filtered down to the school yard where class mates told me how their fathers would view my father. With smirks of superiority on their faces, they informed me that their dads, suspicious of anyone that wouldn't converse in the local Swabian tongue, regarded Dad as the Alien Guy. In their eyes, Dad was a displaced and uprooted man who had run away from his native Russian soil, and simply did not belong here.

It was the unwritten law of the land that in order to belong, and become a respectable member of the community, you had to be born a Swabian. This breed of people is renowned for their work ethic, frugality, and impeccable neatness far and above the high standards of the German people in general. If you wanted to belong to this exclusive tribe, you had to prove your commitment to the land and show a sense of rootedness by owning an apple orchard, pasture with clover, or field with root crops, such as potatoes or turnips. Once you were the proud owner of a parcel of land, you had something substantial to show for and, more importantly, talk about.

It was also important for anyone who wants to belong, to be fluent in conversational Swabian, a highly distinct dialect, in fact a peculiar language all to itself. If you want to speak to a Swabian, you have to be proficient in the use of idioms, sayings, and proverbial folk wisdom, and apply them generously to your speech. This, more than anything else, will delight the heart of any native Swabian man or woman. Once you are embedded in the local real estate and navigate securely the native speech, locals start to take notice of you. They tip their hat as they walk by you, and say, "*Gruess Gott,*" meaning Greet God the all important Swabian way to say hello. And as you greet them back, "*Gruess Gott,*" locals start taking note of you. Now that you've passed the preliminary hurdles, in their eyes you are taking shape as being somebody, versus all the nobodies who come to the blessed land of *Swabia,* not knowing the customs, but still expecting to belong. These Nobodies are known in the local vernacular as those who merely stick their nose into the Swabian way of life.

Once you've cleared the entrance exam, there is a reasonable chance that natives, we're talking strictly men here, will invite you into their sworn-in circles. Brotherhoods that sit together under clouds of tobacco smoke, playing skat, drinking beer, and fermented cider, and eating pretzels. The soft kind made with lye and uniquely Swabian. Eventually, you become one of the regulars at one of the reserved oak tables; at the Goldenes Kalb, the Die Katze, the Zum Ochsen, or any other of the numerous and proud local inns.

Dad never made it into any of these fraternities. With no land to his name and his inaptitude in the Swabian tongue it was a foreclosed matter, regardless whether Dad would exchange personal niceties with his customers or not. As a man, Dad was respected only because he did *a damn good job* at milling their precious grains, so Mother told me. She in turn had overheard these words spoken by peasant wives who discussed town politics at the butcher's while waiting for sausage, liverwurst, and pork roast to be cut to order.

If you bear the Alien Brand on your skin, as Dad did on his ruddy pockmarked complexion, you need to be twice as good as your competition to stay in business. Luckily for the family, Dad beat his competition hands down. His intimate knowledge of machines, and flair with anything electrical were instrumental in making the mill run smoothly around the clock, twenty-four hours a day. He made sure that most of the electric power needed to operate the mill was generated on the premises. At peak times, this homemade power would mill ten tons of wheat per day into virgin white flour. And, on top of that, our water power would lift three grain elevators loaded with grain sacks as heavy as six full grown men right up to the roof granaries, several stories above the loading area.

Electrically, our household was more than complex, it was puzzling. Our electric outlets were divided into those that tapped into the town's power grid of alternating current, a sure-proof and reliable source of electricity, and then we had *wild card* outlets. For my own safety, these I had to memorize. Those joker sockets tapped into the direct current, supplied free of charge by our waterworks, albeit, in my experience, quite unpredictable and sometimes dangerous in its effect on household appliances.

At times when, absent-mindedly, I plugged the radio into the water power socket, fumes started to emanate from the tubes in the radio, and the music of Connie Francis and Freddy Quinn literally went up in smoke. Luckily Dad had a supply of replacement tubes, and I never had to wait too long for the music or radio drama to come back on.

Away from power circuits with alternating and direct currents, standing with Dad at the center of the waterworks, here at the fulcrum of the water wheels' endless rounds, life was still simple and sensually most stimulating. I could smell the mustiness of aged oak shaped into two enormous hoops, both of them so large an elephant could stand inside and work it like a treadmill.

Amazingly, aquatic plant life flourished in this cavernous environment, and gave it a distinctly seaweed-like odor. Around the iron-reinforced rims of the water wheels, that was as daunting as the caterpillar treads of old German tanks. Along the spokes, as big as the trunks of full-sized beech trees, deep-green to olive-black colored cushions of water mosses clung to the hardwood as barnacles attach themselves to seafaring ships. The musty smell was light and clean however, for the busy current of the Ortzan had no patience with staleness. It just kept on washing away and splashing over the wheel-bound vegetation.

I was engrossed by this feast of tingling sensations, like the musty smells and the ice cold mist on my skin. My ears filled to the ear lobes with the deafening sounds generated by the water wheels' wolfing down the Ortzan stream. I listened in on this churning conversation between ancient wood and fresh water, with the aching and creaking troughs, and the moaning of the water wheels' axles. The refrain of captured plunging water being swallowed, and then emptied from the disinterested giants' mouths. I listened intently to this chorus, for I was eager to detect in this song the forever elusive meaning of Ortzan.

The archaic name of the stream that flowed by my home never ceased to intrigue my imagination. Ortzan was an odd and enigmatic word, so far removed from any known expression in my vernacular. Even Mother, always knowledgeable about the origin of words and local customs, had to admit her ignorance when I asked her what kind of meaning this strange word "Ortzan" held in its guttural sounds.

"The name of the stream goes back to the old Alemannen, the original settlers of this valley," she told me. "We're talking ancient pagan times, long before Jesus Christ was born, and people did neither read nor write, and therefore wouldn't leave us any explanation about their name giving of rivers, woods, meadows, and mountains. Linguists and local historians however had looked into the extinct language of the Alemannen, as preserved in the many quaint names of fields and plains," so Mother had told me. And I decided then and there that one day I would look up this research, so I could finally make sense of the word Ortzan.

While the waterworks loomed large and mythical in our lives, and provided the lifeline to my family's milling business, it neither bothered nor thrilled the rainbow trout, the actual inhabitants of the stream. Unlike the trout who had adapted to the constant churning of their environment, blotting this disturbance clear out of their bead-sized minds. To me the waterwheels never ceased to be an object of marvel. The closer I got to them, the more I felt entranced by the hypnotic regularity of sounds and motion. As if I had entered a sacred place, I stood motionless. Only vaguely aware that if I moved only two more steps, I would have been ground up and ripped apart between these giants. They wouldn't stop turning unless Dad would divert the stream in a complicated procedure into a chute that bypassed the water works.

"If you get in between those two," Dad pointed at the water wheels groaning and moaning right in front of us, "there's absolutely nothing I can do for you." He said so with his mouth right up to my ear. And on his warm breath, I detected a grave warning an admission of his own helplessness, and his dread of losing me. Nodding my head, I showed that I was sensible enough not to tempt the fates. By now, I understood on a gut level the danger that revolved just two steps away from my toes. I leaned back, nestling closer into Dad's warm and reassuring body. He held me in a tight embrace, his arms as strong as a vise around my chest.

After Dad's entreating whispers into my ear about minding the dangers that lurked in front of me, we both yelled at our chests' capacity, but the words were drowned out in the heavy din of gorging and disgorging waterwheels. I felt father's grip tightening around my ribs. Just as much as I stood there in sheer awe, he, a seasoned miller who had managed three mills simultaneously in his native Russia, continued to be amazed. He watched the gigantic power tools of his milling trade do their job. Like Jonah in the Old Testament, standing here on the water wheel landing, we got an inside glimpse of the whale's innards.

Indeed the Ortzan had a tendency to swallow up whole beings, just like the whale in the biblical story, and disgorge them literally under our nose. The swift currents of this stream that reached up to my thighs during spring snowmelt, presented us with death in a manifold of ways and always unexpectedly.

Dead beings that were disfigured, smelly, and bloated, visited us far too many times in the form of stiff carcasses of livestock and pets that had drowned while drinking from the stream. These dead bodies of lambs, calves, dogs, and other animals, were stopped on their downstream drift at the wooden rake that guarded our waterworks, from the interference of any flotsam.

It is sad but true that many of these animals had died because cold-hearted men, and possibly even women and children, had intentionally tossed these hapless critters into the river to dispose of ailing animals, the runt of the litter, or the pet that wouldn't mind its master. I knew that fickle-hearted people drowned their pets on a whim, simply because they had lost interest in the companionship of these loyal souls. The darker side of the Ortzan prevailed on Heavy

Days as Dad called them. On days like that, whole litters of kittens washed up against the rake. It was Dad's dirty work to retrieve these bundled carcasses, and bury them in a more decent fashion. Molested kittens, more than any other creature, tugged at Dad's heart strings. Innocent, little creatures, that had been drowned, in a tied up burlap sack, by some callous hearted upstream neighbor.

We knew that Dad was experiencing a heavy day when he, already a man of few words, would hardly speak at all. Whenever Dad had to deal with a bundle of innocent death, he became strangely shy and withdrawn. His eyes were cast to the ground, and his mouth was sealed shut.

Even more ominously, the Ortzan had swallowed up and drowned a kin of mine, who bore the same name as my Mother and Sister. This was Margret Heham, a name that town folks had either forgotten conveniently, or if they mentioned it, they did so behind hands in front of their mouths, so you could barely hear it.

Because of the shame she had brought upon the mill, her memory was much dimmed in the family stories. Aunt Elma would serve me milk and a butter and raspberry jam sandwich. Nevertheless her story came up, between bites of bread and butter. Aunt Elma was not one to hold it in. She just had to pass the oral legacy on, for Aunt Elma was the sole surviving repository of the family myth that these two milling brothers Albert and Hans had created in their lifetime.

Margret, the woman with the hushed reputation, was my great aunt whom I had never met. She chose to end her life prematurely about two miles upstream from the flour mill where I grew up.

If visualized on the family tree, Margret Heham branched off as one of Grandfather Herbert's six sisters. She was born a Stalzer into the midst of a family that eventually counted thirteen children altogether. Their upbringing was so poor, that their family myth held as a centerpiece a true miracle. When starved for a bite to eat, Alfreda, the mother of Margret and Herbert and all the other hungry mouths, foraged in garbage pails for edible discards. All the while the kids watched, and were made to pray so God would show mercy, and provide them with something to eat.

Indeed, the miracle materialized. A whole loaf of perfectly wonderful peasant bread waited there by the roadside only to be picked up by Alfreda who, stunned by the miracle, fell to her knees and thanked God for his endless compassion. This episode must have left an indelible mark in Margret's memory, for she made sure that such poverty would not befall her future family. Still quite young she was wedded to Hans Heham, one of the two brothers who were both notorious because of their cunning business ways. These two brothers jointly owned and operated the Jrosse Muehle, one of the biggest and most modern mills in the upper Ortzan valley.

Hans and Margret's betrothal caused an uproar in the gossip circles in town, mostly because of a large, almost indecently wide age difference between the two. Not to mention the fact that Aunt Margret was a penniless lass. Granted though, she was a pretty looking girl. Hans Heham had steadfastly remained a bachelor for such a long time, mainly, *so they said*, to stash away even more money. The rumor ran that Albert together with brother Hans had over the years of wheeling and dealing stashed away a veritable treasure of gold jewelry and precious stones.

Even Mother raised her eyebrows when she gave me her version of Aunt Margret's sad story. She knew, all too well, from her own experience, the embarrassments that a large difference in age creates. Dad was 15 years older than Mother, and people who didn't know them as a couple occasionally referred to her saying, "Now you must be Willy's daughter". Dad, for unknown reasons, felt flattered by such observations. Possibly he looked at Mother as a trophy of youth that he was lucky enough to call his own. Mother, however, inevitably blushed and became awkward and self-conscious when people made such remarks.

This large age and social gap between Great Aunt Margret and shrewd miller Hans may have been a contributing factor to Margret's tragic ending, this much I could read from Mother's animated expressions on her face. Neither storyteller, Aunt Elma nor Mother, would delve into speculation as to why Great Aunt Margret chose to take her own life at such an early age. It was up to me to arrange the bits and pieces into a meaningful composite which would satisfy my appetite for cause and effect. Aunt Margret's terrible ending needed, in my imagination, a substantially terrible cause for her to take her own life.

I held the chronology of her last months in my mind, and pondered its significance. In due time after her marriage, Great Aunt Margret became pregnant with her husband's seed. The delivery of the boy child was difficult even by the tough standards of those times, when pregnancy and childbirth was still a major risk for women as well as the unborn or newly born baby.

When, after hours of labor, the doctor finally held the baby in his hand, he shook his head. The blue-purplish pallor of the skin told him that this delivery had come to a bad ending. The midwife wasn't ready to give up though, and held the baby close to her chest. All the coaxing, cooing, prodding, tabbing, slapping, shaking, and numerous other tricks she applied, did not make the baby boy live. The child that was meant to continue Hans's proud line in the milling trade was stillborn. And Margret survived the ordeal by the skin of her teeth.

All along the gossip mongers in town had figured it out. Margret had made this catch of a rich husband mainly because she was young and strong, and there was an excellent chance that she would provide Hans with a much wanted male heir. He had felt his power base crumble, and saw himself outnumbered in the family business by his brother Albert, who had produced two strapping male heirs to join in the milling trade.

When he was told about his stillborn boy, Hans entered the nursery forcefully and looked at Aunt Margret, *still in shock from seeing her baby dead*, with such contempt, it could have frozen the Ortzan over. This had never happened in recorded history. The midwife later circulated her impression that Hans must have been taken over by an evil spirit to produce such a menace toward his wife. The fact that he didn't say a word made it all the more ominous.

While recovering from childbirth, Margret fell into a gloomy state which turned blacker every day. Neighbors were frightened by her ghost-like appearance. Gone was the rosiness of her cheeks. Her skin was as pallid and slack as that of an old woman. The spring in her walk had changed into a listless shuffle. She kept her eyes cast to the ground. Gone was that sparkle that once radiated her expectation of having a good, that is prosperous life ahead of her. Her vivacious speech had dried up into gloomy silence.

One afternoon in early March, the sun still a faint glow in the sky and the air prickly cold to the skin, she slipped out of the mill. Nobody noticed her, as the place was as usual buzzing with business. Later, neighbors remembered seeing a furtive figure, slighter than her own shadow, slipout of the towering mill garage and hurry toward the water meadows. A stretch of land along the Ortzan that was being flooded during early spring, for more verdant grass to sprout. She walked as if in her own dream, and glided by the water-logged meadows. But then she would stop on the graveled path and turn sharply to the left where she entered the marshy lands, a forbidding zone at this time of the year.

The mud sloshed and gurgled under her sinking steps. For the occasion, she wore her Sunday church going outfit. A wide woolen skirt, set into innumerable pleats, bellowed around her slight body during this gusty afternoon. She wore white lacy stockings now studded with muck. As she slowly and arduously made headway in the water meadows, her black, lacquer shiny, ankle high shoes looked like mud slinging mules. Whoever saw her on that inhospitable March day, must have wondered why, for goodness' sake, this young woman had entered the swamps in her church outfit, where she staggered and lurched toward a mysterious destination.

During drier seasons, I have gone many times the same route as Margret did, on her last day. Deliberately, I wanted to retrace her steps, so that I would get a notion of the forces that drove her into her own undoing. Maybe she had heard voices come from the old gnarled trees that stood like crooked signposts in the wetlands. "Come hither fair lady, and yonder where the river forks we will show you a peaceful place to rest." If I tilted my head in a certain direction into the wind, I myself could hear luring whispers that drew me into the uncultivated shallow land where the wet meadows meet the Ortzan's Horsetail. With piercing leaves and unyielding stems, obstructed access to the point where the Ortzan divides into two. Even shielded by my denim pants, I could feel the poking of these plant daggers. They made me run the gantlet before I would get to the divide that had swallowed up my great Aunt Margret. I had the idea that the plant and animal inhabitants of this godforsaken piece of earth had conspired to forbid my venturing further into the secret lair of the spirits that reign over the Ortzan stream.

The destination point on my journey toward greater understanding of the unfathomable finally lay before me. In terms of man's figures and names this was a sobering place. At this junction, the Ortzan stream separates into two unequal canals. One, amounting to three eighths of the total volume, ran through the turbine of the Armbruster cloth dying plant, and emerged beyond. In all shades of purple and blue from the plants' effluents. The bigger branch, called officially the Five-Eighths Canal, flowed by our mill and drove the water wheels.

As I stood on the embankment's un-mowed grass, so high it obscured my searching gaze, my attention was funneled into the turbulent flow. Swelling into angry waves right before the pointed wedge of the meadowland that drove a dividing angle into the heart of the stream. The willows at this juncture were sweeping the crests that foamed with rage.

These drooping old bystanders of Margret's demise appeared particularly sad and weepy. As I watched their gliding branches with lancet leaves riding astride the foamy peaks, I felt transported into a trance like state. I could have sworn something, that was invisible to my eyes, was tugging at my feet so I would step closer to the borderline. In my daze, I vaguely sensed that someone nudged me with sweet persuasion. "Come closer my dear. Come and take a good look at the swirling waters. Maybe you can see my face and my long hair floating on the waves."

In a startle, I awoke from my entranced gaze at the most beguiling spot of all spots that I knew along the Ortzan stream. Tall reeds had guarded the drop-off into the water, as a line of soldiers and had poked me, of all places, in my tiny nipples. I was glad for this rough wake-up call, for I had felt a magnetic pull toward the stream's cleavage that gaped open like the frothy maw of a rabid animal.

The inexorable spinners of fate had spun a short yarn of life for Margret, and she had arrived at the end of her tether. I literally saw her life unraveled into a string of yarn, and Margret stood there totally alone, drenched, and shivering with fear as she was about to jump off, from her last inch of life.

Did she bother to take off her mud-clogged shoes and soiled stockings? So I wondered, as I gazed into the turbulence that raged over rocks. In March the Ortzan will reach up to a full grown man's waist. Dad had told me so. He knew from experience, since every year when spring rolled around, he would go out with a crew of hired hands and dredge the Ortzan's stream bed. Some time before he scheduled this expedition, he would traverse the stream right where it forked, and wade across to assess how high the sandbanks had grown since the last cleanup. Dad could only do this by hanging on to a rope that two men held on either side of the Ortzan. This railing safeguarded Dad's passage across the stream, for otherwise the strong spring current would have pulled him under. Just like it did with Margret.

When I peered into the stream right beneath me, I became aware that Grand Aunt Margret couldn't even see herself reflected by the water when she contemplated that last motion. The Ortzan is laden with silt during spring snowmelt and turns the color of coffee. Usually the stream's current was one straightforward swift motion, but here at this junction, the currents going to the fork were agitated into rapid whirls, and it looked to me like the Ortzan had turned into one big bowl of coffee. An invisible hand stirring the dark brew-laden with silt and brown as coffee. She herself peered into the whirlpool right at the fork. I imagined her slowly lowering herself into the swirl. Possibly shivering and screaming, *Oh my God*, shocked by the icy sting of the water. However soon her scream would be muffled, for I knew just by feeling the incantations of the spirits of this sight that she must have dunked her head as soon as the ripping stream embraced her shivering body. Once submerged, she let herself drift and be pulled under like a willing piece of driftwood. Her wide skirt may have welled up like a descending parachute, and her long hair wrought into a bun must have come undone and floated on top like those long strands of mosses that undulated around smooth river rocks.

In my imagination, I saw this woman float coming up against the wedge, the dividing point. Which way would the stream take her? Three-eighths of the water passed through the dying factory, her turning into even deeper blue and purple. Or would the current take her home, on Five-Eighths Canal, bringing her right up to her husband's water works. There she would get caught in the long wooden teeth of the rake that screened the stream for dead trees and shrubs, drowned livestock, and Sunday garbage that had been dumped by upstream neighbors.

Chapter 16

Birds

Seen from the top of the nearby mountain range, we had by far the hugest trees in the whole town. Next to the stream, they thrived on a boundless supply of water.

Birds of all kinds congregated in these ample canopies. My favorites among them were larks and blackbirds with their yellow bills. Their ecstatic chirrups gave me goose bumps and made me shiver. The joy of their song was infectious.

Invisible in the dense foliage of willows and poplars, they called out to friends and neighbors in the dark, gothic-looking spruce trees of the neighboring sawmill. I had figured out that the birds' call and response was their way to broadcast any news and also to locate potential mates.

These happy creatures didn't have to wait long for a response. Just a few seconds after the trills and warbles fell silent, there would be a cheerful chirping coming from somewhere in the four directions.

And so it went back and forth. Each bird trying to sound louder and happier than the one before. Over the course of the day, the bird concert grew and subsided like waves, but during sunrise and sunset it was a veritable raucous symphony.

Unfortunately much of the birds' activities like their mating, nest-building and feeding of the newly hatched offspring remained obscured behind multi-layered drapes of lancet-shaped, silver-green willow leaves.

Chapter 17

Trout for Dinner

Whenever the weather was fair, I could be found outdoors. I might be checking for grubs under rocks, studying spiders building webs and enshrouding their prey, or I would be lining up slugs to see which one of them was the fastest.

Meanwhile, forced by circumstances, I wasn't much of a birdwatcher; I made up for it by studying the drama of aquatic life at close range.

The stream that passed through our property was my favorite playground. It was lined by poplar trees so high their tops appeared to scratch the sky, as they lined the riverbed. And the willow tree next to the river branched out wider than our wash house, and the trunk was low enough so Sister and I could climb up and build ourselves a cozy bed. We wedged cushions between the arms of the tree, and piled bedding into the bottom of the trunk. Then we stretched out, our feet hung over the edges of tree's limbs. "This is a comfy place," Sister would say. "And nobody's check-in on us," I would add. At times we would bring dishes and foodstuffs to our hideaway. We would have afternoon tea, and sip it with gusto from our miniature china.

Our favorite snack was buttered Laugen Brezeln. We looked through the twisted loops and discussed their shapes which resembled that of the number eight or that of a set of eyeglasses. Mother had told us the Brezel shape had its origins in pagan times when these intertwining circles symbolized fertility.

"The more we eat of these the more fertile we'll become," I told sister. And she looked at me wide-eyed. "We might have babies twice a year like Muschi." She wondered and sounded scared. Our cat Muschi was unstoppably fertile. "Every time the neighbors' tom cat slings around the woodshed, Muschi grows a belly again," Dad had remarked every time Muschi got pregnant. "I don't want to be fertile," Sister said. "You know what happens to kittens," she insinuated.

"They grow up to be full size cats," I said, just to tease Sister. To make her spill out the whole story rather than just roll her eyes. With experience, I had developed a trick to make Sister spill most any of her stock of secrets. So I pointed up at the sky "Wow look at those cloud castles! I'll bet you we'll have an electric storm that will shake us out of our tree house."

Sister wouldn't even look up, but continued with her story. I noticed she was barely breathing, and the color of her cheeks turned pale. "I was there when Dad pulled them out of the river." I didn't respond and kept still for her to continue her story. "When Dad opened the burlap sack, I counted them one by one, they were six of them. Their eyes were glazed over like frosted windows. Three of the kittens were black with white markings and three tabby." I tried to find Sister's eyes, but she kept her gaze cast down. "Dad said that some peasant upstream must have tossed them into the Ortzan."

I couldn't hold back my curiosity any longer, "you mean somebody would toss live kittens into the river and drown them in a sack? That means they had no chance, no chance at all" I said. I pulled a handful of lancet shaped leaves from the tree, wadded them into a ball, and tossed them into the stream to our left. Sister looked up and stared blankly into the distance. Mister Valcon's smoke stack belched forth blackish smoke banners that drifted in the direction of Mount Ursual, to the East of us.

"I took a close look at them," Sister said, and paused. She grabbed a handful of dried leaves from the pit of the tree trunk, crushed them into powder and tossed them into the air. When her arms fell back into her lap, I saw that her hands were shaking. "Their bellies were full of water like water balloons. Their mouths open and stiff. Their tiny tongues hung over their lips, like this," and she hung her tongue from the corner of her mouth. I shifted in my seat. Sister liked to delve into unsightly details, the ugly spots, the puss, blood, and slime, once she had decided to tell her story.

"Dad tied up the burlap sack and buried them under the cherry tree. Now the dandelions and violets growing there will be bigger and bushier than anywhere else in the garden."

On breezy days, we'd just snuggle under our down comforters and gaze into the billowing canopy of our willow abode.

Countless leaves shimmered in an ocean of sunlight. Sunlight bounced off of millions of green mirrors, and blasted into emerald fireworks. Right below us the Ortzan stream rushed by at the sped of a tall man walking briskly. As the Ortzan rippled past us in its gravelly streambed, it had already travelled from the springs in the foothills of the Alb mountain range. The Ortzan's source was a whole day's hike away from our home. In my hometown Seiffingen, the stream was divided into three channels, the biggest of which flowed right by our grist mill. Downstream from us, after the Ortzan's channels rejoined, it still had to travel as far as a three hour ride, in Dad's old Opel car, until it finally drained into the stately Neckar River. A busy waterway dotted with barges and ships. Only the gravely and speedy headwaters of the Ortzan teemed with brown trout, known throughout the valley as the most formidable and crafty game fish around.

When we lay in our willow's tree trunk, the stream beneath us spoke to us about its inhabitants, the newly hatched tadpoles, millions of them. And only a handful would make it into adult frogs. The sound of rushing water reminded us of schools of minnows the size of our pinkies, dashing to-and-fro near the bottom of the stream. They were as frisky as the kids of our gradeschool during a field trip.

While I didn't know a thing about sexual intercourse between man and woman, and still imagined that a kiss sufficed to make a woman pregnant, I had observed just about every animal on our land go into season and mate. However, breeding among fish is an eventless procedure. They have no courting rituals like birds, they neither sniff nor hump like dogs. And the trouts' soundless coupling is far removed from the high drama of cats in heat. There's no biting, hissing, clawing, or scratching in our Ortzan stream. Through my daily observation, I found out that trout prefer late fall and early winter for breeding.

When the stream is awash and blazing with fallen leaves of all colors, female trout dig with their tail fins a shallow depression into the gravelly stream bed, and hover over this hole, with as much patience as our hens in the chicken coop. The male trout would sneak right behind her and squirt his sperm to fertilize the fish eggs.

In those moments of procreation, our stream trout, the most ferocious predator the length of the entire Ortzan, had a vulnerable look about it. On most other days, the trout in our stream were suspicious of any shadow that would cast while approaching the river bank. But during spawning season, I could walk up close and even move and they would remain in place, their beady eyes aware of my presence.

I never ceased to be amazed at the countless numbers of eggs produced by fish, and I was even more astounded that only two dozen minnows, at the most, would make it into adulthood. It showed that life in ponds and streams is perilous.

But still, the Ortzan was alive with brown trout, the size of Dad's forearm. Mister Egbert Valcon, our sawmill neighbor kept them stocked for his own pastime, and that of his well-heeled angler friends.

This trout had me hooked in many ways. I marveled at the fish's clever color camouflage. Their silvery sides dotted with black spots that faded into lighter ones mimicked the river, right down to the silvery play of light across the swiftly flying current. These bodies swept like transparent shapes across the gravelly stream bed, where rocks and mosses of all sizes created a backdrop of light and darks spots. Just like the dots of varying sizes appearing as dark and lighter shades on the trout's flanks, back, and fins. Their chameleon-like appearance allowed the trout to travel the stream like the mirages of light and shadow. Trout are the wariest of fish. They register any sudden and jerky movement. The mere shadow of my arm would arouse the fish's suspicion, and send it scurrying for shelter under the overhang of the river bank. Or in a split second it would flick its tail and dart upstream like a silver rocket. Invisible to the untrained eye, trout would slide sideways, drift down-stream, dash forward, or sway their tails among the undulating strands of sunken weed beds.

For most of their lives, the Ortzan trout thrived unharmed. Partly because of their camouflage and also because those who held fishing permits were busy business men, who would find time to cast their hooked bait only on weekends or holidays.

Over the years, I had become an expert trout watcher. But first I had to learn the rules of the game. Trout came alive when clouds hung in the sky and diffused the stark sunlight, and also in the twilight hours of the evening or wee morning hours. I could see their dashing performances. I saw them break through the surface and shoot up into the air like missiles; mouths wide open to inhale whatever living matter came across their orbit. However, under clear skies and bright sunlight, trout would prefer to languish near sunken logs, undercut banks and hover near bridges. Like cats, trout dallied away and dozed most of the day.

If I would stand still for a while and train my eye on the water, squint to block out the glare of reflected sunlight, sort out the fleeting shadows of clouds and willow branches from among the shifting shades of rocks and water plants, only then would I get a glimpse of a sleek muscular body, as it streaked by me, or lounged in easy suspension among braids of water mosses, the face of the trout, bare of any expression, other than lips set in a defiant smirk and eyes frozen into a detached stare.

Trout have been around a hundred million years, my grade-school teacher had told us. If we mess with our streams, trout are the first to go. Trout like the coldest, cleanest, and clearest water of all game fish. If factories drain their polluted waste water into the Ortzan and farms discard their stable effluent into our river, then you just watch for bloated trout to belly-up, washing against the shore. I took my teacher at his word and walked the length of the Ortzan, a mile up and down from our grist mill looking for signs of morose dead trout, and I did find them belly up floating in eddies amidst grimy foam and foul smelling waste. The main polluters were large size plants that sent their waste water straight into the Ortzan. Luckily, we lived upstream from Gerhart's factory where fabrics were dyed in all of the rainbow colors, and the industrial effluents dyed the Ortzan opaque. And we also lived upstream from the paper mill that spilled noxious chemicals into the river. As long as I can remember, the Ortzan that rushed by our property was as transparent as spring cleaned window panes.

However, the grist mill operation posed a different kind of threat to the trout population. Our hydraulic turbine caused many a trout to get pounded against the iron grill that covered the flume so no rocks or other debris would run through the turbine. Because of the pull of water plunging into the chute, those trout that hovered near the grill were forced to battle against this strong pull until their fighter spirit broke. And as their strength weakened they would get sucked against the iron grid, and here they would fling their battered and bruised bodies in desperation. They would squirm and writhe, open and close their mouths in silent alarm, and finally give up in exhaustion.

By the time Dad would come to fetch trout for dinner they merely flapped their tails, and fanned their gills. Even though Dad had trout every other day, unlike any of Mr.Valcon's well-heeled angler buddies, he never had to cast to get the fish. They virtually got washed into his frying pan, that's how he would put it, and omit part of the gruesome story that I am about to tell.

When I looked at the face of a trout it appeared empty, not revealing any emotion. I couldn't find a trace of sympathy in their beady-looking eyes. The angle of their jaws reaches way back behind the eyes, like a mean grimace. Having its mouth thus emphasized gives this fish a menacing look. You can't tell by looking at a trout's facial expression whether the fish is in good spirits or close to dying. This made me wonder whether looking so Aztec stone-faced was just one more facet of their ingenious camouflage.

At the time, I was convinced that trout had a mean streak in their personality. Besides their stone-faced grimace, they sport a mean looking tinge of orange on one of their dorsal fins. The color of scorpions, orange in the animal world signals danger, and trout like pike, are the cannibals among freshwater fish.

I have seen trout *feed on each other* and even devour small fry, *their own babies*. And worst of all, if one fellow trout is wounded, the others will sidle up to it, just like they do while spawning, and bite off whole chunks of its body. Then they proceed to devour these chunks of cannibalized fellow trout right on the spot, all the while showing no sign of shame, or embarrassment.

The victim usually hovers close by, *enduring being eaten alive without flinching*. It merely watches its own undoing with beady eyes.

At least twice a week trout were washed against the grate that screened off the chute of the electrical turbine. The suction would hold them like glue to the metal grate. Routinely, I would go and check if the trout was still salvageable or not. This also gave me a chance to touch them. I knew the subtle difference in the feel of a trout that was dying because of exhaustion and one that was still vigorously fighting for its survival.

After having been battered for hours against the cutting edges of the metal rake, by the swift current of the stream, trout would lose their fighting spirit. This giving up of spirit became apparent in the rapid deterioration of its body. Under stress the slick and resilient feel of a healthy trout changes, and turns into a more slimy and sticky texture. Also, the high gloss of their skin turns into a milky opaque that screened off the chute of the electrical turbine.

Judging by those signs, I would decide whether I should rescue the trapped trout and throw it back into the water further upstream, where immersed in a more gentle current it could recover from the trauma.

While I found trout cold-natured and callous, I was still intrigued by their mystery, their hardiness, vigor, swift movements, and particularly their warrior instinct.

Dad's predilection for trout meat, gave me an opportunity to experience at close range the indomitable fighting instincts of this killer fish.

Father loved trout, for he was a serious connoisseur of trout. I knew the trout's ways and tricks, whereas he knew every nuance of how they were supposed to taste.

I looked at trout cheeks and found them to be the only soft, rounded, and amicable feature in their faces. If you asked Dad what he thought of trout cheeks, he would have told you that they are the tastiest bits of meat on the whole fish. He saved the cheeks for the very end of his trout dinners, and then placed them on his tongue with a gleam in his eyes. Sometimes in those high moments of trout feasting, he would wink at Sister and I like boys on the street who wanted us to join their games.

Dad was not a fisherman who catches and kills the fish with a sense of art. In comparison, Dad's method of securing fresh trout was plain gross.

About once or twice a week, he would pull out a trout that I didn't get a chance to rescue. By the time Dad would get it, the fish was often sore from the constant banging against the metal of the rake.

If I was around, I'd watch with keen interest how the fish reacted being taken out of its element. With its powerful muscular body it would wind and wring itself into all kinds of rounded and oval shapes, and sometimes it succeeded in jumping out of Dad's grip, landing with a flop back in the water. However, Dad would generally prevail and toss the fish into a bucket full of water.

Curious, like the bystanders at an accident site, I watched closely every stirring of Dad's catch. Captivated trout show agitation by opening and closing their mouths. I imagined they were screaming, but my ears couldn't hear their screams since the frequency of fish calls is beyond the range familiar to my ear drums.

When I was still younger and less educated, I assumed fish were gasping for air when they opened and closed their mouths. Once I had learned that fish have gills instead of lungs, I understood why captive trout acted the way they did. Restrained in a plastic bucket, the gill flaps bulged and kept fanning water over the gill filaments to supply fresh air. As the oxygen content in the water decreased, the trout's gill flaps would get more and more agitated, and the mouth would fall open.

Sloshing around in the bucket, the trout kept its beady eyes peering in one direction only. No matter what happened on its side or approached it from behind, trout's eyes always stared straight forward. I figured that it must perceive danger through other sense organs.

Trout don't show pain, no flinching, trembling, or submissive posture. However, their battle for survival was fierce and endless it seemed to me. I witnessed the slaughter of trout on the kitchen sink many times. I saw their bodies toss and slam, when Dad thrust the sharpest and longest kitchen knife into that collar slot between the head and the rest of their body.

The killing of the trout was a bloody mess, for blood spattered on the stone top of the sink whereby it stained the tiles, and Dad's hands and wrists got bloodied.

Even though I watched from a distance, I felt the agony of the fish palpable in the air. In the throes of death, the fish bent its body and wrung itself out of Dad's hold. Like a taut spring, it hurled itself up in the air, flip-flopped, slapped against the wall by the sink where it left another bloody trail. Dad's hands groped and grasped, and the moment he thought he'd finally caught the jumping slick beast it would slide right through his hold, and eject once more like a missile. By then the whole kitchen smelled heavily of fish.

The battle always ended with one dull thud, and the fish landing next to Dad's knife. In one last spasmodic jerk, the fish twisted its head with the mouth reaching for its tail. I wondered did it want to bite its own tail? The very last sparks of life were faint ripples, nerve twitches that would travel the length of its body. Finally the fish lay still, having spent all its formidable spring.

I don't know how long this battle lasted. Possibly it was just a couple of minutes, but it truly seemed like hours to me.

In one swift and elegant motion, Dad would slice open the belly of the fish, and scrape the guts out of the belly. The entrails of a trout are purple, the color of like wild grapes. The mere look of it gives me a bitter taste in my mouth.

If Dad found the ovaries of the trout swollen with eggs, he would discard the whole fish. "Trout that are getting ready to spawn taste nasty," Dad had told me, with an expression of disgust. If he happened to get a pregnant female, he would mutter some cuss words under his breath for having gone through all this mess, only to find a damn pregnant fish. In those instances, Dad would be mad at himself for having overlooked the telltale sign of a female that is about to spawn, the swelling on the sides of the fish near its tail.

After this prep work, Dad washed his hands with soap and rinsed them thoroughly. It appeared to me like he needed to cleanse himself of all the blood and gore the fish had spilled on him. With a look of eager anticipation, Dad would get busy at the gas stove.

This gave me a chance to approach the dead warrior, who lay still, being pinned with a knife to the chopping board. Was Dad suspecting this gutted trout might still jump off the sink?

The bloodshot eyes of the trout looked vacant, and, as always, straight ahead. Lips turned down in a defiant smirk. The trout's defiant look, notwithstanding its belly slit open, always puzzled me. Could it mean that the fish felt victorious in a sense, by having wrestled with Dad until it had totally exhausted each and every muscle fiber in its body?

"What do say?" Dad asked casually as he dropped a tablespoon of butter in the cast iron skillet and lit up the gas flame. It was his way of making conversation as he sensed my uneasiness with the killing of the fish. I usually kept my thoughts to myself, not wanting to upset Dad.

The sweet dairy smell of the butter mingled with the fish flavor. Dad looked happier by the minute. With great care he placed the fish in the skillet. Dad had the timing of his fish fry down to a science. He considered it a major sin to overcook fish.

With a sense of ceremony and great expectation, Dad sat down at the table. He would cut a couple of slices of fresh rye bread and place the whole trout on his plate. Evenly distributed over the length of the fish, he placed curls of butter that started to melt immediately. Then he squeezed a wedge of lemon, sprinkled salt and pepper and took his first bite.

As I had refused his invitation in the past, he no longer would ask me whether I wanted to join him. Having watched the ordeal of the fish's killing, there was no way I could eat it.

Instead I would run out into the open air and play with the dog, who sniffed the fish smell on my clothes. Like with taking in a deep breath, I would take in the bird's ecstatic chirping and feel comforted and reconciled with the order of things.

Chapter 18

Winter War Zone

Twice every generation an extended Siberian cold front throws Central Europe into the deep freeze. I remember it as if it had been yesterday. Record lows had frozen all our pipes and we had to get water in pails from the stream. People in our town huddled around their wood-stoves, drinking mulled wine so hot that it would burn your mouth.

After the cold front had made its way across the Iron Curtain, it lingered over our Ortzan Valley for about two weeks. Under the clutch of sustained day and night freezing temperatures, the Ortzan stream that powers the water wheels of our grist-mill put on an icy mantle of haunting beauty. Locals called it the Ice Castle. Since the Ice Castle depended on global factors, only the Farmer's Almanac and an old gap-toothed hag of a neighbor, who had been demented by syphilis, ventured to forecast its coming.

In the past, half of the time, one or the other had guessed wrong. This time the old witch with the ugly sore on her upper lip had correctly intuited the coming. "Twelve days after Christmas, give or take a day," she predicted, and spat through her gapped teeth. She handed Dad a wadded bill that she kept in her woolen stocking, to pay for a sack of chicken feed. And sure enough, the day of Epiphany, the ice castle had reached the height of its glory.

Unlike the seasonal color splash of autumn foliage and spring blooming, the Ice Castle's coming was capricious like a meteor. It attracted the naturalist photographers, those who appreciated that beauty is as fragile as a snowdrop poking through the frozen ground. They knew that the best things in life are made precious by the long time we have to wait for them. And the waiting for the ice palace required a special kind of patience; one that stretched beyond the certitude of the yearly round of seasons and festivities. Santa Claus, Christmas, and New Years came and went, nine, ten, eleven times, and sometimes more. Until sometime in January, the Siberian cold would clutch the mill stream in its vise and congeal the boundaries of the swift Ortzan and its steaming effervescence. (The Ortzan was actually steaming, and was considerably warmer in temperature than the frigid air.) An ice show of haunting beauty.

Monday after Epiphany, I awoke to a jungle of frost flowers that covered all the window panes and created a milky luminescence on an already wintry gray day. Mother and I were still sitting at the kitchen table chatting over breakfast when Dad flung open the door. Briskly a cold rush of air streamed in from the chilly hallway, and fanned open the napkin next to my fork and spoon. "Here read this," he said, and tossed the folded paper onto the center of the table, it landed just inches away from the jam jar. "We made front page news," he added and left again. Mom unfolded the paper and I noticed a faint tremor in her hands. She read the headline, "*Gristmill Is Formidable Ice Fortress.*" Then she showed it to me, a picture that ran smack across the width of the front page and a headline in letters as large as the announcement of war. Just like the frost flowers had grown overnight, so our home had become a regional landmark. By virtue of the ice palace, the water wheels beneath it had turned into local celebrities.

The editor of the paper had rung us up that morning and inquired about the dimensions of the largest icicles. Shortly after that call, Dad pulled out his longest ladder and positioned it tightly against the west wall of the mill. He pulled out his measuring tape and reached for the peak of the tallest icy spire. Just when he had hooked the end of the tape on the very tip of the icicle, the ladder slipped on the frozen ledge. Only by holding on to a branch of a willow tree did Dad avoid falling into the stream. I said: *"Thank you God,"* when Dad shifted the ladder back into balance, and slowly descended the rungs of the ladder. A plunge into the Ortzan would have been near fatal, given the forbidding cold of that day.

Once the news had spread, the bridge over the Ortzan swarmed with curious spectators like an anthill. Some had seen the front page headlines, others had heard it through the grapevine. In any case, by mid-January the bridge that leads across the Ortzan stream provided full panoramic view of the ice palace, and was as busy as the town's market before Christmas. Amateurs rubbed elbows with professional photographers. The men, (and there was not a single camera-wielding woman among them), set up their Leicas and Hasselblats on tripods. They often blocked traffic on the bridge, which narrowed the street into one lane, and required gestures of hands, grimacing, and other motions, to negotiate who has the right of way to enter the bridge first.

I was seven years old when the Siberian cold front settled in our valley. The Ice Castle grew steadily as temperatures fell below minus twenty. During those days when our grist mill was a regional landmark, every member of our family walked taller, for we were the proudest bunch in town. But, just as Dad liked to predict when things went well for us, *what goes up must come down.* And so did the fame and the pride. Just as the Ice Castle had reached its full splendor, it came under relentless attack. *They say, "pride goes before the fall".* Our family's stature had grown with the spires, and it collapsed as the boys toppled the proud structures. Glory and fall from grace came full circle within less than a fortnight.

The Ice Castle abutted against the west wall of our grist mill, and created a rampart around the waterwheel house. It leaned against our business and home, grew on our land, and sprouted around our waterworks. Rightfully, the Ice Castle was our property. And yet, we neither could buy nor sell it, or even claim title to it. Its nature was as elusive as the falling leaves of autumn.

Everything was frosted like a cake: the volcanic rock foundation of the mill that skirted the Ortzan, the oak-wood encasement built around the water wheels, moss-covered pumice that parted the stream bed in two, willow branches that dipped down into the water, shrubs and grass on the embankment; every blade and plank that lay within reach of the stream's vapors had been iced over.

By Tuesday, after Monday's headlines had been digested, the bridge over the Ortzan Stream had turned into a veritable circus. It was shutterbugs' winter heaven. I watched these men blow into their stiff fingers before they positioned their equipment at just the right angle. They had long lenses, fat lenses, and one old man whose white hair flew like a whirlwind around his forehead, had an antique camera over which he draped a cloth. To my bemusement, he stuck his head and unruly hair right under the cloth. This made me wonder why he had to hide taking pictures. The sting of the cold air crept into people's bones, and the men on the bridge looked like they had stilts welded to their feet.

Photographers had but a couple of minutes to position themselves, signal the oncoming traffic, and appease the occasional truck driver, who swore and yelled Sacrament, Christ, and other blasphemies at the castle and the crowd, for delaying his delivery tour. Invariably, one of the more congenial photo amateurs would step up to the door of the truck, greet the man behind the wheel by tipping his hat, and offer the guy, still glowering under his workman cap, a smoke while waiting. Miraculously everyone relaxed once the first smoke curls floated in the frigid air. Having successfully stalled the traffic, shutterbugs would resume their business and peer through the view finder only to be delayed by a fogged-up lens. "Damned", some would swear. The nipping cold had a way of slowing down every action to a snail's pace.

I noticed the expression of relief on their faces whenever they pressed the button on the camera or tripped the remote wire control. "Ah," they would exhale, and send forth a vaporous cloud. Then they would rub their hands as if they had won in the lottery, and without pausing they would rush into the next shoot advancing the lever, viewing, adjusting, and clicking, and on, and on. Every time they deemed the shot prize-worthy they would straighten up their bent backs and grin with satisfaction. Another picture for the family album, or perhaps a shot good enough to be enlarged, put in a gilded frame, and displayed above the sofa next to the bellowing buck and his massive antlers.

In their excitement, men tripped over their tripods, coasted like checkers on the icy road, stood on their tiptoes, and squatted near the ground. It was a free-for-all photographic hustle and bustle on the icy bridge. Unintended by the players, it frequently turned into slapstick comedy. I had seen two men careen out of balance and land haphazardly on their rumps. They had smashed their expensive looking equipment. Always the exclamations of anger and grief were louder than the clanging of hard-hitting cameras or lenses shattered on the blacktop. Swearing and cussing provided momentary relief: "Jesus Christ, Sacrament, shit, and shit" again, as they hissed and rumbled, patting their ruffled clothes back into shape.

Others who were less concerned with their looks and more worried that they had broken their equipment, didn't care about chunks of snow, ice, and dirt still clinging to the seats of their pants. They walked away hugging their camera close to their chest, as if such demonstration of tenderness could mend a broken shutter. A few of the men winced and grimaced when they landed bottom first on hard packed snow and ice. These more expressively endowed men showed drama in their faces, they bit their lips and knitted their eyebrows in pain. They limped off the scene of public humiliation, dragging one foot behind the other as if they were unsure whether to leave or stay.

I feared for their lives when I saw some daredevils climbing on top of the landing. Equipment dangling from their necks, they did a tightrope act on a narrow ledge covered with icy snow. It looked like an uneasy jig. Knees jittery, they teetered on the brink of disaster. Vapors from the stream billowed up and enfolded the figures on the landing, now obscuring and then again revealing their arms held out to the sides like balancing poles. Some even stuck out their tongue and pointed it in the direction they hoped to go. For all their derring-do, they barely scored a shot.

Siberian cold demanded mummification to the point of burrowing under ten layers of clothing. It inflicted pain, blue noses, and frostbite. It froze your snivel, it made your eyes water, and tears freeze as they rolled down your cheeks. It encrusted eyelashes and mustaches, and made them as stiff as broom bristles.

This disabling cold was something and, with the exception of a few people, it appeared that the majority among the photographic enthusiasts were taking the climatic adversities in stride. To keep themselves out of harm, they blew into their palms, rubbed their fingers and ears, stomped their cold feet, and cajoled their stiff knee joints. Some of the jollier ones had flasks of plum schnapps in the inside pockets of their coats and shared the spirits with those who looked like they were suffering the most.

If you had around thirty-something years under your belt, and were in proud possession of a respectable camera and the capricious Ice Castle happened to come around at that juncture of your life, more than likely this posed the last opportunity for you to preserve an image for posterity. It was obvious even to the uninitiated bypasser, that the gristmill was a representative relic of the past; antiquated by modern milling standards. And compared to the modern hydraulic turbines that sprung up on the waterways across the Swabian Region, our oak wood water wheels were museum pieces.

The whole shebang could be razed tomorrow. Without the waterworks, there would be no chance for an Ice Castle to sprout forth and thus the miracle would have vanished for good. Our family and the larger community of my town were dimly aware of the fleeting nature and questionable return of the Ice Castle. So it was no surprise to me that the men on the bridge went crazy trying to capture the Siberian ice fortress on film. It was a generational opportunity, something to show to your children and grandchildren, and reminisce about the miracles glimpsed and framed through the view finder of their cameras.

One of the high points of the ice castle came when my grade school teacher hauled up the entire class in front of the spectacle. "Now here, boys and girls, you see at work a physical process similar to what is happening in the caverns of our beautiful Alb mountain range." The tall and lanky man spoke carefully and pronounced every syllable extra-clearly, as if the frigid weather would muffle his speech. Secretly, I had to chuckle, for once again his glasses sat crooked on his nose. It was clear to me that the man needed a wife to keep him tidy and straight.

"Who among you has been to the Bear Cavern," He asked. Everyone flung up their arms and hands. Our teacher grinned widely, pleased that we had all ventured beyond our backyards. "Do any of you know the official names of those limestone structures," He continued. "We have two different names distinguishing between the ones that grow from the ground up and their cousins which drop from the ceiling down," He said, and pushed his wire rims to the other side. They still fit crooked though. A couple of kids raised their hands. I realized there was no time to diddle around; I had to spout forth my expertise concerning this matter, before these two were given a chance. "It's stalagmites and stalactites, Mr. Bernhardt." I shouted with great confidence. I had been to the Bear Cavern not too long ago and had been all ears and wide eyes, when the guide had given a walking tour of the caverns.

Mr. Bernhardt grinned from ear to ear, took his glasses off his thin nose, and pulled a handkerchief from his coat pocket to wipe the condensation off his glasses. He pulled some coins along with the handkerchief and they dropped to the ground. Several kids, in the front row, swooped down on the change and offered what they had collected back to the teacher. He dismissed their offering in a sweeping gesture, and they appropriated the teacher's coins faster than any pickpocket could hide his loot.

"Now, how would you know which is which," He asked. I itched to answer this one too, and jumped on my tiptoes for my turn. "The fat and lumpy ones grow up," I blurted out, before I even bothered to shoot up my hand. "The skinny and pointed ones grow down," I yelled and looked triumphantly around me. I was on a roll. No one else had even attempted to tackle this question. I embellished my expertise, and started to draw the outlines of fat cones going up and skinny ones pointing down. My class mates parted left and right of me to allow me ample drawing space.

While in the act of illustrating the interior of the Bear Cavern, all the heads swiveled in my direction, and the teacher's myopic eyes dwelled on my radiant and flushed face. I had successfully demonstrated my expert understanding of the cave's natural history, and, on top of that, I had merited my teacher's highest laureates, Ice Princess, he called me and winked. "You are excused from writing a field trip report, now you've done your homework right here on the spot." I curtsied with a flourish to Mr. Bernhardt, and basked in my newly-acquired celebrity status. It felt as delightful as if I had been served a cup of hot chocolate with Mother's scrumptious currant cake, smothered under whipped cream and butter-roasted almond slivers right here on the wintry bridge under a steely sky.

But days like the field trip, when I stood in the limelight of my classmates attention were the exception. During the rest of the time, throngs on the bridge had no use for me, this girl with the frost-bitten purplish nose and the pointed woolen cap, from which, dangled two red pompons. Other than those pompons, my looks were inconspicuous, whereas the huge German Shepherd dog at my side appeared downright dangerous. Together, we were an unlikely combination that kept onlookers at bay, and on their guard.

I thought these men were peculiar in their one-directional focus on the Ice Castle. These photo-crazy mobs were unlike the townfolk who would pass me on the street and make eye contact, usually smiling, sometimes frowning, but always acknowledging my presence. *"Gruess Gott"*, they would say which freely translates into Greeting God. This common greeting that is part of the *Swabian* dialect and heritage had always enthralled me. *I assumed that God*

was actually residing somewhere between my toes and my skull, and
likewise inhabited every person that I greeted.

The crowd on the bridge was too preoccupied for greeting
God, too busy to even notice my existence. The men wore blinders
to anything else but the photogenic ice display. Indifferent to the
world at large, their vision was tunnel-narrow and, much like their
lenses, trained exclusively on the Ice Castle.

While the hordes "wowed, ooohed, and aahed", always
jockeying for the best position in front of the Ice Castle, I stood and
watched, my hands covered in woolen mittens that Mother had
knitted for me. I held the mittens over my ears to prevent the
chilling air from giving me an earache. Father had told me to keep
my feet moving, for he had seen too many prisoners of war lose
their legs to gangrene after frost had eaten its way into their numb
limbs. Heeding Dad's urgent advice, I constantly trampled the
crunchy snow as if I was pressing juice out of grapes. When I
exhaled large puffs, my breathy mist configured into fantastic
shapes, ghosts and fairies and floated and drifted away.

Although I stood just within a stone's throw from the Ice
Castle, I remained invisible to the camera-toting men. Indeed, I
could have stood at the center of the bridge and nobody would have
noticed me. The Ice Castle was so spellbinding. It eclipsed the rest
of the world. The sheer size and glamour of the Ice Castle outshined
me. In its shadow I felt like a dwarf, a homely field mouse. At times
my invisibility made me feel insignificant, and I wondered how I
could turn the situation around.

After the field trip with my schoolmates, I yearned to be on
center stage, for just one brief moment. This audience of middle-
aged men was much less prone to notice me than my grade school
pals. I realized that if I wanted to be noticed, it would take measures
of an extreme nature, something more gutsy than I had ever done
before. I needed to put on an act, an over-the-top performance,
something so outrageous that jaws would drop open and eyes would
bulge, and then tele and wide lenses would spring into action. The
image that came to my mind was a copious turd. I envisioned
producing it in plain view of the Leicas and Hasselblads. Surely, if
only for a moment, a nicely turned bowel movement would grab
their attention. Those were the thoughts that came to my mind, when
I envisioned myself a police detective or private eye watching the

frenzied action on the bridge under the guise of plain-clothes anonymity.

Once the Ice Castle had blossomed into all its glamour, I recorded every movement on the bridge, as if it were my home assignment to draw an exact picture of the scene. Prince, our family's large German Shepherd dog stayed right by my side. Warm in his heavy shag coat, he rolled in the snow. The colder it got the better he felt.

The two of us held watch from behind three granite millstones. Dad had retired the gigantic round granite rocks because the surfaces had been worn so smooth over the last twenty years of service. They would mash the grains, but no longer grind them, a distinction that was paramount to Dad's milling trade. To move these stones out of the millworks, Dad had recruited the strongest men in the neighborhood - the dads of Franz, Gunther, Johan, Maynor, Heinrich, Max and Wolfrik.

Before they embarked on the venture, he had produced a bottle of Schnapps made from prunes that grew unattended in our orchard. He let the bottle go around a couple of times, then he intercepted it, even though eager hands were still groping. As the men tackled the job, and felt emboldened by the alcohol in their blood, I heard them chant in rhythmic unison, *hau ruck, hau ruck,* again, and again, moving one mill stone at a time, inch by inch; bracing it with crowbars, so it wouldn't tip to one or the other side and crush anybody's toes.

I heard grunting too and farting, and saw the men spit right and left as if a glob of saliva would slicken the *hau ruck* operation. Thus, they goaded the stone slabs out into the open to the designated spot. Dad had always prided himself that he could lift three times his own weight if he made a loud sound. Preferably he would count one, two, and three in Russian. Sounds and vocalizations of all manners were luring me into the thick of the action during the millstone removal. I heard the men groan and grunt louder than Dad could count to three. In fact, Dad's vigorous Russian counting was nothing but a murmur compared to the chorus of his work gang. Once they had the mill stones in place and installed in a shady corner, between the oil mill annex and the main gristmill, Dad insisted that they be stacked irregularly. It was his idea of creating a stone sculpture.

But before they had finished the structure and hoisted the third stone on top of the preceding two, an accident happened that might have set the stage for other accidents; it might have seeded the beginnings of cold and hot rage in the heart of the victim and those who were among his family. Franz's father had brought along his own flask of schnapps and drained it by the time the men stood equally divided in numbers on either side of the third mill stone.

The rest of the guys braced the last rolling granite rock, as heavy as a hay wagon, their faces strained and drawn into serious expressions. They braced all of their individual weight against that milling stone with an array of crowbars and tire rods, and then an accident happened. Out of the blue, and to everybody's dismay, this schnapps-emboldened man, gripped by utter stupidity, jumped jauntily in front of the rolling slab. Franz's father declared against his team's chorus, No, you fool, step aside! And other hoarse and urgent warnings. I am Atlas, I can hold up the world on my shoulders.

Other than being hunched over, his shoulders were safe and secure alright, but his foot was in for a crushing awakening. In his alcoholic craze, he managed to wedge his left foot under the moving slab. He howled like a madman. Within less than a couple of seconds he had three of his five toes smashed under the moving mill stone which no longer had the cutting edge to grind but plenty of weight to mash anything that came under its tonnage, including the many various bones that make up a man's toes.

During the heydays of the Ice Castle when Prince and I were embarked on our lonesome sentry duty that exposed us to the withering elements, these millstones provided a welcome windbreak, and gave me a chance to gaze at the gazers with impunity.

From the day that I was born, Prince had been my steady companion. He had sprawled like a big shaggy rug next to my pink baby skin when Mother had put me out on a blanket in the grass. Her intention was to condition her newborn to the outdoors. Prolonged exposure to the elements, so she assumed, would give me a hardy and healthy constitution. It also provided Mother with plenty of time to be by herself, and sit for long stretches gazing out of the window, or watching the fingers of the grandfather clock move.

Unbeknownst to herself, she was in the grip of a postpartum depression. Everything was indifferently gray to her, even the pink in my cheeks. Paralyzed and inert, mired in a bog of feelings, she was able to provide minimal care only. She barely managed to uphold a semblance of motherhood. After long intervals of introspective reveries in the house, she would step out to check in with her firstborn, take care of bare-bone necessities like changing an overdue diaper, or pressing a bottle of baby food into my groping hands; and then she'd fly off like a bird and retire to her interior world.

Again she would leave me for hours on end to my own devices. Pictures that Dad had taken of me showed me as an insular figure. A baby that looked at the world vacantly, for hardly anybody had bothered to fill those eyes with reassuring glances. Our family albums had pages and pages that recorded my various stages of infancy, and every page was a study of the different angles of a motherless child, a lone island surrounded by a sea of grass and sky.

Even dad was conspicuous by his notorious absence. Other than short visits with his Leica, when he would shoot me in exposed situations, such as my butt bared during diapering. He too was gone most of the day, laboring hard to make ends meet. The only living soul other than the chickens, was Prince, who had a noticeable amount of wolf genes in his pedigree. Prince stayed close to my blanket nuzzling my tiny body with his moist black snout.

In the days of the Ice Castle, Prince might have given the appearance of a proud and happy dog, but in reality, however, he was nearly blind. His keen vision had taken a turn for the worse on the day of the rabbit carnage.

On that Whit Monday, two years before the Ice Castle appeared, Dad had successfully diminished the once so proud Prince into a fearful and submissive doormat. That day had been a turning point in Prince's life. From then on the dog's eyes started to get dim and dimmer. An opaque veil descended upon Prince's keen and watchful eyes, much like the wintry frost flowers that blossomed and spread across our window panes during the reign of the Siberian cold. Often I wondered how much of visible reality Prince could still make out. The shutterbugs, the lenses wide and long, the squatting and tip-toeing men angling to the right and the left, and never quite finding the perfect frame. Did they register as dots in a maze of gray? A fuzzy haze maybe? Darting specks on a snowy television screen?

Even though he was nearly without sight, Prince recuperated from that severe flogging and in many ways returned to his old self, which was an intrepid yet loyal wolf - dog soul. Over time, he adapted to his misfortune of waning eyesight by doubling his sense of smell. Thus, although nearly blind, he was still a formidable watchdog.

Any man or woman's privacy was a public library to the dog's nose. If Prince had been given words, he could have informed me who among the guys on the bridge wore the cleanest underwear and who had the stinkiest ass. Prince was a connoisseur of body odors, sweet or sour smelling sweat, the musk, and the manly smells, the foul or spearminted breath. They all registered on his radar scope.

Prince's snout could read you as if it were an open book. Before you knew it, he could smell through you, know who you are, where you've come from, and place you as a friend or foe. Thanks to his extraordinary nose, our dog knew more about people's drives and motivations than any shrink.

Prince never tired of scanning the air for warning signals. A hint of fear, or any mal-intent, and he'd jump to attention, his hind legs shaking and his forelegs ready to pounce on you. If he was alerted by a suspicious whiff, his shaggy tail would stand up erect like a flag, his hair would bristle, his teeth bare, his blue-black lips shone moist and rich as shoe wax, and a deep and ominous growl would rise from the pits of his being. All the while his dark eyes remained veiled, serenely detached, and void of expression.

Icicles came in all sizes; small, medium, and large specimens that rose upward or descended downward, wherever stream and earth met. They grew phalluses of the most inspiring erections. I seriously doubt that those camera-toting amateurs saw penises when they gazed at the ice colonnade. I imagine they probably recognized something loftier than genitals: The steeples of churches, balustrades of royal staircases, colonnades of Greek temples, or the shapely legs of a movie star.

To me however, the icicles were astonishing replicas of the male sexual organ. I was puzzled and equally intrigued by this law of nature, for each icicle that I recorded in my notebook was by far longer than it was wide. Why wouldn't they come in round shapes like hoops, loops, circles, and crescents like flowers, beehives or the moon? In my role as the proud princess of the Ice Castle and avid naturalist, I kept daily track of the phallic squadron. On my way to school in the morning before the photo shooting crowds took over the bridge, I would check to see if the icicles had grown overnight. I would write my observations into my notebook, "Looks as if the fat and bulgy cones grew about as much as my pinky while the skinny spears added a full hand span of length." It never failed that the thin and bony ones grew faster, similar to the kids in school.

During my morning inspection, with no one else around, dirty thoughts would creep into my mind. No matter which way I looked at them, I couldn't help but see an arcade of phalluses. Men's and boys' dicks, and replicas of the huge penises of horses when they get excited, as the blacksmith pulls off their worn horseshoes and fits their hoofs with singing-hot new irons. Not that I had actually seen this. Mother had told me in detail of her own childhood experience of such an equine erection, which had left an indelible impression in her memory.

It had been during one of our breakfast sessions when Mother veered into the past and told me stories of family, legend, myth, and those of her own invention. "Catherine the Great, the German-Russian empress who invited your Dad's ancestors to farm in Southern Russia, was a lover of horses," Mother had said, one day over breakfast while I was piling home-made blackberry jam on my whole wheat toast and smelling the cup of coffee under my nose. "She would love horses so much that she would lie on some wooden platform and have herself hoisted right under her favorite steed. They employed a winch, or pulley, or some other mechanical contraption to get the Czarina positioned just right. And then she and the horse would make contact." Mother paused after the word contact, and her keen eyes searched my face for any reaction. "They say the horse actually got off and the empress of Russia was in ecstasy." She paused again and her eyes were fixed on the blackberry jam that I had piled on my toast. Her eyebrow drew up into a severe arch, especially as she pronounced the words "in ecstasy." It appeared to me that Mother was so captivated by this tale that she was actually envisioning Catherine the Great together with horse winch and servants, all trying to make something work that wasn't meant to work by natural design.

I didn't quite get the implied scandalous gist of this story, for at the time I was still blissfully ignorant of the mechanics of love-making. I hadn't seen a man's live prick yet, neither had I observed any horse that had an erection. In fact, I had no idea then that pricks were meant to enter women. All I knew was the pre-pubescent anatomy between my legs which I had studied by means of a handheld mirror.

Mother had entered the bathroom one day after I had taken a bath, and had caught me in the act of holding a mirror between my legs looking at the pinkish opening between my legs. "What are you doing?" She had asked, and the surprise in her voice made me feel self conscious.

"I'm looking at the inside of my pussy," I had told her. Mother had a concerned look on her face, and motioned me over to the chair. She sat down and I stood close to her, wearing only a short top. She made me sit down on the foot stool next to her to educate me about the meaning of those pinkish folds, that looked to me like a couple of overlapping fat lips. She said, "Now listen up carefully that which you call pussy, and by the way where did you hear that rude word, is a woman's greatest treasure. In the future think of it as one of your most precious gifts, keep it private, and hidden from anybody who wants to get close to it. Think of it this way: If you had a treasure chest full with gold, you wouldn't show it to just anybody on the street, would you?" I shook my head.

"No way," I said. "I wouldn't even show the change in my pocket to anybody."

Her concerned expression changed into a smile, but her brown eyes maintained a stern gaze. "If you want to be happy in your life, you keep that treasure of yours shut closed, secret, and hidden until the day that you meet a very special man. And you will know if it is the right man because he holds the key to your treasure chest."

"A key?" I repeated and wondered how a key would open my pussy since I hadn't seen any keyhole during my mirror exploration. "Now don't be silly. It's a figure of speech. When you're older you'll understand what I mean. And don't you worry, before that special man comes into your life, we'll have another talk."

If women were in proud possession of a treasure chest, it dawned on me why the stills of movies that forecast upcoming shows at the local theatre featured men and women forever engaged in territorial drama. I could understand now why those handsome movie studs were groping and reaching to get into the heroines' treasure chest, while the women would arch back, hold out their arms and hands to keep them from getting any closer. Their cheeks flushed and lips parted, they would bashfully turn away their faces, close their eyes, and bar the men from further entry.

By the time the Ice Castle came into my life, I knew about horses' huge erections. I had studied the stills in depth and I had perused all of Mother's art magazines where large glossy pictures of ancient Greek statuary piqued my anatomical interest. Most importantly, I had seen up close and experienced on my skin Franz's prick, limp as a worm and then thick and upright like a full-size pine cone. Curiously, it was a minor fellow among the icicles that captivated my imagination more so than the huge icicles that were sized to satisfy Catherine the Great, or the blacksmith, or *my mother, for that matter*, who loved to watch thoroughbreds get excited.

This modest-sized rascal of a icicle featured uncanny resemblance to Franz's real flesh peter. They could have been twins if it weren't for transparency and the refraction of sunlight along the icy shaft. Moreover, just like Franz's dick, this otherwise inconspicuous specimen featured a bulbous head and a ridge that ringed the tip like a noose, and separated the head from the rest of the shaft. Every time I passed the ice palace, this particular fellow caused me to have flashbacks of a hot and humid August day, during the summer before the ice castle came into existence. A cursed and red-letter day, when under the glare of the midday sun, Franz nearly succeeded in jabbing his dick into my treasure chest.

I had just turned seven then. And looking back at that tender age, I know that I had my first encounter with old man Saturn. Astrologically speaking, he is the authority that teaches unembellished reality. It was Saturn poking at my innocence. Saturn, the universal taskmaster, works us over in a seven year cycle. He had come to visit me in the guise of Franz, accompanied by his eager pecker.

Saturn had stepped into my life, so I would understand the difference between fairy land fantasies where a kiss turns a frog into a prince and the reality of the two sexes. So I would understand the nature of men, whose pride and joy turned long and firm when they desired a female. So I would also understand that lust changes the male appendage from soft and vulnerable into something hard, pushy, yeast and beer-like smelling, and ready to dig in.

The memories of that summer day made me tingle and shiver at the same time. Yet more than anything else, the memories of that day of discovery and shattered fantasies left me feeling a stale taste in my mouth and a sore hollow in my belly. Whenever I passed by the Ice Castle, the staleness and sore memories surged and stung in my throat like bilious heartburn.

Aside from the turning of the leaves, the Ice Castle was the biggest photogenic event in our county. The contrast between the two couldn't have been more pronounced. The fall foliage show was a fire-works of maple, beech, and oak that blazed across the flanks of the Alb Mountains. It turned the half-evergreen woods into a tapestry of flaming red, auburn, and gold, whereas the icicles were delicate, ethereal, and crystalline clear. Ice Castle and fall foliage were marvels of nature, equally thrilling to behold. Both came by the grace of God. And I figured that it must have been the wrath of God that fell on our Ice Castle. His retribution came in the form of the boys in our neighborhood. They conspired against the Ice Castle, and laid siege to the icicles that dwarfed their own male appendages and therefore had to be razed.

So I watched the crowd from my lone sentry post behind the millstones. Not that these men were anything beautiful to behold. I found them ordinary, compared to the beauty standards I had established by studying movie stills posted behind glass at the local theatre, a building which I had to pass during my shopping trips to the dairy shop and the butchers. The men's fleshy faces were pitiful compared to the commanding expressions of Steve McQueen, Tony Curtis, Alain Delon, or John Huston. Their beefy bodies compared poorly to the sleek physiques of Greek gods, such as Adonis and Apollo, whose marble poise and statuesque elegance I admired in Mother's art magazines.

The majority of these shutterbugs were middle-aged men whose beerbellies bulged over belts that were fastened too tight. They were balding, had flaps hanging from their chins, and their eyes were dulled by a dreamless state of being. Their mouths were clamped shut like Grandma's purse. These men had summoned all their guts to steal away from their humdrum jobs. For once they had skipped lunch and the obligatory pint of beer, and had sacrificed the orderliness and predictability of their daily routine to come here and find themselves richly rewarded for such enterprise and courage. If the sun hit the Ice Castle just right it would illuminate even the waterfall behind the ice and create a stunning light show.

No matter how cold it got, the Ortzan stream kept on rushing forward, seamless, never stopping, tumbling over the water wheels as it had done for a hundred years. Like the progress of time, the Ortzan stream knew no standstill, no stopping for the shutterbugs. Not even the Ice Castle could hold the river back. It rather surrounded it like a translucent stage curtain. The rushing mill stream shimmered through the transparency of every shaft, as icicles and falling waters refracted the beams of sunlight giving bursts of spectral luminescence that glowed and beamed back, sending the camera crowd into virtual shooting orgies. Even I was overcome by the dazzle of this light show, and sometimes I would hold my breath, thinking that this would increase the pleasure of the icy fireworks.

Even though it could not stop the progress of the river, the stillness of the ice castle cast a spell on everything that came close. It held people, plants, birds and even the sound of the wind in hushed suspension. Even the perpetual roar of the Ortzan, which dropped some twelve feet from the top of the chute to the bottom of the stream bed, had been muffled, caught like a wild animal and trapped behind the bars of an ice cage.

However, nothing would slow down the camera frantic crowd. Between oncoming cars, clouds that obscured the sun, and children that ran into their visual field, these serious looking men shot away at the Ice Castle as if they were snipers brandishing machine guns. From what I could see, they spared no expenses to freeze the Ice Castle on film. Some went through several rolls during one shoot.

Often they would position their families in front of the Ice Castle. Kids would roll their eyes and screw up their faces and drive their dads crazy whereas mothers would smile so widely you could see the fillings in their molars. I could picture the photos taken and later arranged in the family album next to the palm fringed summer vacation in Italy, and the shots of their weekend trip to the Bear Cavern, where guides would dress in brown and black pelts and wear grim-looking bear masks.

In how many photo albums, so I wondered, did our Ice Castle gleam next to the bear pictures? Photos of man-sized icicles, next to those of bears' fangs. Splendid pinnacles behind parental grins, kids flailing their arms in the clutches of brown bears, and the same kids poking their noses as they stood in front of the Ice Castle.

the thought of so many diverse realities, packed together on one album page, made me dizzy. And yet, I was also aware that none of these treasured photo albums would feature me or my dog. We were less than a supporting cast, we weren't even granted as much as a bit part in this photographic shooting orgy. The thought that nobody had found me worth a single exposure made me feel as gray as a field mouse. However as small and insignificant as I felt, I still had a good-sized dog at my side.

During that record-cold January, Prince was usually glued to my side. I observed and he smelled as the lenses opened and closed, like the blossoms of greedy flowers. Tele-lenses as long as my arm aimed at the Ice Castle. However, during this time, never once did any of the lenses aim at us. Even if I happened to pass by the crowd and walk on the bridge, my appearance only triggered minor annoyance and the readjustment of men and equipment. They would veer more to the right or left to eliminate my figure from their view. I got a hint of minor irritation. These men had no use for me, and if I lingered too long they looked impatient and made motions as if they wished to erase me, and wipe me clear off the scene.

Further upstream from our gristmill, the Ortzan divided into two main channels. The same could be said of the crowd on the bridge. One faction, the most visible, was the avid photographers who hustled and bustled to get the best close-up, tele, and wide-angle shots of the icy splendor. Then there was a bunch of neighborhood kids, all boys. Their names were Franz, Gunther, Johan, Maynor, Heinrich, Max and Wolfrik. They lived in the neighborhood, and were by and large older than myself. While the photo amateurs were mainly busy and anxious to get their shots in during lunch-break or during a mid-afternoon coffee break, these neighborhood kids acted as if the clock had altogether stopped ticking for them. They had too much time on their hands, and as the old folks say, "the devil finds work for idle hands to do".

After lunch, these youngsters prowled the banks of the Ortzan, besieging the castle like waylaying bandits. It was hard to read their minds for most of their faces were covered up, hooded by woolen caps, scarves, and turtlenecks they had pulled over their freezing noses. But I knew from first-hand experience that these guys were up to nothing good. The telltale signs of mischief were written in capital letters all over them. The way, that some of them hunched, and others thrust out their chests; their eyes darting like scared rats. And whenever by chance, one of them showed part of his face exposed, I would glimpse sullen expressions. Their shadowy presence around the Ice Castle made me suspicious, and threw Prince's snout into a virtual frenzy.

I knew most of these boys from grade school, but it was the girls' policy to stay clear of them. By and large the girls my age had no use for boys then. We were happy playing our own games and chanting verses, always giggling adjoining hands to form impenetrable circles. The other sex was shut out, period! We scorned these brutes and considered them nothing better than a constant irritant.

It was the boys' preferred pastime to run by us girls and lift up our wide flung skirts and petticoats. In turn, we would squeal like pigs and cackle like hens working ourselves into a great big frenzy. The boys would deftly defy our protestations and plant spiny hulls of horse chestnuts in our stockings, or toss them down our neckline where they clung to our flat chests and pricked our nipples. We feigned righteous indignation protruding our tongues as far as they would go, and we'd yell, *"icky, gross, disgusting"*. In turn, the boys would get their greatest kick out of watching us pluck those burry critters from various hidden areas of our anatomy.

When the boys approached, we usually dispersed, scattering like a bunch of scared sparrows. However some of us, and I was among this minority, kept our heads held high, noses screwed upward, and lips turned down. We were standing our ground and dared them to come near us. In clear view of the glowering boys, we girls would act particularly intimate, place pecks on each other's cheeks, hug, link arms like fences, and always giggle. Making sure all the while, that the boys wouldn't miss any of our touching and sensual gestures. In response to our amorous sisterhood and girlish games, the boys would huddle in some corner, stick their heads together and hedge new strategies.

One guy in particular had the cold fire of revenge planted in his heart. The glint of cunning in his light-blue eyes was colder than the icicles. This was Franz, a beefy chunk of a guy, built like a closet, arms as long as a gorilla's.

Since the Ice Castle had been celebrated on the front page of the local newspaper, Franz and his gang of loyal retainers hung around the bridge, loitered aimlessly, waiting for the grown-up crowd to disperse. I sensed in their devious looks, those furtive eyes of thieves, the pointing of fingers, and brandishing of sticks at the gristmill and the Ice Castle, the swagger, and their delirious hooting that Franz and his retainers were up to something majorly bad.

Franz and I had unfinished business between us, something shameful that neither of us was able to shake off. It happened the summer before that Siberian Winter. I had just turned seven then, and knew how to write my name in capital letters. It was at that time that I had seen a litter of kittens plop out of our mother cat's behind. I was known as a public menace, for I would behave like a fiend racing my shiny red scooter up and down the street, in clear violation of traffic regulations, of which I was blissfully ignorant. It was then that I had my first good and hard look at the male ding-dong full-assembly appendage, which I had to admit, was a nifty thing to have.

The true life pecker and balls that I had inspected up close, even smelling its odor that was akin to Mother's baking yeast and dad's pitcher filled with beer, was Franz's pride and joy. He was twice as old as I and much more experienced. That memorable summer when I had told him about the kittens being born, he topped my story, and by far, out-did my account. He rendered a detailed eyewitness report of what he had seen peeking through the keyhole of his parents' bedroom door. How his Dad had planted his huge salami-size prick in his Mother's hole, and that he had pumped, and drilled her hard. How she had arched back in pain, and yes, she had screamed as if his Dad had run through her with his sword. In fact, they both had screamed, and his Dad had done it two more times.

And then, his Dad had said, "that was one heck of a fuck". And his Mom had a swollen stomach a few months later. "That night my dad, had pissed his juice into her hole and made her a baby," Franz said, and watched me with greedy eyes, wondering how I might react to his story.

"Don't tell me he pissed into your Mom's treasure chest. It's nothing but a lie. Men don't piss into women, they use a toilet, or a tree, or the corner of a house to relief themselves." His account of his parents' lovemaking had shaken me deeply. For all I knew, babies were made by tender hugs and prolonged kissing. I was so upset that I nearly burst into tears. Franz had dared to burst my tidy fantasy of how babies would come into this world. I pounded my outrage onto his barrel chest. He held it firm like a drum head and laughed and laughed. "That's the grossest, meanest, dumbest thing

I've ever heard!" I yelled and pounded more. Franz hollered hysterically. He had never seen me so sore.

Just a few days after he had revealed the details of his parents' love wrestling, Franz approached me on my way home from school. He proposed that we have a show-and-tell session. "You show me your private parts, and I'll show you mine." It was a straightforward deal. Since I had been made curious about the male genitalia by his eyewitness report of his Dad's large wiener, and since I had been intrigued by the pictures of nude Greek statues in Mother's art magazines, I conceded to the deal.

Franz's nickname was "Hot Sparks" and most appropriately so, since he had maculae all over his body. In August, the year before he and his retainers had laid siege on our Ice Castle, I discovered that there were secret places on his body where there weren't any maculae at all. I nearly stubbed my nose against his peter checking for any macula on the underside, base, and tip. Franz even pulled back a fold of loose skin to show that his dick was macula free. "See! I told you," he triumphed. He took his time to demonstrate every inch of his dick. He even let me have a close-up view of his balls, which I thought a curious addition. "Let me see those," I said, and reached out to touch those wobbly balls.

Hold it, he said, and retracted his genitalia from my groping curiosity. I want to show you how far and high I can piss, and then it's your turn to show me your stuff. He stood broad legged, his pants down to his ankles. Where do you want me to direct my spigot? Since we were right next to Aunt Elma's bed of summer flowers, and well hidden behind a stack of cordwood, I had a choice between dahlias, cosmos, and gladiolas to be hosed down. I chose the red-faced dahlias. "Now girls can't do that," he said and stepped back from the smiling dahlias. Look at this arc! He aimed his nifty hose at the center of the dahlias.

"Now it's your turn," he said. His left eye glowed with the kind of anticipation that kids have when mother opens the cookie jar. "This ain't no fun," I declared, and was ready to get dressed again. My chances in this contest were close to nil. In terms of pissing girls were operating under a severe handicap. I found myself far less endowed. My gender had been short-changed. God had granted the male sex a handy tool whereas females had only two holes, one for liquids and one for solids. I had nothing more to show, but a tiny purse consisting of several flaps of skin, for which I didn't see any purpose. I also had a puny thingie that was ticklish and smaller than the nail on my pinkie. My spigot was internal and the stream of my piss reaches about as far as my toes. Hot Sparks had the grin of a champion while I had been beaten sorely.

"You look like a scaredy cat", Hot Sparks said, and gave me a peevish look. My perennial rosy complexion must have drained out of my face. Already feeling defeated before I had done my part of show and tell, I let my panties drop to my knees and hunkered down. "Take them off altogether!" He said.

"Why?" I asked, and my irritation was growing.

"I want to see it all. Those panties hide half of the show".

He was such a bully, I barely had slipped my undies over my sandals and he yanked them out of my hands. He stuck his big nose, practically one big macula, into the crotch of my white cotton panties. His nostrils flared, he screwed his eyes shut, and deeply sucked in the air. He sniffed back and forth, nose wrinkled in excitement, his nose busier than my dog's. "Smells like bread dough," he said, and tossed my underwear into the dahlias that were still dripping with his piss. "I don't have any piss to pee." I said, trying to find a pretext for not performing my part of the deal.

"Okay then," Hot Sparks said. "I've seen girls piss before, it's a boring little tinkle. Let's move on to the next item." What item? I wondered. There were only two functions to our private parts, pissing and pooping. And I wasn't about to do the latter. For all I knew, men and women alike had to squat down and press to produce a bowel-movement; it was the same operation for both sexes. The show was over, I reached my hand to pick up my panties, but Hot Sparks pulled me back.

"Now you stand here and block anybody from seeing this, because I'm going to perform a miracle for you," Hot Sparks said in a confrontational tone. He positioned me like a Japanese rice screen in front of him, and sat down in the grass. His knees flopped to the sides, his thighs fell open revealing the whole panorama. He spat into his hands, and started to whittle away at his peter. He rubbed it up and down with one hand, and then the other, as if he tried to milk it. I watched closely so I'd be able to tell my girlfriends when school would start back up again.

"What are you trying to do anyway?" I asked.

"I told you, I'm performing magic on my dick. I'm going to make it grow into one big and juicy cucumber. And then you can touch it and rub it, and it will grow even bigger and eventually it'll spurt out some juice, and if I put my cucumber into your slit we can actually make babies."

Sure enough, his dick grew longer and fatter by the minute. He made moaning and groaning sounds as if he was in pain.

"Does it hurt?" I inquired, more out of curiosity than any concern. "It hurts like eating a gallon of ice cream or like going down the roller-coaster, or diving from the five meter board, orooo", he said. But then he got busy moaning again and I watched the tip of his prick flesh out and swell up and get all juicy like a salivating dog snout.

Okay, now you sit down opposite of me and open your legs wide. I'll take a poke at your pussy."

"You sure as hell won't," I said in great alarm. "I don't want any babies. I am still in grade school, what would I do with a baby? Besides, neither you nor any other boy is ever going to piss into my treasure chest."

"You could give the baby up for adoption. Doctors and lawyers pay money for cute little babies", he said, and fondled his prick even harder. "You could take the baby to school, show it around during recess, and pass it to all your girlfriends. It would beat the heck out of those stupid dolls and teddy bears that you girls chauffeur around in your dumb strollers."

He scooted up closer to me. "You gotta lie down and open your legs wide, or it won't work. That's how my Mom and Dad did it, and now Moms' as big as a beer barrel and carrying a baby in her belly."

The head of his dick glistened as more juice trickled out of the hole. While I was spellbound by his dick magic and the feisty look of his juicy pecker, I used arms and legs to keep him off of me. No way, I would not lay myself down flat to have him poke me.

Hot Sparks pulled at my legs. I lost my balance and fell straight down on my rump. My buttocks and tail bone hurt as if a fence post had been rammed into me. For a moment I was dazed by the pain, not alert to Franz's climbing on top of me. He pushed his hot and hard dick up the insides of my legs.

"No, you jerk, I'll never let you get close to my treasure again." I said, and pulled my dress between my crotch so I had at least the fabric to protect my treasure chest. I clamped my legs together tight and had his prick caught like in a vise.

"Ha-Ha treasure", he snickered. "It's just an old piss hole, and meant for men to pump it full with baby making juice."

"No it's a woman's treasure," I hollered at him, my fists buried in my groin as further defense against his stiff poker.

The notion that I carried a treasure chest between my legs had been planted by my Mother

"It's a treasure chest, you shit-head!" I insisted and knocked my knee into his groin, shoved it right between his balls. Dad had taught me this trick. "In case any guy ever wants to feel you up," he had told me, "you just look kind of dumbfounded and shy and then, faster than he can bat an eye, *you draw up your knee and whammo, you shove it into his groin, dead center, right here.*" He had shown me the most vulnerable spot between his pant legs and I had carefully inscribed it into my pectoral memory. "That's where he hurts the worst," Dad had said.

Franz rolled down from the top of me. He pulled his legs into his abdomen, thus shielding his injured male pride. His hands were cupped tightly around his balls to further shield them against any assault by my deadly knee. "You fucking bitch," he hissed through his clenched teeth. His face puckered like he was eating sour prunes, his eyebrows were drawn so tightly-knit there was no space left between them. He howled, and then he fell into a measly whimper. I imagined that I had squashed his balls. In a flash I understood that I had to run, and be out of there before he could get up and take revenge. I had turned a guy twice my age into a whimpering and mewling mess. But at the time, I felt ambiguous about this accomplishment, not sure whether I should relish this as a victory or the beginning of a war.

Ready to bolt, I picked up my panties that were damp with his piss from the drooping necks of the dahlias. I wasted no time to pull them on, and lit out for home. "You're a sissy!" He yelled. "You're a chicken, prissy pussy, scared cunt." Even at a distance, I could still hear him rail against my private parts front and back. In the windows of every house that I passed, blinds opened and curtains got pulled to the side. Franz's foul-mouthed slandering of my female endowments and the lack thereof, his jeers, and taunts, had drifted into my neighbors' living rooms and had fallen onto curious ears. My pussy had become an object of public interest and defamation. I felt a surge of shame like a scalding shower, red hot and stinging.

This was the day when I had been publicly tarred and feathered, like the jealous and indolent sisters in Grimm's fairytale Frau Holle. Astrologically, Saturn had introduced me to the nitty gritty ugliness of reality. And Pluto, the Lord of the Underworld, had darn near ravaged me. Weeks and months passed after the scandalous piss and prick charade, in full view of the dahlias. I wondered whether Franz had forgotten our show-and-tell session. When I had had a chance to inspect his dick from all sides; beneath, and above, and smelled it too. Had he put aside that hot August day when I had refused to piss for him for fear that I might be ridiculed. In great alarm over my treasure chest, I had refused entry to Hot Sparks' peter. Was it possible that he had buried the memory of the shooting pain when I had kneed him in his jelly balls? I concluded that loss of such momentous chunks of memory was highly unlikely, and the withering looks that passed between us, *mine prickly his chilling*, confirmed my suspicion.

Fall had come and gone, and I had built a whole zoo of animals made of the horse chestnuts I had gathered in the school yard. I gave them matches for legs and tails, berries for eyes and snouts, and the shells of acorns for oversized ears. All the trees now were swept clean of their brittle fall foliage. People stayed cozy in their homes, where their water kettles hissed on the coal and wood burning stoves. The apple juice in the large oak barrels had fermented into an alcoholic drink that grown-ups ingested at every opportunity, giving them a slight buzz for most of the day. At dinner time the kitchens up and down our street had the familiar aroma of fermented cider sitting in pint-size mugs next to blood sausage, liverwurst, home-baked bread, and pickles for dinner. Life was good in the fall after the harvest, and firewood had been brought in. We gathered around the woodstove and spoke of the Farmers Almanac's prediction, that come this January, the Ice Castle was meant to come back after eleven years since its last appearance.

Inevitably, winter held its entry and we put on parkas against the stiff wind hailing all the way from Russia. Frost flowers spread across the window panes; snow fell and stalled the traffic. We pulled our sleds out of storage. And the mercury dropped to the teens and wouldn't budge. Frost had an unrelenting grip on the land and the people, and laid the foundation for the most magnificent Ice Castle in the recorded history of our gristmill.

During one late winter afternoon, the clouds were a gloomy slate-gray-blue and their low hanging bellies scraped the tops of the trees. The setting sun cast too scant a light for any photographs to turn out, so the camera bugs wandered off, tripods on their shoulders.

From behind the stack of mill stones, I spotted Hot Sparks, and his gang of friends, come up the narrow trail that skirted the Ortzan stream north of our property. Since last summer an eerie truce had lain between us like a frozen lake, treacherous in its smoldering silence. Hot Sparks had buried the hatchet and so had I. When we had passed on the street he had usually a band of boys around him, buffering him from all sides. They would yak it up, cajole, and be loud, and boisterous. His retainers would screen me out of their visual field similar to the tunnel-visioned camera-toting hordes who eliminated me from their close-up, wide, and tele-shots.

But the truce was over. Prince sensed danger too. I could tell by the way he bristled his hair and rooted around in the air to catch a drift of Hot Sparks' squeamish scent. Hot Sparks and his tribe congregated on the bridge, and stuck their heads together, and separated out whooping and hooting vicious-sounding war cries. From behind my lookout, I watched them gather rocks alongside the Ortzan embankment.

As Prince and I watched the conspirational activity of Franz and his band of loyals from behind the millstones, I grew more and more wary. Prince's muzzle mirrored my suspicion. It was going faster than the seconds on a wristwatch. For Prince, his zest for life hinged on his nose. It was the springboard for every move he made. He could tell the difference between an individual who was a harmless gawker on the bridge, to someone who was up to something wicked. Prince was electrified by his zealous snout. His hind legs kicking up the snow, his tail as bristly as Mother's lint brush, everything about him was electrified.

In one sharp inhale, It became crystal clear. The hooded gang's motive sprung into my consciousness as clear as the images of Prince's rabbit raid. That had come up for me, even though I had not been privy to the actual slaughter. These hooligans had come and besieged the Ice Castle for no other reason but to take out our family's pride and joy, to raze that which my Dad and Mom had waited for more years than I had been around on this planet. The Ice Castle was the very epicenter of my life in those days, the high point of my social and natural studies. It had provided me with the rare opportunity to be on center stage; the celebrated and knowledgeable ice princess among my grade school friends. It had catapulted my home location into fat newsprint and into countless family albums, and now these hoods were on the brink of destroying all of that. The mere anticipation of that menace paralyzed me, just like the rabbit raid had shut me down.

While I sensed that disaster was imminent, I did not dare confront Hot Sparks and his buddies. I stayed glued to my spot next to Prince who was so charged up by the clandestine preparations on the bridge, he looked as if high voltage was running through him.

After they had scoured the embankment for good-sized rocks, they gathered their loot into a tin pail. I had counted the rocks that they dropped into their bucket; there were twice as many rocks than there were icicles on our ice castle. Their pail had filled up fast.

But they weren't done yet. To increase their armaments they dove into the bushes and pillaged our elderberries for good-sized branches which they stripped of any remaining leaves and side limbs. They piled their sticks near the landing. Each one of them took turns carrying the brimfilled bucket to the bridge. Franz Hot Sparks, the ringleader, stuck two fingers into his mouth and let forth a blood curdling whistle that aroused Prince's ears, and had a rallying effect on his scattered pals.

Once they all had formed a tight cluster opposite of the Ice Castle, Franz tossed his arms up toward the gloomy sky followed by a quick chop of his hand aimed at the ice sky followed by a quick chop of his hand aimed at the Ice Castle. The guys let out another hoot, and Franz bent over to pick up a round rock the size of his fist. He tossed the missile dead center at one of the largest and most majestic pillars of the ice fortress. The rock hit solidly. The ice chimed, clanked, and toasted its own demise. As it tore off I thought I heard it moan and wail, but that could have been my imagination. The splash was loud and the guys let out another curdling jeer.

For me there existed no physical boundaries. The boys' razing of the Ice Castle was equal to them ravaging my own body.
A few oblique rays seeped through cracks in the slate-colored clouds. They hit the remaining spires of the castle, and they also highlighted Franz Hot Sparks. His maculae and his beaming chums. I so utterly resented the fact that this late wintery sun had put a spotlight on these lowlifes. I could have puked right on the spot.

Franz spat into both of his palms, wrung them together, and reached down to grab another fist-size rock. He spat on the rock also, walked backwards across the bridge, took to running and swung his arm back behind him, as if he was going to throw the discus in the Olympics. At the very instant that his arm was half-way through the swinging motion, I bellowed from the depth of my belly, *"You asshole don't you do that! - Stop it - Quit right now!"*

Franz stopped his throwing action, looked over his shoulder to locate my voice, but since I ducked behind the mill stones, he could not see me. I thought he wouldn't, couldn't, shouldn't dare such a monstrous thing. After a few startled looks among his retainers, some shrugs and nodding heads, he resumed his attack, swinging wide and far behind himself releasing the rock. And then I heard another clanking, clinking, moaning sound. His cohorts jumped and burst into demented laughter. Franz bowed to his visible and invisible audience.

Prince's muzzle was on red alert. In turn, his olfactory scopes were trained at Franz, and Kurt, his sidekick Then at the pail of rocks, sticks the boys brandished like swords, then he zoomed in on Heinrich who peed against a utility pole. Even during these, the coldest days in my memory, Prince's snot remained fresh and moist. It gleamed blacker than the tele-lenses. Small droplets formed around the edges of his nostrils. On that particular dim and wintry afternoon, I could tell by his pawing the snow and other nervy gestures that Prince was on the ready. His whole body quivered and shook in anticipation of a major engagement.

"Prince, you go show them what you've got!" I said, to my dog, who bristled at my side, his muzzle already way ahead of him, his tail whipping up a gust. He bounced out of our hiding place like a revved up ring-fighter, and drove a wedge into the tight cluster of sneering boys. "Don't take off he's just a blind dog!" Hot Sparks yelled at his buddies but they dispersed like firecrackers. Hot Sparks dumped the bucket which obviously belonged to him, and got ready to run too. Prince bared his two rows of perfectly sharp teeth, and his snout had snarling folds ripple up and down. His growling came from the most furious gut in his belly. I saw Hot Sparks shudder, wanting to beat a retreat, step sideways, shield his dick with the bucket, and shout defensively, *"get away you fart, beat it!"* Prince pulled his lips up higher and the white enamel gleamed with menace. I was watching it all from a safe distance

I was tickled to my bones. Prince grabbed ahold of Hot Sparks' pants, tore at them, shredded them, leaving a gaping hole right where the crevice of his buns showed like an upside-down smirk. Hot Sparks screamed as if he had been set on fire, he covered his ass with one hand and his dick with the other. I thought I saw blood, and felt exhilarated by the thought that Prince had sunk his teeth more than skin deep. Hot Sparks dropped the empty bucket, and dashed off faster than the smartest moped on our street. Thus our secret had sprung open like a foul egg. Its smelly content had offended Prince's olfactory sense so much that he had to take action, set things straight and rip into Hot Sparks' smug posture.

I flew up three stairwells to the fourth floor where Dad was sitting in the kitchen having black forest smoked bacon, on big chunks of Mother's home baked bread, and a glass of red wine. "Dad, Dad..." I gasped still out of breath. "Dad, they threw rocks at the icicles, smashed to pieces the longest ones..." I grabbed his hand, pulled him off the chair, and took him down the stairway almost as fast as I had come up. "Look at this Dad, isn't it a shame?" Tears rolled down on both cheeks. A pale moon peaked through the willows and bathed the damage done in its silvery light.

"And here's the bucket, we've got proof of their attack, Dad!" Dad stood frozen in silence for a minute or two that seemed longer than at the dentist's. Then he squeezed my hand, and came down to my height as he kneeled next to me. He looked deep into my eyes still full of tears. "Stop your crying. Time heals everything. Come next year around this time, the ice castle will grow up again and be better than ever."

That night Hot Sparks' father came over, puffed up and bristling like a hedgehog. "Now you've got to understand that I am a peace-loving man. I happen to be your neighbor, but I am pissed at you and your Goddam dog. That dog of yours is a fiend, meaner than a wolf. My son's been traumatized for life. No telling what this vicious attack will do to him in the long run." And on he railed.

Dad let him finish his tirade. "You don't stop people when they need to crap," he once had told me. "Don't waste your time talking back. Let them shit to completion, then get up and leave and do what you need to do." So he let Hot Sparks' Dad rant and rave until he ran out of steam. At that point, Dad dug into his pocket, fetched his wallet, and pulled out a couple of bills. "Take this and buy your son a pair of decent new pants."

Three days later, the pack of hooligans were back at the landing. Hot Sparks sported new pants as green as the grass in spring.

I thought it showed poor taste, and regretted that Dad had shucked out the money which he could have spent more wisely on Sister and I.

Once the bridge was clear and no adults in sight, the band of warriors seized their armament which they had kept hidden under some bushes. Proudly they wielded sticks and branches, two of them had broom sticks that they brandished like guns. Hot Sparks held a ski pole up high above his head. Watching from behind the millstones, I noticed that they were entranced by their combined daring. Hot Sparks was the first to strike. He climbed up on the landing, stood there with two of the guys on either side of him, then he thrusted the tip of his pole at the closest icicle. The boys were so absorbed watching Hot Sparks at work they didn't notice how the main door to the grist mill had opened, and my dad appeared.

He wore his usual work outfit, but at his side he wore something altogether unusual. Dad sneaked up on the gang. And without them noticing it, he was within striking range. "You better take off fast as you can, or I'll take you out, one by one, with this gun of mine." He yelled, and Hot Sparks swiveled around to face Dad toting a big old gun.

Never again did the street gang assemble in full force, and take aim at the Ice Castle. There were sporadic attacks here and there by a couple of intrepid warriors. However, no longer did they wield sticks to ramrod pinnacles and anything else that was longer than wide. Instead, they got their thrills by throwing rocks at the rainbow trout which undulated their tails, ever so slightly, to camouflage themselves among the long strands of swaying water mosses.

Chapter 19

Twins

Mom made a virtue out of our needs. We didn't have enough money for Sister and I to have store-bought clothes. So Mother made it her major pastime to sew and knit pants, sweaters, dresses, caps, really everything on our skin except our shoes and underwear. When Sister and I were going to bed each night, after the "Goodnight Uncle" had talked to us on the wireless at 7:45 pm, and before the World News, Mother was getting ready to leave the kitchen. She sat down at her sewing machine to work on new outfits until way into the night. Often she'd still be there at midnight, passing material under the needle, stitching away ferociously at seams and hems.

While most of the time I put on Mother's creations without feelings of pleasure nor disapproval, I have to say I took her for granted. But machine-knit grey wool pants that fit as tightly as leggings managed to throw me into great confusion. Leggings at the time during the late fifties, were unknown to fashion magazines, unseen and unheard of in apparel stores. When Sister and I first took our grey wool knits out on the street, it seemed to me that a hush fell on the pedestrians; really on all the traffic passing us. We were such an unbelievable curiosity wearing something that nobody had ever seen, much less dreamed of parading in public.

I don't know how Sister felt about staging a public spectacle, but I didn't wait for her to have her own feelings. As soon as I brought up that we were so unique in our grey knits that we actually caused a stir in people's perception, I laid out my feelings to her with such urgency she couldn't help but adopt my point of view as if it had been hers. "Did you see neighbor Loraine stare at us?" I continued. "She looked us over like we had just dropped in from some unknown planet. Actually she stared. And you know why? It's these pants. Nobody in the world wears these pants; it's just you and me. That's what I believe. And wearing something that does not exist is worse than being naked on the street." So I had spilled my guts on Sister, and she looked wide-eyed down her legs where her home-knit pants clung so tightly to every curvature of her legs from ankles, over calves, adhering to her thighs, and even closer to her buttocks. Her eyes started to well up and big tears ran down her cheeks.

Now, I felt bad for having dumped on Sister, who was 18 months younger than I, and had so much less maturity and insight to deal with the role that we had been cast in. Yes indeed, for the first time I felt the shame of being a social outcast.

I was aware of fashion trends at the time. Every girl in our class, really most every girl in school wore these winter ski pants made of some synthetic fiber, knit in some huge clothing factory. These pants were all alike, except for the colors. They all had a strap around the heels so they would not slip out of the boots. The good thing about these pants was that they looked anonymous; yes indeed they were like a uniform. Where as every inch on our grey knit pants screamed, "Look at me! I'm one of a kind! I have imperfections for I was manufactured by Mother during midnight hours. Mother does not go by current fashion trends and the prevalent vogue; she follows her own drummer and that drummer is a loner."

The major advantage of the stretch pants that everybody wore, besides the security of them being anonymously fabricated for the masses, was that they did not cling to every muscle fiber. Our grey knits outlined every twitch in our quads, every wrinkle in our socks, and every ounce of flatulence protruding in our stomach. The pants emphasized our buttocks, and made them look like the kind of double buns many bakers fashioned in our town. It seemed to me that these grey pants served like a looking glass so all the curious bystanders could see exactly what was going on in my body. And that was the worst because it filled me up with a sense of body shame. Even though I was entirely clothed, I had the feeling of standing stark naked in a circus arena, for everyone to gape at this world curiosity.

And it wasn't much of any comfort to see that Sister was the exact same walking curiosity. Mother made a point of dressing us like twins, though in bone structure and facial expression we were quite unlike. I was several inches taller than Sister and quite lean. In fact, I had so little cushioning on my bones that at the school's yearly medical checkup the nurse talked in a hushed voice to the doctor. I overheard her saying that they will send me off to a spa on the North Sea coast so I would gain some weight. That very day, I rushed home in total alarm, and told Mother that the medical team wanted to send me away from home to fatten me up. Mother intervened, and I believe she told them that she was feeding me nutritionally balanced meals three times a day. It was my hyperactive constitution, and she expected me to put on pounds as soon as I would go into a different stage of maturity. She called it puberty, and I didn't have a clue what that was.

I was blonder than Sister too. My hair was so blond it was truly platinum-golden-white. Sister was slightly darker with a brunette tinge that later developed into chestnut as she entered that wondrous state of puberty. Sister had altogether a more rounded look, plump. I would tease her for having that plump good-natured look about her; while I was lean, mean and mischievous looking. In fact, when she was still a baby, she was even chubbier compared to her size now; and I would call her, with much good intentions, "Maggi".

When my parents inquired what this term of endearment was all about, I would tell them with a straight face that it meant a little round ball, the stuff that you retrieve from your nose and then roll between the tips of your index finger and thumb into a pill shape. Then, depending on your mood, you either eat it or throw it away. My parents were so impressed by my straight-faced explanation that the nickname "Maggi" stuck with Margret to this day. She still prefers it over Margret, the name she inherited from Mother, or Meggeli, the cool Anglo version of Margret, which I gave her after my second lesson of English when I entered the first grade of grammar school. Once Sister and I wore our curious outfits to school, I felt cold contempt in the eyes of Padma, Ebba and Hansine; the tight-knit core of our recess games. I heard whispers behind hands that shielded busy mouths. I imagined their smart evaluation of our outfits. "Did you see what Anna and her Sister are wearing? It's long underwear! They're coming to school in their long johns! Can you imagine! My mother would never send me to school like that."

Every whisper, every scant look, every schoolgirl that walked by and made a beeline for the next cluster of whispering girls, all enlarged into one sordid conspiracy aimed at excluding

Sister and I from the playground and its social niches. It made us lepers because of our different looks.

Our grey knit pants were just too different for any of our school mates to bear our companionship any longer. My Sister and I had to rely on each other for a bit of comfort, but the awkward feeling of being in everybody's misgiving eye made our generally tight sisterhood a precarious coalition. How could I comfort her? When I felt all the pain of finger pointing and social undesirability piled on me like a mound of bricks that were meant to crush me into a pile of dirt? All the comfort I could offer Sister was to walk in tandem with her, making wide circles around the tightest gossip clusters of what used to be our playmates, and who now looked like henchmen of the Spanish Inquisition.

Clad in these pants, we no longer had that spring in our steps. We walked heavily like a team of old horses with huge blinders to shield out the world's mockery. Each step felt like stepping into quicksand. Clearly the world was no longer a welcoming place.

In the afternoons during the winter, we used to join some of the most of daring of the sledding kids in town, who rode over moguls and let themselves be thrown up into the air when taking the bump full blast. Being outcast among our sledding pals was the greatest humiliation of all. Margret and I coasted down the mogul run as if it was our own funeral procession. Gone were our customary loud and brave war cries. And, with envy, we heard our pals yippee twice as obnoxiously as in former days.

After so much shame something shifted in both of us, and we felt anger, even rage surge up in our bellies. Why couldn't Dad just go with us to a clothing store, the big department store Santur that promised to have something suitable for even the smallest budget? Why not take us there and pick us out two exceedingly normal stretch pants? Black, for that was by far the most inconspicuous color.

Sharing our torture over being fashion outcasts, seemed like climbing the Daemmer Mountain, barefooted, such a daring and painful thing to do. Deep in our hearts, we both had a notion that our parents had given their best. Mom had worked until the wee hours on our wardrobe, giving us a semblance of plentitude and choice, even through there was no cash to buy any clothing items ready-made. And Dad was the hardest working man we'd ever seen.

At the time when he was in charge of the flour mill, it ran like Swiss-made clockwork, 24 hours a day, without ever stopping. Every little gear had to be greased, and in top order for the machines to run ceaselessly.

But then everything changed. A phone call from Grandfather and Dad's craftsmanship turned from being a proud (and by many accounts) the best miller in the valley, to a humble lot. He began selling sacks of flour to housewives. But the flour wasn't milled by him. It had been factory milled in one of the few remaining mills in Germany.

Grandfather needed money to pay off creditors, who lurked like hungry sharks for Grandfather to fail on one more promissory note. Waiting to throw him into bankruptcy, and waiting to dig their sharp teeth into his real estate holdings, and get them dirt cheap.

So Grandfather was in dire straits money-wise. The German government publicized the economic program that gave incentive payouts to mill proprietors who would agree to have their old fashioned or small-to-medium-sized mills shut down. Then the flour business would be handled efficiently by just a dozen or so modern flour factories. That was the plan, and it got Grandfather hooked. That's when he called Father who had operated the mill successfully for years. Fifty thousand German marks was the price tag the government held out for the shutdown. Too good of a price for Grandfather, besieged by credit sharks, to pass up. So he told Dad on that phone call that changed his life forever.

When Dad received the news, he couldn't speak. And he didn't speak for days. It was Mother who told me that soon Dad would be without a job, and that at his age in his mid-fifties, it was almost hopeless to find a skilled job.

I had almost forgotten about the doomsday plan, since weeks passed with the mill humming away as regular as a fine-tuned steam engine. But then strange men, half a dozen of them, came with trucks. They held crowbars, monkey wrenches, axes, and hammers twice the size of any hammer I had ever seen. Dad let them in, his face as pale as the white cotton sheet that covered me every night.

The demolition crew got to work without much acknowledging my Dad. He was made a bystander; a hapless audience to the undoing of his livelihood. Like a huge centipede, the demolition crew got into the finest of machines, indeed those machines that Dad had kept in meticulous shape through daily maintenance. They ripped and gutted the machines with their tools of destruction. They left holes in the floor where the machines had poured and sifted the finest white flour into cloth sacks that held as much weight as Sister and I together.

When their week's work of demolition was completed, the floors of the mill had gaping holes, virtually every machine or transmission wheel that had any function in the milling process was pried out. The mill resembled one toothless woman who had a handsome face as long as she kept her mouth shut.

In one way, the shutdown of his pride and joy was like Dad's funeral. I had never seen Dad so helpless as in those days. I didn't see him cry, but I cried for him at night, tucked under my feather down comforter. When the Milky Way peeked through the wide open window, and the wind blew the lacy curtains like the sails of a dream boat.

It had been a year since the demolition crew had razed every one of Dad's beloved machines. Meanwhile he had been checking the employment ads in the paper for any job that would fit his milling expertise. But soon he found out that millers were obsolete in Germany with the national shutdown program in full swing, just as the dodo bird was an extinct species.

I remember him putting in a work stint for an Uncle who owned a stone quarry. Dad came home dead beat tired and demoralized. Mother explained later that most young men in their twenties were working for uncle, men who were mostly muscle and much less brains. They had given Dad the hardest and meanest jobs to do for they knew he was related to Uncle, so Dad had been a scapegoat of sorts. They vented their discontent against this old guy who was an oddity on the job market, and the boss's kin on top of that.

Day in and day out, Dad was scouting out job opportunities, and day in and day out he came home empty handed. Younger guys were given preference. Finally the manager of a large and modern flour factory called Dad. He told Dad that he had heard good things about his craftsmanship and that he felt sorry for Dad having lost his business. He had a business proposition to make. You work as a salesman for our flour line, and you can be as independent in your work schedule as you like. We'll let you be your own boss, just like you were before. Dad tossed the idea around in his head during several sleepless nights. Then one morning he called Mr. Hoffman, the big guy in the flour factory, and told him that he would take on the salesman position.

That was the beginning of Dad loading his delivery van with five kilo sacks of flour, going door to door in the suburbs where women were still mostly housewives, who made pasta, and baked their own bread and cakes. Dad was a different man then. Gone was the bravado and ruggedness of his milling days. When he wheeled and dealed with peasants who respected that he had much pride in his trade. They knew that giving Dad a hassle would risk getting to know his hair-trigger temper, and this they wisely avoided. Dad, as a salesman, was a much humbled man and aged, too. He looked and felt like he was my Grandfather. I knew how hard it was going from door to door. Climbing countless flights of stairs up to the highest floor with three or four flour sacks in his arm only to find nobody at home.

Because I knew how much sweat went into every mark that Dad earned, I didn't tell him about the humiliation Sister and I suffered with those home-made knit pants. So I didn't pry into him and plead for him to go shopping with us. Sister and I decided to keep wearing the knit pants but to change our attitude. We faked that we didn't notice the slurs and derision. We pretended that indeed we too were wearing those highly desirable and super normal stretch pants, in black. The more we faked, the more we believed.

And one Friday afternoon the miracle happened. Dad summoned us to the delivery van. No, he didn't need us to help out on the sales route, like we've done so many times before. This was going to be a shopping spree he announced, amused by our mystified expressions. And so we went to the biggest, best, and most expensive sporting goods store in the city. Dad treated us like princesses, opening the store's front door, ushering us in, calling a salesperson to serve us, and serve they did. Dad had put out the grand order. "Two pairs of skis for the ladies, poles and all. The best boots to go with it." And we didn't believe our ears when he said. "Some of those stretch pants that every female seems to wear these days. I don't like them, but I think sometimes it's wise to go with the flow." We could choose what color we wanted. I chose green, and sister said black would be just fine for her.

Chapter 20

Learning to Ski

Our neighbor and his wife were of Polish origin. The spelling of their name Obernowski would screw up your tongue. Although as a child I had fun playing with all those consonants bunged together, and the *ski* at the end amused me. All Polish people seemed to like to ski! In fact skiing was on my mind as soon as the leaves dropped and carpeted the ground in a mosaic of fall colors. When we got our first skis, Sister and I went to the slope that was part of Aunt Elma's house and which was adjacent to our garden. A Polish couple was renting the basement apartment from Aunt Elma and peeked through the lace windows when Sister and I tramped through the snow on our wooden slats. We waved to them for we were innocent and naive. Little did we know that when people chose to look at you from behind the curtain that they wished to remain unnoticed.

Our first runs down the slope were mostly on our backsides. In the pristine snow every bit of accident that we had had showed. After only a half an hour the whole slope with knee-deep snow was as smooth as Mother's white table linen, and looked like a herd of moles had decided to throw up a colony of molehills. This is how the snowy hill looked after our skiing debut. Pockmarked by patches of earth thrown up by countless falls; cross-hatched by our sidestepping uphill; scraped bare so brown tufts of grass poked through like an ancient beard. In short, it was our battle zone. Our wobbly knees, after failing to balance, were precariously bent over Sister and me, atop those thin, long skis. Even from behind the lace curtains, we must have caused our Polish neighbors some chuckles.

The invitation was more than welcome. For the first time we gathered speed under our skis. Who could make it to the house first? We unclamped the skis and left them right by the doorway and rushed upstairs. Aunt Elma opened the door to her apartment, and looked us over. "You first got to take off those boots," she said. She continued, "You brought half of the snow that fell last night with you." The smell of cinnamon floated from Aunt Elma's kitchen, and spiced the air. It smelled festive. We followed her into the kitchen, where a jolly fire in the woodstove crackled and the tea kettle hissed. The fat black and white tomcat purred under the kitchen stove, where a dozen cookies piled on a silver platter smiled at us from the center of Aunt Elma's kitchen table. "Make yourself comfortable. Take off your socks, and I'll dry them on the line over the stove. Meanwhile you can rub your feet and make them feel toasty warm!" Aunt Elma was the epitome of all that was cozy, comfortable, and downright homey.

We plunked ourselves down on the chairs at the table. "Can I light the advent candles?" Sister asked, having already grabbed the matchbox. "Of course you can. And what about a Christmas carol?" Aunt Elma suggested. We lit the four red candles as fat as my wrist, and sung Silent Night for Aunt Elma. We made up some of the words, but she didn't mind. Humming alongside our chorus, she heated a pan of milk, and got the cocoa powder out of the pantry. "Mmmmhh, hot chocolate Sister!" I ejected, and that was the end of Silent Night. "You guessed it!" Aunt Elma said grinning. "Start on those cookies while I'm busy here preparing our hot chocolate! There's lots of almonds in those and coconut flakes and loads of butter!" The cookies melted in our mouths, and created a sensation on my taste buds that was like ten hugs, and a thousand kisses. But then I've never received that much love anyways. Not even over the course of my seven years of life! Sister's eyes gleamed, and with the candles flickering, looked back at me from those pupils that were happier here than at home when we sat around the Christmas tree, and caroled together with Mother while Dad sat aside and watched.

Tomcat stretched under the stove, and arched his back as high as Aunt Elma's knees, and then he brushed up against her fat calves that needed special support stockings because of her varicose veins. The clock on the wall measured the seconds in a steady unrushed tic-toc; the fire made little hissing sounds, and Aunt Elma stirred the hot chocolate with a wooden ladle. Those were the sounds that surrounded us. As well as the crunching of our teeth cutting into cookies shaped in moon-like crescents. Stars, and thick "S"s, and "O"s which you could hang on the Christmas Tree.

I saw an old and tattered book lying on the bench and grabbed it. Possibly it was a mystery book. And mystery to me then was any story that had taken place before my birth. The further back, the more mysterious it appeared. Adventures in the Amazon, read the title. I started to leaf through the yellowed pages. I saw pictures of the wild indigenous people who looked into the camera with crazed eyes and wild tattoos. Then I read of headhunters and natives who ate the flesh of their captives, and the flesh of Christian missionaries. "I don't believe that people would eat other people," I announced.

"How do you think human flesh tastes anyway?" I asked, and I didn't expect an answer. Sister put down her cookie and wiped her mouth clean of powdery sugar. "It tastes like pork," she said. As if she knew from experience. Then she said, "Maybe a bit sweeter." I looked at her in disbelief. Five years old, unable to read, and already had an idea of the taste of human flesh! Aunt Elma stopped her stirring and turned her head. Aha, you've got the book on cannibalism. My stepsons read that book to me before they were sent off to war...and never returned.

Chapter 21

Near Freezing

The sun beamed straight down on my nose. My cheeks glowed. With the snow echoing back the incandescence of the sun, fir trees appeared like black-hooded thieves. The cheeriness of this late wintry afternoon slipped away as shadows grew long fingers.

Unaware of the shadowy encirclement, and still blinded by the gleaming light streaming from the snowy slopes bathed by the western sun, Sister and I were oblivious to our exposed skin registering that the temperature was dropping by the minute, like sand dropping in the hourglass.

The ice-crusted snow hissed crunchy sounds under our wooden skis, and the metal points of our sticks pierced the ice where birds' feet had left faint cryptic messages; freezing cold crept up like icy vapors from the ground. It penetrated the soles of our tightly laced leather boots, sneaked through the loops of our wool socks, and started to worm its way into the bones. Like a parasitic bug, frost nibbled and chewed at our toes. But our eyes and minds were still slope-bound, and pulled us forward stepping and v-stepping up the long belly of our hill; that belonged to us, and only us the fairies that must have been hibernating in the trunks of snow-laden apple trees.

"Toes could freeze off without you even feeling a thing," Dad had told me. He had seen it happen many times in Siberia, where he slaved away in the lead mines as a prisoner of war. Grandfather Frost is a treacherous thief. He injects you with an anesthetic of numbness and weariness, and the blood withdraws from the extremities leaving them exposed. Once the wary men returned to their cabins in the evening and the warmth between four walls allowed them to thaw their icicle beards, their nerves in the frost bitten limbs ran amuck. The pain was so excruciating. Dad's comrades would scream in agony for grandfather frost had sawed off their toes. Inevitably gangrene would soon start eating away at their feet like a carrion-eating beast, and the smell in the prison camps was nauseating.

Images of frost sneaking into the body, and the loss of limbs in Siberia passed through the caverns of my subconscious mind. It left me with a vague feeling of discomfort. Still, I wasn't panicking yet, for I intuited a veil of creature and elemental benevolence draped around us. And evening mistress Venus shimmered in grace on her steady ascent in the east. Squinting against the glare of the low wintry sun, I made out the silhouette of Sister. In an assiduous effort, she was side-stepping her skis up the snowy hill. I leaned over my poles, and just watched her insistent ascension. Vapor clouds curled up from her mouth like bubbles from cartoons. She said, "I'm going up this hill no matter what. Even if my knees crumble, I'll still drag myself up there." Her skis drew V shapes into the slope. Every step marked another victory driven by the desire to have yet another downhill fix, the scary exhilaration of jumping over moguls, and weaving through the trees like the wind.

For most of this afternoon, our downhill skiing and uphill clambering, in the foothills of the Schwaebische Alb, had been a blast. We had zig-zagged the fruit trees in this ancient orchard so close by we could knock off the bark with the metal points of our poles. Again and again, we'd thrust ourselves forward steering our thin wooden slats by shifting our weight from one foot to the other. Our bones and muscles instantaneously adjusted to the topography of snow embankments, moguls, and sheer drop offs. Our downhill ventures were all instinct and little style. When we'd take a rock lopsided, or come within a breath of banging into the trunk of a sturdy apple tree, we'd either apply our bottom brake, or twist our bodies like corkscrews thus releasing the grip of the bindings.

Crystalline white snow with its icy crust crackled under our glide like a benevolent witch. Go faster, plough through me. Sweep across me, and I'll teach you the thrill of speed! Ah, it felt so good to skirt the danger zone. And again and again we went bursting into the force of the wind. We relished the power of being ski knights the ancient fruit orchard being our battle field. Trees cheered us on, come and dodge my branches. Make a sharp turn, and zip by my aged trunk!

Time impressed itself on me as the rays of the sun were cast at a shallow angle. The warmth had fallen from his rays as he was getting ready to disappear in the gold, rose and pink splashes of his descent. The cold felt like biting at my fingers and toes as it progressively sharpened its teeth.

"When is Dad going to pick us up?" Maggi hollered urgently from the top of the hill. Her body was slumped over her poles. The thrill of going downhill had seeped out of her bones. "He won't forget us," I assured her with little conviction. She must have noticed my strained fortitude. I needed to be stronger than her, she being my junior sister and I in charge of making her feel alright.

I saw her come down the slope. Her knees were wobbling, and her weight off-center. Clearly she was no longer in the thrill mode. A big weight of doubt had settled on her sagging shoulders. She must have noticed the feigned assurance I had injected into my voice. "How do you know he won't forget us?" Her skis made a braking noise in the harshness of the snow as she parked parallel to me. The vapor trail came off her questioning face, and blurred her eyes that had turned veiled. Tears in Sister's eyes? Or were the icy fingers of frost making her teary-eyed?

"Do you think that possibly the clock stopped running, and he thinks it's still in the middle of the afternoon?" She inquired, desperately seeking for a plausible explanation for that empty and cold feeling in her stomach. We both now shared the bitter sensation of a world neither of us had yet encountered at the time. The fear of abandonment crept into our chattering teeth, and hollowed our bellies.

"No, the cuckoo clock must be keeping time alright. I pulled up the weights this morning, just like I do every morning," I said, still trying to sound as if I was in control of what increasingly felt like a sinister void engulfing us. "And you know Dad has a watch on his wrist. It's impossible that he could miss the time." Sister started sobbing. It was worse to be left without any reasonable explanation.

The silence around us became menacing. It appeared like the fruit orchard was holding its breath. The clicking sound of our teeth made it worse. Thinking of frozen toes in Siberia, I disengaged my bindings, and started to stomp my feet into the ground, huffing and puffing into my fists. "As long as we keep moving, we're alright," I told Sister.

In the west the sun had sunk below the horizon line, and the hues of rose and pink turned steely grey. I envisioned Maggi and I as Hansel and Gretel, my favorite figures in fairy tale land.

Deliberately they had been abandoned by their parents, given up as prey to the wolves and bears in the dark forest, since there wasn't enough food to go around to feed the four of them.

Would I be as clever as Gretel, and save Sister from the witch's cooking cauldron? Sister having plump cheeks, she'd be the one that would whet the witch's appetite, and make her want to fatten her up like a Christmas goose.

"Why do you think, Mom didn't remind Dad that it's long past the time to come and pick us up?" Sister inquired. She was crying now. "She's probably busy bagging sacks of flour and weighing them. Or maybe someone came to visit." My answers sounded hollow. My voice was quivering under the strained attempt to fight back tears myself. Even though I wanted to, I couldn't join her crying for there wouldn't be anybody left with a level head to reassure us that things would turn out ok.

"Did you hear that sound?" Sister asked. "I can't even hear the wind move in the trees it's so dead silent around us." Still, I did sense danger lurking in the twilight shroud that enveloped us, and made the fruit trees look like an army of black-hued ghosts.

"It's wolves howling," Sister said. The words drowned in her tears, and the way she whispered *howling* sounded like the wolves had already encircled her from the back. "I can't hear anything," I said, and straightened up, so I'd look more like a senior sister protector. Hardly had I spoken those words, when the wind brought to my attention a sort of howling chorus still faint in the woods higher up. Sister and I looked at each other like Hansel and Gretel when they awoke and found themselves so utterly alone.

"Start stomping your feet," I yelled. "Or your toes are going to freeze off." I deliberately made my voice sound full with authority, mainly to let marauding wolves know they had someone to contend with, and secondarily to shake up Sister who was slumping, and sinking lower in her body. "I can't feel my feet, they're just heavy. The stinging and burning from the cold is gone," she said. This reminded me of Dad's account of the insidious father frost who creeps in the deepest when you least feel it.

"Wiggle your toes," I said in alarm. "I don't want to," Sister said with indifference, her eyelids drooping, her head lopsided, with her knees angled precariously over her feet. It looked like any moment now she was going to lay herself down in the snow, and go into the comfort zone of sleep.

"Wiggle just once for me!" I pleaded with her, remembering feeding techniques with babies who refuse to open their mouth. "Just one little spoon full for Mommy... and one for Sister."

Despite the pep talk, my spirit was flagging. Why bother wiggling our toes when our parents had forsaken us out here where the wolves were lying in wait, eager to stalk us by nightfall. If they didn't care, nobody else in the whole wide world would give a toot whether our toes froze off. So went my inner defeatist voice while I kept this erect posture exhorting sister to keep it up. "Lift your toes Maggi. You'll see it tickles!" Her tired glance out of those small disheartened slits that grew smaller every time I looked at them gave me great alarm. I wasn't able to shake her out of her resigned state.

Possibly my lips were as purplishly pale as hers. Just to counter her defeatism, I drew my mouth into a faint smile. I wished so much that she'd smile back just to reassure me that she still registered my sisterly concern. *I wanted her to defy the cold, so bad*, just so that I could draw strength from her faith.

Why couldn't we reenact our up and down see-saw game we played all summer long? Our indomitable balancing act centered on the fulcrum of mutual trust. When I'd be down she'd be astride and high up in the air all giggles. And when she was down on the ground I'd holler "Push off" so roles would reverse again. But the red see-saw, dad had installed in the garden, was in storage now somewhere in the bowels of the mill building, and we were stranded here with father frost eating at our fingers and toes.

"Take your gloves off, make a bowl with your hands, and blow into it!" I demonstrated to Sister, and puffed out a cloud of breath vapor into my urgently cupped hands. But Sister barely noticed. Rejecting any effort to keep warm and alive, she slowly crouched down, and got ready to sink into a bed of snow. "I'm so tired. I'm just going to lie down and wait till Daddy picks us up," She said, now almost serenely surrendered to whatever would pass.

Spoken words no longer functioned in this twilight zone. I looked at Sister softly bedded in the fetal position, snow crystals twinkling as the very last sunrays licked over them. I had an image of Mother bedding us down under our plump down bedding. "Guten Abend, Gute Nacht..." the song formed itself on my lips and I hummed softly Mother's lullaby so the snow princess would be quiet in her mind.

"Remember the next verse?" I asked. Sister shook her head. "Dad forgot us and Mom forgot to remind him," she mumbled to herself. It had become her chant. The solar hues of red-orange and gold dissolved to the west, where the steeple of the Bonifaziuskirche pierces an index finger into the sunset glow. The shroud of dusk was upon us, dark and heavy, and it whispered thoughts of doubt and resignation. "Father, Mother don't love you. They'll leave you to be eaten by the wolves. There is not enough food for the four of you. Just lie down and ride on the wings of slumber before they tear you up..." The whispers turned more insistent as the cold kept needling me. I shuffle a silent path toward Sister. Not feeling that any love came into our forsakenness, I summoned a gesture of love, and rubbed Sister's sunken, hollowed shoulder with my stiffened mitten fingers. I increased the pressure at my fingertips to draw warmth from in her, as well as me. My finger's pushing and pressing tried to persuade her that one individual was left *in this inhospitable place, called the world* that still cared a lot about her.

"It's coming closer," She whispers, the anguish in her voice bleeds through with a quivering tremble in her throat. I hear the silent approach of hungry wolves in her anguished voice. My fingers stiffen into a vise grip. I'm probing for the return of sanity in her resigned muscles. Should I lie down next to her, and hug her closely so our body heat would serve us mutually rather than dissipate into the callous dusk? But with us huddled on the ground would Dad find us once he drove up on that long serpentine road; that lifeline which stood out starkly bluish white against the steel-grey horizon. Stars popped up as the evening shroud turned denser. They glinted with the aloof detachment of being millions of light-years away. Some of these stars might be twinkling by the force of the light traveling incessantly onward while the star itself had long since vanquished in the cosmic void.

In my mind, I traveled back to Hansel and Gretel, the mythic protagonists of this, our experience of being cast out into the oblivion of the wilderness. I envisioned Hansel and Gretel making it back home against all odds, pushing open the door to their parental cabin; and then the moment of the unfathomable encounter. Children returning back to the home of parents who had forsaken their roles. Would this girl and this boy, wizened by the battle against the elements of evil, strafe their parents with eyes colder than this wintry night sky? I couldn't find an answer to this question but it seemed that the roles had reversed. Hansel and Gretel in their distress had sharpened their wits, and became father and mother unto themselves. Their blood parents at this point had lost their function. Their role was to launch brother Hansel and sister Gretel on their heroic journey.

Snuggling up to Sister, and sending her some of my body heat, I asked "What do you think Hansel and Gretel in the fairy tale did when they returned home?"

"They killed them," She said emphatically and the breath vapor from her mouth warmed up my nose.

"You don't really mean that! You're just saying that to get a reaction."

"They killed them, just like they did with the witch," Sister insisted, and looked squarely at me, her black pupils large with a fearful kind of defiance.

"You really think they did such a thing...?" I said and started to imagine for myself how Hansel and Gretel would go about killing their mom and dad. There was the logic of getting even in Sister's proposition.

After all, the parents in the story had deliberately misled their children, making them believe they were just going into the woods to harvest blueberries and mushrooms. Once the kids were all tired out and falling asleep, the parents left them lying deep inside the wild woods and returned home so they wouldn't have to share their gruel and bread with their offspring any more. In terms of a justice equation, the deception of the parents of Hansel and Gretel was just as mean if not meaner than the witch fattening and stuffing Hansel like a Christmas goose.

The image of a fiery conflagration consuming a peasant cabin of the dark Middle Ages, with children watching, and parents sizzling like bacon in the frying pan superimposed itself over the dark wintery scene that now utterly engulfed us.

Sister cocked her head like a magpie from side to side as if she perceived some jewel to be gotten in the midst of the black canvas of spruce and pine woods that appeared to approach us like the battlefront of an army. "There's a wolf hiding behind the bush over there," Sister declared. "I can see a pair of green eyes gazing at us."

The wind stiffened under her gaze, blowing the last of the pear and apple leaves that hadn't fallen down from the trees yet, sweeping gusts of fall rustled ominous incantations. You're two parent-God-forsaken babes. Hear the wolves skirting the edge of the woods. They've picked up your scent. They're on the advance. Just keep lying there and they'll find you, and sniff you, and eat you alive.

"I can't feel my toes any more, and my fingers are stiff like icicles," Sister said, her voice choked up by the flood of tears she was holding back. Quickly I directed my attention to my own toes, and checked out whether the nerves were still alive. "My toes burn like the feeling when you bite into a scoop of ice cream," I told Sister; another attempt at lightening up the gloom that had settled upon us, but Sister failed to react one way or another. The emboldening effect of our homicidal conspiracy against uncaring parents dissipated rapidly as the icy gusts that hissed from the west carried on.

A waning moon disk slowly rose over the east horizon casting groping greenish-white fingers through the gnarly branches of fruit trees that had been planted when Napoleon's armies roamed Europe. With its light the snow-covered lay of the land looked cold as a sepulcher. Sister looked as pale and frozen as one of Aunt Elma's porcelain figurines.

A trail of vapor lifted and curled upward in the distance of the snowy road. *"Dad's coming!"* I yelled. Every fiber in my body's muscles twitched and stretched with this discovery. Sister slowly turned her head and sharpened her pupils to see the advance of our rescue.

The motor noise of the approaching delivery van, that Dad drove, drowned out the whispers of branches and menacing wolf noises that had been carried on the wind.

I slowly gathered up my achy bones, with my muscles hanging like lead. Sister wreathed in the snow like a half frozen reptile. There was moaning and sighing, and I didn't know whether it was coming out of her throat or mine. The van's headlights beamed over the wintery landscape, canvassing this way and that, however the serpentine road directed it. The shadow world that had encroached on us dissolved in the lights' roving search.

Finally we made it up to our feet, and stood wobbly. There was little sensation in our extremities to reassure us about our balance now having contact with the ground and the bottoms of our feet.

balance now having contact with the ground and the bottoms of our feet.

"I'd burn them alive like the witches on the stake. Make them sizzle and burst like saveloy (pork sausage) over a camp fire," Sister mumbled under her breath. Then she took in a sharp breath that filled out her body into an upright posture. Thoughts of revenge had surged up again, and I too felt the tingle of inflicting cruelty in the quest of the only justice that made sense to me, the eye for an eye of getting even. I'd lock them up in a walk-in freezer, and double bolt the door. They could scream their souls out; nobody could ever possibly hear and rescue them. Our imaginations were on a mutual feeding frenzy as we glanced squarely into each other's eyes. For the first time since we had felt the full extent of our God-forsakenness.

Dad's van was now within smelling distance of its exhaust. The rev of the motor reassured us in that neutral automatic regular matter-of-fact way only a machine can. If people could only function like machines, this world would be a trustworthy place, I thought to myself.

We stood at attention like the only soldiers left in the battlefield coming face to face with the Commander-in-Chief.

Leaving the motor running in neutral, Dad swung his door open, and came up to us with swift determined steps that showed his body had been warm and comfy while we were turning into human icicles. "It's gotten dark just like that," he said, as he snapped his fingers. "In one moment I still could see the sun, and you wouldn't believe it, when I looked out the window again it was night. So girls jump on in, you must be freezing. I'll take your skis to the back of the van. For God's sake take off your boots. We'll have to give your feet one big bear rub."

We crawled into the van not knowing which emotion of the watershed of feelings to express. Sister finally let loose. Her sobbing at first just lifting her chest, and locked behind a stony Aztec face now exploded into one big outcry. "You forgot all about us, you... you... you... left us out in the snow for the wolves to get us... you." Dad looked at her with firm and compassionate eyes. "The cold will do that to you. It just gets to your head, scrambles your mind. Here, put your feet into my lap, and I'll draw warm blood back into these footsies."

"No, no, no... Don't touch me," Sister said, and curled herself into the shape of a small boulder "You left us here to die,

Anna Louise Haman

you, you, you...." And with the gushing of tears and sobbing she barely could gasp for any air.

Dad drew back away from her, and situated himself in the driver's seat shifting the van into gear. "Mother cooked up your favorite meal, lentil soup and pasta with big beef bones, and red beet horse radish. The bones have extra lots of marrow to blow on your bread." I couldn't help but imagine myself bringing a hot beef bone to my mouth with the hollow inside plump filled with that greasy rich substance that nourishes our bones, and blood, and tastes better than goose-lard.

Once at home, installed around our cheerful dinner table I'd blow into those bones as hard as a wolf trying to get to the goat kids and then spread the heap of marrow on Mother's freshly baked rye bread. Visions of comfort foods stilled my heart, so tightly knit into a bitter sulk. Sister's sobbing softened, and the steady rev of the engine did soothe our urgent feelings with its onward steadiness.

Chapter 22

Having Period

I had a circle of pimples around my mouth, and my face was pale. My hair looked oily. I got irritated at Sister, the cat, and a wobbly chair. I ran out of the kitchen and banged the door when Mother told me that I had over-looked food specks on the dishes while washing them. Everybody thought I was a mess that month of my eleventh birthday. Sister started to avoid me, even Father made large circles around me. Mother observed me with her keen brown eyes as if I was some chemical reaction that was about to explode. One morning, I believe it was the middle of the week, when I got up I noticed blood on the white linen sheet. I looked for scratches on my legs, which so far had been the only place I used to bleed due to mosquito bites, briars, and thorny bushes that I liked to explore, and because of numerous bicycle crashes. But my legs showed only a few scabs and no traces of any blood. When I took off my pajamas I noticed the crotch of my trousers were solidly stained by fresh blood. Now I was more than perplexed, I was scared out of my wits. I must be hemorrhaging, I thought, bleeding from my belly. What did I eat that would cause such a bloody disaster?

I went to the living room with my pajamas down to my knees, and stood there in the center of the room waiting for Mother to come and look at this emergency and call an ambulance. When Sister entered the room I pulled up my pants. She gets dizzy spells and wobbly knees when she sees blood. "Call Mother," I said. "Tell her I am very sick." She looked at me with searching eyes, "So why are you not in bed?" She'll resist any order until she finds out exactly why, where, and what for. "Never mind," I said, and waved her off. "I'll just wait here for Mom to show up." This prompted Sister to call at the top of her voice, "Mother come here, Anna has a disease!"

Mother came with a concerned smile, and in her hand she held a package of diapers. "What's that?" Sister asked. "You're not quite ready to wear these, but I think your Sister needs them right now."

"Mom I'm bleeding out of my stomach, I mean I'm bleeding hard."

"Yes, I saw it coming," Mother said. "Those pimples and your foul moods were accurate predictors for your first period."

"What's a period?" Sister asked. "When a girl reaches a certain age, she starts bleeding for a few days every month, and that marks that she's growing to be a woman."

"I don't want to grow up, if I have to bleed," I said, and Sister agreed, "me neither."

Mom handed me a feminine napkin and some special panties into which the feminine napkins were tied. "Let me show how to do this!" Mother said; and took the napkin, and fitted it into the crotch of those panties, and tied the ends of the napkins onto loops on the front and the back of the panties. She handed me the thing and said, "You'll have to change the napkins every so often, depending on how much you bleed." I looked with disbelief at the napkin and the panties. "You mean I need to wear diapers like a toddler?"

They're much smaller than diapers, but yes they do protect your clothes from getting stained, and in the public you don't want to have blood running down your legs, do you?"

"No," I said, and took the panties she was still holding out for me.

Chapter 23

The Witches Dance

Empty stomachs can create delusions. At times hunger allows us to enter into a crack between two worlds that usually stay separated. I once entered another dimension of space and time and peered through a crack. What I saw made me believe that the past goes on amidst us as if the modern world didn't exist. It all happened during the height of the carnival season. After six hours of school I was a bit bleary-eyed, and my stomach was growling like a wolf.

As I stepped out into the open, I heard the bells of the Narren clanking across the field where the ruins of the ancient monastery lay in different stages of decay. A brisk wind flew into my face; shredded cloud banners raced across a blue March sky. In my head I was still doing noun declensions of Latin words. The accusative and the ablative were still ringing in my inner ears.

Nobody else shared the path through the field that I passed through, my legs walking by somnambulant memory. My stomach growled. I was more than ripe to sit down at the lunch table and smell Mother's cabbage rolls. In my mind's eye I saw my Latin teacher's gaze, critical of my leaky memory, but nearly amorous of Bettie who sat in front of me and knew her vocabulary better than I knew my way back home. To be a teacher's favorite is something major to accomplish when you're 12 years old.

For one year now, ever since I had blood run down my legs when I had gotten up one morning, the monthly menses had absorbed much of my energy. Two weeks ahead of the onset I was already worried whether this time I would bleed through my pads again and have an alarming red stain oozing through my clothes. It had happened to me twice, and the shame of having blood on the seat of my pants for everybody to see and snigger about seeped deep into my bones, and made me brittle in my self-consciousness. Having been one of the first girls in class to have her period, it aroused public curiosity. The fear that I would soil myself again, the image of renewed shaming became a thought that crowded out Latin vocabulary and its numerous declensions. Bettie had not had the bloody experience yet; it was easy for her to retain everything our teacher said.

On this day when my stomach growled like a hungry wolf, the bells of the Narren rang as if the cow herds of the Swiss Alps were flying past me, and the wind caught my hair and tousled it like a grandmother would, I met three people who left an indelible mark in my memory.

He came toward me, made large steps, as if he were gliding above ground. The type of clothing he wore was not like anything I'd seen on the streets of my hometown. His trousers were wide and bulging around the thighs and pleated around the waist. The shirt he wore was shimmering white like Mother's pearls, and the sleeves were as wide as his pants and gathered into a million pleats at the cuffs. He wore a brown gown that had green threads in it that gleamed like the emeralds on Aunt Elma's ring finger. This is carnival I told myself. The Latin chatter had been swept clear by the arrival of this figure.

His long stride came at me faster than I had anticipated given the distance at which I had just glimpsed him. He passed me like a silent train. His stature grew tall as he glided by me. So tall, I was looking up to see his face. Nose, mouth, ears, *everything being in its proper place, except for his eyes.* The eyes were red as if fresh blood had been poured into the sockets. They were wide open and had a liquid expression. Even after he had disappeared behind my back, I still saw those large red marbles as if suspended in front of me. I couldn't recall whether he was grinning, crying or sullen looking, and the blood-filled eyes made the particulars of his facial expression moot.

All the way through our passing encounter I was neither frightened nor unduly surprised. It was Fastnacht after all, things were meant to be off kilter during carnival time. But why didn't I hear a sound as he whisked by? Why were his feet about a foot above the ground, and why the bloody look of his eyes? That was beyond any Narren costume, no Narren could conjure up such an unworldly performance.

I was still dazed by the man's blood-filled eyes. Thinking that this must be the look of someone who had his eyes poked out, blinded as part of torture. I thought of the martyrs, witch tales and local lore that tell of the agonies of being blinded. In my mind's eye I could see a red hot poker being thrust into the eyeball, and the piercing of the cornea, and, like a broken egg, the spilling of the eyeballs, now a running mess of goo, and the horrific screaming.

I was still immersed in these visions when two more figures ran toward me. This time they were women, old hags that galloped like wild horses. They approached me swift as the wind on this blustery day in March. Similar to the bloody-eyed guy, their feet were not touching the ground. Their long dark skirts billowed in the wind, black flags of mourning that trail a funeral procession. Their tops were equally somber-looking, with worsted shirts. Like the man's clothing, the women's dresses were not of this century, nor like the Middle Ages, when common people wore scratchy and rough fabrics from handspun wool and linen, and laundered their good Sunday clothes maybe once a year.

These two women were willowy and lank in their appearance, and so tall I had to look up as if into the top of a tree. I searched their faces and found their eyes in place, except the gaze was beady, eagle-sharp, focused on the far away and not on me. They glided by me like hearses. Their flaring skirts were within reach of my hand. I could have touched them, felt the rough woolen fabric of their skirts to find out whether they were for real. The thought didn't occur to me until much later. They blew by me like the wind and not a sound was made.

It was this absence of sound that startled me more than anything else about these three figures. I was walking on the grounds of the monastery that had been founded some 800 years before. The ruins to my left had housed nuns at one time. Girls my age were mandated by their parents into the Holy Mother's lap so they would pray all day long. This would guarantee God's grace as well as a favorable reputation for their families.

Chastity was a key issue when a girl was given to the convent, so Mother had told me. If she had a soiled reputation in the village and was not getting married, parents would send her off to live behind convent walls, so she could do no further harm to the family name. If she was still a virgin the monastery was best guarantee to keep her in that blessed state. Over the centuries the lay population of my town had spun a web of tales around the keeping of her in that blessed state. Over the centuries the lay population of my town had spun a web of tales around the monastery's past - some of them sinister and frightening to a girl my age.

The grisliest piece in the monastery puzzle surfaced one day when bulldozers arrived on the former monastery lands and cleared the holy site to install a soccer field. During the earthwork, shovels uncovered a rock wall that led to an underground passage, which in turn opened into a walled subterranean chamber. In the recesses of the rock wall they found sarcophagi, and in a sarcophagus *they found the skeletal remains of infants.*

Rumors had spread like a wildfire, and many among the Catholic churchgoers in our town were deeply shaken. Mother told me the story when the news broke. She sat next to me while I was eating lunch after my six hour school day. These days, because of my Latin elective, I came home after our family's regular noon lunch. My stomach was in knots, and my appetite almost past the peak. All morning long I had survived on nothing more than the freshly baked roll I had bought during recess from the baker who set up his baskets in our school yard.

"Did you know that they found underground chambers near the monastery?" Mother asked as she ladled borscht into my plate. I shook my head. The beets were so hot I had to blow on them for a bit. Mother resumed her story. "On your way home from school, as you pass by the ruins, haven't you noticed all these serious looking people poking around at the monastery?" She asked. I hadn't been aware of all this activity, shook my head, and shoveled the borscht into my hungry mouth. "Archeologists are digging around there, and historians and clerics are looking over their shoulder," She said, and sat down again passing me a slice of her freshly baked bread. "You want me to butter it?" She asked.

"No, I'd rather blow bones," I said. This was one of my favorite mealtime diversions. Whenever Mother had cooked stews like borscht she would put in thick beef bones which had globs of marrow in their holes. I loved to blow on the narrower side of the bone and pop that jello-like wobbly stuff onto my bread, spread it with a knife, put some salt on top of it and devour it with the greatest relish.

Mother smiled seeing me go through my food ritual. She wiped a wisp of her fine hair to the side of her head, and then secured it in a fist-sized knot in back. Her voice turned lower. "They had the skeletons and remains of fiber tested in the labs. Scientists have determined that trauma to the head and neck caused the infants to die. They had been killed," She said, and sighed deeply. I stopped eating for a moment, holding the bread with marrow halfway between the plate and my open mouth.

"Babies? Killed by who?" I asked. It sounded too absurd to be credible.

Close to the convent there was the tallest man on the school staff who had read one thousand books on local history, so he had told us, which in turn had made him so shortsighted he had to peer through glasses that were as thick as my finger. "Why did they kill babies at the monastery?" I asked my history teacher.

I put one and one together and the outcome would have been pregnancies and babies which had to be disposed of before the church authorities would find out.

Babies born to nuns who had taken up the vows. Or perhaps to pregnant women who were sent off to the convent because the father was a nobleman, and the bastard child would have caused great scandal.

Chapter 24

Black People

Only Mom knew what her mission would be in black Africa. It seemed she was taking up the torch her father had handed her in a relay. He had never been able to fulfill his life's dream, and be a missionary in the former German colony of Cameroon. With its defeat during World War 1 Germany had lost all its African territories, and Grandfather was a fully trained missionary without a mission.

Like her father, Mother loved African people and black students were welcome at her dinner table.

How did Father feel about this? After all, Mom's black friends were one of the most exotic things to happen in this small town where they lived. Neighbors would register young black men coming in and out of the Jrosse Muehle. Sometimes they would go for a walk with me or my sister. The miller's two blonde daughters walking with dark men! What an outrageous sight for neighbors who think that people from Berlin or Hamburg are foreigners.

Not wanting to look like he was racist, Dad let Mom indulge her exotic friends. They were just friends he thought.

When I was thirteen Mom invited the first black man to our house. She envisioned him and me getting married - the perfect ticket for her African mission to become reality.

On this brilliant Monday, that already had a hint of the crispness of fall, I thought I'd swing by the Jrosse Muehle and say hello. I had been with Mom and Dad on Saturday. They both were in a gloomy mood then. Mom, who usually was talkative, had hardly said anything and Dad spoke of the weird look he got when

The computer disk that this story is on had technical problems – lost storage, and Anna did not have a written copy. My feeling was to publish the incomplete story. David Froebel

Chapter 25

Beliefs Create our Reality

Beliefs create our reality, or let's say they create what we see. We get our beliefs set into place mostly by our parents. And these conditionings were some of the basic beliefs that my Mother and Father instilled in me at a young age and which in turn framed my understanding of reality. An additional profound influence on my belief system and therefore my reality was my reading years of subscriptions to Walt Disney's Mickey Mouse comics. In fact I learned to read before I went to school. It was the combination of cartoon frames and the talking bubbles with words in them that taught me the meaning of words.

"Men with long noses also have long penises," my Dad postulated this when we watched a political round-table one Sunday afternoon, after I had remarked that the journalist from Tel Aviv had such a long nose. Even though I have tried to look at men's noses objectively, Dad's observation always came up like a red light (or a green light). Let's just say men's long noses have a special meaning to me.

"It's easier for a camel to go through the eye of a needle than for a rich man to enter the kingdom of heaven." Mother had told me that very early on. Surely she said it in the correct biblical phrase, but I soon turned the saying into something short and more intelligible for me. I had this belief confirmed by several sources. Dagobert Duck, the richest man in all of Mickey Mouse's world, surely would not make it through a needle's eye with his bunkers full of money. He also was a strangely lonely man, no wife or children of his own and his only pleasure time was to visit his bunkers and walk-in safes to view his hordes of money. This was not a life that appealed to me.

Grandmothers enjoy their grandchildren more than mothers enjoy their children. I experienced this firsthand, my mother's mother never tired of me, except once that I can remember. Even on her death-bed she would listen to my reading Mickey Mouse stories, and I also enjoyed her stories, which she read from the Unity Church newsletter. In fact Grandma did my home work assignments for needlework class. She knitted my gloves, crocheted the protective cover over coat hangers, an asinine assignment if you asked me. She also crocheted more pot holders than my mother had pots, and she showed me how to cross stitch in a neat way, the only stitch I can remember of a dozen that we had to memorize. All the while she was busy with my homework, I read to her about Goofy's mishaps and Tick, Trick, and Truck, the nephews of Donald Duck who I found extremely clever. We were the best team, *combining work and pleasure*. I wish she were still alive.

Again Walt Disney corroborated this positive experience of grandmothers and their benevolence toward kids. Grandma Duck was by far the happiest person in Disney's Mickey Mouse World. She had a neat farm with all the animals you could possibly want. A picket fence and a homey farmhouse behind it; and Tick, Trick and Truck never tired of visiting her and having adventures on her farm.

"If you're an outsider a mask won't do you any good." Mother told me, when I deplored the fact that my sister and I were not given any masks or costumes during carnival. Other kids in school dressed up as witches, the boys especially liked to do that, and cowboys and indians, an equally popular costume among girls and boys, where as Sister and I remained in plain-clothes, nothing more nor less than Anna and Margret Haman. Thus the carnival season made me feel doubly estranged from the rest of the kids. I told myself, once I was a grownup I'd wear the most outrageous mask of all. Well, once I was an adult I had no clue what to wear. I never had practiced dressing up and masquerading during childhood. The only costume I have come up with so far in my life is being a sun flower during the celebration of my hometown. Mind you I was just one sunflower among about a hundred kids. Still, that was one of the better costumes.

When I was a teenager and dating a very smart kid, I went to a carnival ball with him and asked Mother to sew me a costume. She suggested going there in a burlap costume, with me representing a sack of potatoes. The proposition upset me, for at the time I had the urgent need to look attractive, appealing to my date. So I asked Mother to sew me an-extra short mini-skirt out of some shiny fabric, and a floppy hat with a wide brim from the same material. I painted my boots white; at the end I looked like I was freshly imported from Carnaby Street, London, which at this time was the center of the Beatlemania fashion world. Among witches, and warlocks, magicians, and pirates I wore the only contemporary outfit. My date told me that I could have at least worn a face mask, the thing they wear at the opera.

There were two more times I masqueraded myself, *both in America where carnival is more of an adopted custom*, hardly a custom at all. It was at a Toga Law School Party where I painted big freckles on my face and had two braids sticking away from either ear. "I am Heidi," I told Roman men and women, wrapped in bed sheets and laurel-crowned. Again I was a misfit, out of line with the rest of the crowd. At a pagan wedding in the woods of western Massachusetts, USA I finally came full circle. My earliest costume had been a sunflower and here I stepped into the circle and declared I am the sun. I had bought seven yellow silk scarfs and managed to flutter them in the wind like sunrays. I was a success, but nearly starved because the bridegroom and his bride couldn't get enough of our costumes and forgot to feed us.

Chapter 26

The Hole

What is a parental home in your dream? A parental home is a house where I grew up. In the dream I am an adult in my parental home. How is a parental home different from another home? This is the place where I spent my childhood; all my memories are connected to this place.

How do you feel about your parental home? I feel much sadness. I lost both my parents in my parental home, my dearest Grandmother died there and my baby brother. I was with them as they died or came shortly after. Also my parental home, or the mill, is a huge old building that needs repair in so many places. And my family does not have the money to even start repairing leaking roofs and the like. So my parental home is like a constant reminder that we don't have the means to afford proper upkeep. It's very difficult to keep clean, because it's so huge and old. And we have an ancient toilet that does not flush and it is an embarrassment to me. As a child I always wished my parents would be able to remodel the mill. But it never happened.

Is there anything in your current life that reminds you of death of dear ones, that is huge, and in need of repair? My family saga chronicles my tragic origins in the old Europe. And I often doubt whether I can pull it off, since English is not my native language. And I would need someone to do the editing and proof-reading for me. And then I don't know whether something as non-commercial as a family saga will ever get published. I could publish it myself I guess.

What is a bathroom? This is a place where people take baths and showers, brush their teeth and dress. It's a place to get clean and nurture yourself with water or in water. How does remodeling change a bathroom? It makes it more pleasing visually. But most of all it allows me to have a warm bath whenever I want to. There is tile all around me. The room is just right in size so it is comfortable and warm.

Is there something in your life that reminds you of a place that you would want to change so it is more pleasing visually and you could enjoy its warmth and clean yourself in warm water whenever you want to? I guess I would like to have a warm and comforting relationship. But in order to have that I would need to remodel some of my possessive ways and my need to overdo it.

What is a kitchen? A kitchen is a place where you prepare food and eat it once it is done. How is a kitchen different from a bathroom? A kitchen is a place for community. In my bathroom I'm alone most of the time. What was the kitchen in your parental home like? Mine was a place where Mother made delicious foods and we very much enjoyed all the meals that she prepared. It's where I found my parents lying dead on the floor; after my Father shot my Mother and then killed himself.

Is there a place in your current life that has delicious meals and community and where you have long discussions with loved ones? I cook my own meals and they are very simple and healthy and I eat them by myself alone. So I do miss community in my life.

What is a blue-collar worker? This is a person skilled in manual labor. He gets the job done according to what the contract says or what I tell him. Is there any person in your current life who gets the job done accordingly to what you ask him to do? I need to be my own blue collar-worker. I need to be more disciplined and do what I plan to do.

What is Falstaff like? He is a Shakespearean character who overdid it and the structure of the house is about to collapse. Is there anything in your current life that holds up the structure and is about to collapse? My recent workshop collapsed when one of my two participants walked out, my being the astrological-physiological consultant/coordinator. How did I feel when that happened? I was close to tears, but I held them back because I felt I needed to take care of the other remaining participant who said that she felt terrible and unsure and *collapsed*. I don't know. Well, the remaining member would have been even more disturbed and would have left also if I had not kept it together whereby the whole workshop would have collapsed.

For Closure

by Anna's husband David

Look peoples, this is not exactly the easiest stuff for me to write about, but I do believe the book needs closure. Anna had a vast, very vast, knowledge of spirituality. She did lean towards Native American Spirituality; you will see in the coming pages of the next chapter, where Anna wrote of partaking in a *Native American Long Dance.* Also, hopefully, to be published in the future in her second book, "Anna's Spiritual Path in America" her intimate friendships while living at Sufi camp in New Mexico. Someone once told her she had been a Southwestern American Indian counselor in a previous life time - I believe it - I remember her last days prayers.

The time span when Anna was fifteen to the nineties is vacant, I know, but hopefully the coming pages of her 1995 – 1996 journal and a variety of her short stories to be published within, "Anna's Spiritual Path in America" will help clarify matters. Presently I could connect with Anna through trance medium asking questions, but I don't think or feel to, I refuse to for Anna's sake etc. Concluding my writings, well, I will say something about her past sex life. She was heterosexual, but she once had two female room-mates, in Massachusetts, one lady lesbian and the other lady bisexual. This was after she was married for twelve years. As a result, her marriage had ended traumatically for her.

After being married she went on a vast amount of dates, shall we say, and half of the time, yes, there was intercourse. After she told me, of the number of men that had similar physical characteristics (black hair) and were healthy, I asked her, "How could you do that?!" Anna's reply was "I learned how to seek them out" I think the average woman, having had so many sexual sharings, would have most definitely contracted AIDS, but not Anna.

When Anna was 19/20, she went to North Africa and held hands with men in a community dance ceremony. These men's hands had never held any women's hands in an Islamic dance ceremony. Anna also had in-depth experience of astrology and Sufism and was a certified Kripalu Yoga teacher; she even wrote about her thoughts and feelings of going to an American Indian Long Dance, which is included in the end of the book. She wrote, "Balls and penises"; again I had been advised to change her words, but I refused to.

She once told me that in the seventies, she peddled her bike wearing no bra through the black section of conservative Waco, Texas. She found it refreshing, but she also said, "I did not consider myself a hippie." She called herself a warrior in private (to me). In fact, during the last week she was alive, one morning, she told me that she had killed a bear in her dream state.

Now, Anna and I have never discussed this subject of her reincarnation. Only recently, I have read in her 1995 – 1996 journal that she composed while she had her psychological / astrological counseling business in Albuquerque, New Mexico and also lived extensively at the Sufi intentional community in the mountains of New Mexico: "A_____ laid another trip on me saying that she saw me in her past life in a concentration camp. I became defensive and told her the bit about the resistance to the Nazis in my family." Twelve days later Anna wrote in her journal: "And last night there were many sleep interruptions caused by A_____." Four days later Anna wrote: "Last night I dreamed of vicious dogs and I stuck knives into their heads. The night before I dreamed of sick dogs which I had not fed for a while and their legs were hurt and I treated them with Johannis Oil and they healed. Forgetting to feed the dog is a recurrent theme." And, "It was very hard to get up this morning." Nine days later she wrote: "Finally dreamed last night that I fed the hungry dog (Prince). I even held some of the meat between my teeth. I slept in this morning and still took a nap." And seven days later she wrote these interesting sentences: "But it doesn't need to be another near-death criss situation. I have experienced so many. If I decide that I don't want these situations any more, possibly they won't wind up in the same manner as they did before in my life." Thirteen days later Anna wrote: "Looked at the charts of the Oklahoma bomber, Anne Frank and Jane Austin!"

I have chosen to put Anna's favorite photo of herself on the back cover of this book. Originally it was to go on her second book, that I named *Anna's Spiritual Path in America*. Her only request was not to show any nude pictures of her; there will be no nude pictures of her as an adult. If these words are upsetting for you, it is understandable; the paths of our lives pass through many fears, insecurities and confusion; our intent is for honesty, truth, and mental healing, and not to offend anyone. Embracing these dark moments is necessary for the completion of our journey. As the saying goes, *the truth shall always prevail*. Anna lived a tremulous life with many ups and downs. She traveled many miles in her pickup truck - having visited most all of the states, and by air, for example, to Germany and back to America. While traveling extensively, she accumulated knowledge for her writings - mainly this book. Luckily from the help from God / Jesus / Aristotle / Mohammad / The Great Spirit / Rumi / Mira / Buddha / etc., Anna spent an enormous amount of money to write the book. And I can attest to the fact that she was extremely frugal with her money in some ways.

Chapter 28

Native American Long Dance

We had come to dance all night around a fire at the center. We have our hopes and wishes, neatly wrapped up in prayers that we cast in the four directions. Many among us are stuck in careers that pay the mortgage but leave the heart starving. Men and women alike are at their wits' end when it comes to relating. Men want to howl like wolves and so do we women. Female and male are out prowling each other. Neither one knows any longer how to fill the role.

"Create a banner that is representative of you life's journey," Linda tells me over the phone when I asked what I needed to bring to the Long Dance. She and her husband are the leaders of the dance. And bring something that is precious to you to the give-away. It's an exercise of letting go, she said. Otherwise, you need to bring your own water, for there is none at the site where we hold the dance. After getting all the details and directions, I hang up, take a deep breath and know in the pit of my stomach that after this dance my life will never be the same.

We brought banners of all sizes: as small as placemats and as large as a sizeable flag. The banners bear images of our childhood, broken dreams and most of all broken hearts. We hope for mending, and new designs to unfold during the Long Dance, which as a time-space event is a lifetime compressed between nightfall and the birds' songs during pre-dawn.

My banner is makeshift, a one-hour affair of compressing the milestones of my life into a crayon sketch: I as a baby the color of salmon. Brother who died of Leukemia, under a smudged black cross. Sister, inveterate playmate and then rival in romance and beauty. Artistic expression, an outline in pink that bloodies into red. The German Shepherd that lay next to my crib and shared twelve years of my childhood - tail up, big muzzle and blue and black. My parents who died together on one day. Will I be able to speak to the group about the horrid circumstances of their dying? I paint them lying next to each other, trickles of red crayon smudges where the blood dripped from their gun wounds. My grandmother angel in yellow. The memory of her gentle intellect and caring I paint as a bright yellow arc that beams right into my heart. The man who *fifteen words omitted because of defamation of character*. The second half of the picture starts with an airplane taking off, jetting me from the old world to the heart of Texas. The tremors of the culture shock are little black and orange wavy lines, only after twenty years of my residency as an alien are they starting to become solid ground. Finally the outline of myself, mid-aged, naked like I was as the salmon-colored baby and a big question mark dangling over my head. Not knowing where I'm headed next and therefore a participant at the long dance, where answers emerge like fish that are ready to bite.

I had decided in the last minute to join the long dance. The date for the three-day event I had marked with faint pencil in my appointment calendar, clearly overshadowed by underlined appointments that wouldn't shake my performance by an improvisational troupe, an appointment with my massage therapist - all occasions where I knew I'd emerge safely intact, my belief system still in place.

I pack my camping gear with list in hand. As I drive on the interstate with Peter Gabriel on the fm radio I notice that I left my straw-hat back home. The scorching sun is bound to make inroads through my thick skull.

I pass through (*Stoneway – a very small town in New Mexico, USA*), once a thriving community sprawled alongside the Santa Fe railroad tracks, now a sleepy place where ranchers wear oversized Stetsons and the convenience store beats the pulse of the town. After this sleepy community, it's nothing but dirt roads in National Forest land and jackrabbits darting across my path.

I come to a gate. A stocky woman with curly black hair gathered in a ponytail that reaches down to her buttocks opens the gate and flashes a welcoming smile. "I'm Maria the camp cook," she says and her wide cotton skirt billows in the hot breeze. I smell charcoal on her skin. Just pick yourself a nice spot and join us for dinner. We're barbecuing ribs and have a ton of potato salad and coleslaw.

Someone howls and grunts behind me. I whirl around and look into the furry mask of Wolf our dance leader. He wears a loose shirt of feathers and flaps his feathers. "Looking for a tent site?," he snarls at me. Stay away from the men's quarters. Celebrate solitude when you most crave company and you'll soar by the end of the dance. I sigh. The wish to escape the cold grip of loneliness has brought me here. Possibly I would find a dancer who would spark my chemistry and we would cuddle at night under the full Moon. Wolf just burst my bubble. While I scanned the valley for a secluded spot, Wolf laughed so loud his belly wobbled along with his feather garment. Then he spreads his wings and slinks away.

I park my truck at the far end of the camping ground and decide to raise my tent next to a big cedar which would break the wind and give me shade when the sun scorched the land.

As soon as I started to unfold the canvas of my tent and lay out the poles, a tall guy with cowboy boots and an east coast baseball cap sauntered into my construction site. "Hi I'm Charley!" He stretched out his squarish hand. His palms felt warm and a tad clammy. "I'd like to get it up all by myself. These days I'm practicing self-reliance." Charley took a step back and folded his arms in front of his black t-shirt. His right boot tip drew a circle in the ground and kicked pebbles to the side. "You've been to the long dance before?"

"This is my first time," I said and tried to figure out which poles I should insert first. "What about you?" I ask.

"This is my third time. The stuff that happens during the long dance is so potent; I can coast on it for a long time." I lay down the poles I just picked up and stand up straight. Charley got my curiosity engaged.

"I've heard that people break through their fear threshold, kind of like in a ropes course," I say.

"That's just the beginning." Charley adjusts his baseball cap and spits to his left. "I'd say a better description is that you dance your whole life - birth to death. I've had three deaths so far and I'm ready for my next one."

"That sounds scary. I didn't really want anything drastic to happen. I mean I came mainly to find answers in this time of transition. Dying wasn't on my list when I signed up for this." I pick up the poles again and insert them through the sleeves of the tent.

Charley relaxes his posture and puts his hands to his sides where he hooks his belt with both thumbs. "You'll get what you need during the dance and after. It's not so much a question of what you want. In fact I can almost guarantee that something diametrically opposed to what you expect is going to happen while we dance all night," Charley says and spits right in front of his right boot tip which is wrinkled like the laugh lines on his face and slightly turned up like his stubby nose.

"I'll catch up with you at the chuck wagon," he says and roughens up the spot on the ground that he had just smoothed into an empty circle.

For dinner I have burritos with grilled chicken and beans. I stuff my mouth to capacity for this mountain air and the excitement of seeing all these new faces around me makes me hungry.

Late at night we gather under the full moon that hovers like a rising balloon above the canyon wall. Wolf lights up the ceremonial pipe and makes his round. He blows spirit into every man and woman. "Be mindful as to what you wish to encounter in this sacred place," he says. "During a long dance in the past, we have had a B 52 jet fly low over us, so low I thought it would cut off the tips of the trees. One woman admitted that she had prayed to see the biggest bird ever; she had been disgruntled that only sparrows and other small birds would visit her during the long dance. The Kachina spirits of the ancient dwellers of this sacred site have been seen numerous times by participants. They are friendly and curious spirits, glad that we are dancing on their sacred land." With this, Wolf bows to the circle and dismisses us into a peaceful night. I walk back to my tent and cast a dim moon shadow in front of me. As I crawl into my sleeping bag, I sense that I am not alone. I feel a cool and spritely sensation on my skin - a Kachina blowing spirit breath at me?

Next morning we gather into a circle for a name game. Some thirty men and women - a majority of us are men. We look puzzled and expectant like grade school students on their first day of school. Unspoken question marks are painted on everybody's face. Our facilitator Tom tells us to move our names. Make you name a statement in motion, an impromptu dance, an expression of where you're at. I'll start out introducing myself. He makes a salute-like motion, snaps his heels together, tips his hand to his brow, and yells his name - Tom - short, tidy, and efficient. Then everybody in the group snaps into Tom's salute and belts out his name so it is flung back by the canyon walls. The round starts about ten heads ahead of me. I have time to think of my performance, but once it's my turn, I discard the pre-conceived idea and move as the Spirit moves me. I have finally arrived in the moment. I swing my hips like a belly dancer. The motion sends ripples through the circle. My name travels through thirty-some throats. I feel larger than life-size. Once we've completed the circle, I know just about everybody's name, and even more significantly, I know the way they move.

In the late morning we're building the sweat lodge from the bottom up. Clearing the space, we pray to the four directions. To the ancestors of the north for wisdom and the loneliness and cold nights that bring insight; to the west where we are challenged to make tangible the idea we have formed in our mind; to the South where the heart sees the truth and allows the truth of others to unfold; to the East where new beginnings jump into the arena like unbridled colts. Every stake we drive into the ground, every knot we tie to fasten the willow branches, every blanket we drape across the scaffolding, is a vehicle of prayer. I experience work as ceremony and it makes me contemplate a world where work is prayer, where dirty dishes create an occasion to invoke the directions. I shiver at the possibilities of such a world and I know that it's up to me to make it happen in my own life.

We go into the hills to gather rocks for the sweat lodge. They have to be the right size so they hold and radiate the heat; like stars once they glow in the midst of the sweat lodge, in the pitch black. I turn over rocks and discover dozing lizards and beetles of iridescent colors. I say thanks to all my relations for the ceaseless stream of wonderment they create in my life. I carry every rock like a baby to the fire pit where the sweat lodge leaders judge which rocks are right. I lay my rock into the fire pit, next to other rocks and lay down a prayer as well. "May I find the courage during the sweat lodge to speak my truth," the words tumble from my lips and I place the rock on the shoulders of others as the leader nods approval.

Years ago, I, David partook in a five person sweat were we didn't really know what we were doing using rocks that <u>were not volcanic</u>. A rock exploded – literally exploded in the bottom, (Thank God), of the sweat-pit hole. It exploded like a grenade going off. In *essence, never ever use rocks that are not volcanic for a sweat lodge.*

I am bleeding and this creates a vexing issue. In other sweat lodges that I have attended women who were bleeding were not allowed inside the sweat lodge. I decide to ask the leader and be up front with my situation. She puts her arm around my shoulder and pulls me closer to her side. We have no such rules, she says. Women who bleed are purifying and sweat lodges are meant to purify body, mind and soul.

I am relieved that my condition does not create a hindrance. When I squat down behind a bush and look at the stream of liquid gold interlaced with threads of dark red blood, I feel blessed to be a woman.

We have two rounds of sweats back to back. As I lie in my tent I hear the first group chant in the lodge. They bellow Native American chants, songs by Susan Osborne and Rock'n Roll tunes. I notice the edge to their singing, a tinge of desperation, but even more so, a quality of lament. Their bodies cooking, they must be down to baring their souls.

It's time for the second group to sweat. Those who just finished the process crawl out and emerge humbled. The sinking sun streaks across their glistening skin.

I undress while the men and women of the first round dry themselves off with towels. When I, dressed down to nothing, I notice my stark nudity and that of my brothers and sisters. I see balls and penises of different sizes dangling, breasts that lie flat on women's chests and breasts that are perky and plump. I don't feel excitement exhibiting my nudity nor do I get thrilled seeing so many genitals at arm's length. What unites us is our desire to make it through the extremity of temperature, get past the fear of dark and claustrophobic panic, to experience the very edge of what we can tolerate. We start crawling into the sweat lodge going counter-clockwise until we butt up against a seated buddy in the dark, and sit right next to him. This is a large group and we sit tightly packed, knees knock against neighbor's knees, shoulders against shoulders. Once we're all seated in a circle the rock carriers exit through the flap that serves as entrance and exit door. On a pitchfork they thrust glowing rocks into the pit at the center. "We're pulling down the galaxies," Wolf says. And indeed, the night sky's aglow. Every rock comes alive, sparkles and beams from every pore. "Let's sing a song," Wolf suggests and we break into a chorus of Native American chants. The first jug of water splashes onto the rocks and fills the lodge with thick steam. Newcomers to sweats are gasping for air. The singing keeps us energized, as we burst into the refrain, my fear of suffocation is quelled. Wolf invokes the sweet medicine and ancestor spirits of the four directions. "Let's pray to the north, where wisdom dwells, where delays and obstacles make the going hard, and loneliness makes us freeze at night." Several brothers and sisters speak to the north and ask for spirit's guidance, an infusion of patience. I speak to the North, so its spirit guides will help me break away from the seven-year spell of solitude. "I've had my share of cold and lonely nights. I'm ready for some loving touch, hugs, and snuggles," I say and choke, tears well up and merge with sweat dripping from my brow. Others speak to the north and invoke clarity where their vision has been blurred by doubt. "Now let's turn our attention to the West, where we shape our ideas into tangible reality," says Wolf and throws the door open so the rock bearers will bring in new fuel. Every red-hot rock that glimmers at the hub of our legs intensifies the heat. And more water on the rocks make me duck low to the ground where the air is cooler. We break into song; the beginnings of a panicky butterfly sensation near my solar plexus dissipate as I harness my voice to the strong team that thrusts forward like a locomotive. The last direction we invoke, is the East where beginnings take shape. I am no longer fighting discomfort of my dry mouth, the sweltering heat envelopes me like a sticky shroud. I am in an altered stage of awareness, as if I sat next to my body, like a bird perched next to its partner.

I'm in no hurry to get out when the crowd spirals out through the flap. Still I follow the snake movement of bodies on all fours. The prayers, urgent pleadings and sweet words of gratitude along with the Native American chants and the songs we pelted against our lurking fears, still ring in my ears. When I step outside, I'm so dizzy; I have to lie down on the cool ground. The full moon swims overhead through shreds of clouds. Brothers and sisters hug. People take refuge in their towels. Everybody rubs and strokes their skin. Bellies wobble and breasts dangle following the vigorous action. Charley squats next to me. "You're all right? Need a swig of water?"

"Yeah, I'm fine. Just resting my bones. It's been a whopping sweat for me." I say and he strokes my forehead.

"No kiddin'. We all have this dazed look. I think Wolf cooked us well."

As I start to shiver, I muster up enough energy to wrap a towel around me and trot to my tent where I'm too exhausted to arrange my sleeping bag. I lay down my tired bones and I'm gone the moment I close my eyes.

Before sunrise I hear the drumming. Wolf must be climbing up the hill to greet father sun. I get up in a hurry to follow the early morning pilgrims who step to his drumming beat. When I catch up with Wolf, I'm taken aback by his wild get-up: Coyote pelt draped over his head, a ring of feathers makes him a pagan saint. Heya, heya, ho... We chant in our rusty morning voices and the sun's red halo crowns the eastern mountain range. We chant louder and faster and the flaming chariot rolls into its full splendor.

On my way down the hill, I come across a curled up diamondback rattler, still in it's morning stupor.

For breakfast we gather around a camp fire, our mugs filled with coffee and plates of hash browns and scrambled eggs with bacon make us feel homey in spite of the early morning chills. The curls of steam rise from my mug, the fire crackles. The chatter around the fire blends into a benevolent drone like that of a bumblebee and rosy fingers of the rising sun reach up to fissures and cracks of the canyon wall.

In the late morning we arrange the bamboo bars in a large circle and stake them to the ground. They form the skeleton of the long dance containment area. Weavers lace yarns that represent the elements by color around the stakes. "You want to weave passion into the circle?" Wolf asks with a sly look on his face. "Passion?" I repeat and ponder whether I want to take the green ball of yarn. "Sure I'll do it," I say. The proposition suits me. Passion has been a desirable companion for me throughout much of my life. Images of past passion pass by my inner screen: The way I stood there seeing eye to eye with the reaper when my baby brother gasped his last breaths dying of Leukemia. The irresistible pull of the tides on the shores of North Africa where a beautiful Arab man waited too wrap me into his arms amidst the din of drumming and the chants from the minaret. I took the green yarn into my hands and my left hand unwound passion above the black thread of death that Jim, an engineer from Oklahoma City, weaved into the long dance circle just in front of me. I kept entangling with passion. I looked behind my shoulder to see what part of life would follow above passion. Linda, a biochemist from Minneapolis, smiles at me with an intertwined yarn of light blue and pink. I'm doing birth, she says with a toothy smile. Baby boys and girls made with much passion.

In the shade under a clump of juniper trees, a drumming ensemble starts up a spontaneous jam session. I boogey my behind and create a wavy line of passion. The driving beat captivates us weavers and Jim's death and my passion get entangled. "Don't bother to straighten them out!" he says and winks at me through his black framed Buddy Holly glasses.

The circle is woven by a dozen strands of life's ingredients. I look at the green, how it rides like a sea serpent between death and new birth, and I wonder how passion will weave into my dance tonight.

Wolf spins through the center of the dance ground and announces, look around you. Check all directions and the in-between places - north-west - that might suit you best. Once you've found the perfect spot, raise your banner to one of the bamboo poles. Tonight, during the dance your banner will mark your spot in the universe, your station in life.

I walk around and look at the different banners that brothers and sisters are tieing to the poles. I come across Bob who raises a flag like banner as big as his diminutive stature. The black heart at the center is cracked through the middle. He hangs his banner on a pole due south, where hearts are broken and mended. Tom's banner features buffalo, eagle and other medicine animals within a circle of hawk feathers. He hasn't changed the scenery since he created this piece of personal tapestry three years ago. "What do you think of this one?" Lisa asks, and tosses her ash-blond shoulder-long hair as if she had to get rid of something. I gaze at the magazine cut-outs organized into a collage that reminds me of Rachel in the Alps." "Do you want to live in the mountains?" I ask, for the visual message seems evident. "I grew up in Colorado where I did a lot of skiing as a child, but now I'm all boxed in, spending all of my days and many nights at the research lab injecting rats and mice with flu viruses."

I scan the whole circle. Many poles are already claimed. My feet take the lead and I walk to the south where one empty pole calls me - it's right between Bob's cracked heart and Michael who raises a blue fabric banner with a black cross painted on it. "What is the meaning of the cross?" I ask. Michael, a tall and burly guy with a salt-and-pepper beard and the smile of Winnie the Pooh, turns toward me. "Oh, it's the fourth direction and my desire to make peace with all of them. But there is also the quest for the Holy Grail;" he points to a moon-like crescent riding on the top of the cross with its hollow side pointing up. I stand on my tip toes to reach the highest point available to my fingertips, there I affix my white and pink cotton scarf which has kept me warm on many winter nights. It flutters in the stiffening breeze like a sail. Right next to it I pin my oil crayon painting of the losses in my life: Mother, Father - both dead on the same day. Baby brother, "Prince" the German shepherd dog who lived with me from day one when I was born until he was put to sleep because of blindness at age twelve. The loss of my beloved grandmother and the golden memory of her that protects me like the wings of an angel. Divorce from *ten words omitted* to share. And finally, a single figure painted in peach and pink, all naked with a large question mark hovering above her. This is Anna as I see her today. Her future is all wrapped up in the unknown. The long dance tonight - so I hope - will sweep me up like a swift stream and give me pre-view of that which life has in store for me.

All our banners are fastened to poles and the long dance arena looks like an *old world May Dance circle* with multiple maypoles staking out the terrain. We have free time to get dressed for the occasion. Wind gusts hurl through the canyon and we look warily up into the sky. Thunderheads the color of black ink are bulging against the canyon rim. "The deluge can wait until tomorrow morning," Tom yells and his echo travels up and down the canyon. Master drummer Ammar from Palestine sends drumming torpedoes and passionate invocations to Allah.

For the dance I brought a maroon silk skirt that flares out as wide as a parachute. I wear a matching vest that shimmers with silver threads and I wear a tight, ribbed cotton t-shirt that gleams as white as the teeth in toothpaste commercials. No bra. I let my hair fall wherever it wants to. This is a night where everything goes. No dress code or any other protocol. "Just do your dance," Wolf had said earlier that day, "and remember life is nothing but a dance too!"

Night falls and I see torches lit up - a sign that the group gather into a silent procession. We form a line and I wonder who is that person under the wolf mask? Tom wears a tuxedo complete with hat and gloves. Lisa came in her wedding gown. "You want to wear the veil? It goes with your white t-shirt," she asks. I decline Sshhh now! The woman's voice from under the wolf mask growls. We proceed with measured steps, torches flicker and light up the canyon shadowland.

Wolf is waiting at the eastern entrance gate to the long dance circle. He is bedecked in plumes and coyote fur. Only his wily grin remains undisguised. One by one we step up to him in full ceremonial costume. I am (name omitted) and I will safely convey you across the river (name omitted) that separates the Netherworld from the World of Illusion. Once you're past the threshold you will dance your remembrance of your life from the day of birth until today. Wolf puts his arm across my shoulder and directs me to the pole where my banner flutters in the breeze. It greets me like a flicking tongue. Wolf pulls at my ear lobe and whispers. At first you remain close to your banner, dancing your childhood. I will tap you, once your dance shows that you've graduated past your groping childhood days. The tapping is a signal that from now on you're free to roam throughout the circle. Wolf disappears light-footed and initiates the rest of the group into the circle.

Four people are drumming the heartbeat, loud, steady and in sync. The man with the large broken heart banner and the man with the black cross against a blue background stand on either side of me. I see the light of the bonfire dance across their faces.

Due to computer problems the rest of the file was lost I presume; *or a act of God??*

Adios Buenos Dias Nuevo Mexico

New Mexico, Land of Enchantment, you have bewitched me with your blue green occan of sage brush and mequite

You bedazzle me in your arid sparseness

Your soil lies in shades of red and ocher

And the shadows of clouds race over your badlands like herds of wild horses

Your land is a sacred land

Anasazi, Zuni and Taos Indians have stampcd their prayers into your soil

Your dry air had healed those with wheezing asthma and consumption

The wind dances in funnel clouds over ravines and sand banks

It hurls through canyons and echoes in ancient cliff dwellings

Endless mesas cradle the wind, hold the sun, and thirst for eight inches of water every year

The smoke of cedar and pinon hangs over pueblos where elders hold council and youngsters smoke pot

Mexican wetbacks roast chile on parking lots

Hey Miss, care for green chile fresh from Mesilla valley

So hot they'll burn holes into your stomach?

Pueblo Indians sell pinon nuts, two bucks a pound

Their Children worked all day to fill the bag

New Mexico I miss you

I miss the rattlesnakes and jack rabbits in the Sandia foothills

Where the sunset douses the land with shades of purple and rose

I miss the cholos with their Aztec faces void of any signs of emotion

I miss the lowriders with their car bellies scraping and sparking fire off the asphalt

I miss the Rio Grande with the cottonwoods arranged on either side

One thousand miles of its blue green artery undulates toward the Gulf of Mexico

I miss your houses made of earth

Houses cozy with passive solar heat, brick floors, heavy beam ceilings and Spanish tile

Red chileristras swaying from rafters and over front doors

Chimes singing all over Santa Fe

And most of all I miss the sky with its light so intense it could cut diamonds

Your sky makes love to the land every day in one dazzling light show

New Mexico is Sun Country,

It's mostly masculine and spirit

But where the water strikes and the rain gathers

The feminine arises in luxuriant shades of green

And the Indians invoke the Great Mother to grow corn, squash and deer for tacos and carne adovada

New Mexico, I miss you

Author Anna Louise Haman

In the sixties American Indians and dope-smoking hippies were doing a lot of teaching of "love nature's gifts". There is a big new wave of people teaching appreciation of Gods gifts of nature in America people from Mexico some of the people can only speak four or five words of English but they teach by example. If you cannot understand this some-day or some lifetime you will. Well now the choice is yours you can either pass on the book or throw it into your fireplace. *David A. Froebel*

Anna's Modified Serenity Prayer

GOD GIVE US GRACE TO ACCEPT

WITH SERENITY

THE THINGS THAT CANNOT BE CHANGED,

**COURAGE TO CHANGE THE THINGS WHICH
NEED TO BE CHANGED,**

AND THE WISDOM TO DISTINGUISH

THE ONE FROM THE OTHER

"Here Is What I Am Itching To Say!"
Anna's Husband's Comments

Now most, but profoundly not all, of my fellow writer friends that are older than myself, me being 67, have at times been very perturbed with my attitude of expression. Particularly in what has been written by Anna, that I have not published yet and, what I have written about myself and society.

Anna once said to me, "You can do whatever you want with the manuscript. You can even burn it if you want to". She was calm and very mentally competent when she said that.

My thinking is that in her family there was covert incest to her and her sister in the story telling. Her insistence for expressing honesty started after high school, writing about musicians and actual rock stars as a journalist. Anna's purpose was to expose truth, love as she understood it and, if necessary, raise the muck to the surface, using sharp words for tools when needed.

I believe God, Anna, my Grandmother, etc. have gifted me with teachings to be daring. Well, I think it is time to change so called "normal formalities" and express the following.

We both had some unusually freaky experiences back in those days that we both survived. When I was in Viet Nam, I didn't particularly obey all the rules and regulations, but I did leave with the Air Force Commendation Medal. Later in life, I got to experience part of the famous Woodstock Rock Festival in upstate New York, 1969.

My wife, Anna, was my incredible intense love who spiritually healed me from a Viet Nam experience. She listened to my buried remembrances which I had kept deeply hidden. People can think what they want, but I try not to care what people think about me if the truth helps in the long run. Well, as the saying goes, as long as you are still worried about what others think of you, you are owned by them.

Hopefully, this book will help a lot of people regain hope and inspiration with a new perspective/outlook towards humanity after- shall we say - hard times.

I feel blessed to have been able to co-author and publish my wife Anna's book. Again I'd like to thank Anna and all of my diverse friends for their patience, teaching, and compassion *after Anna's transition*; this book would not have made it to print without this group effect. For me to do it by myself, ah forget it. I used to be a college educated automotive technician, not a literary person – but I do have a love of writing. Well, now I gotta give my heartfelt comment *Pride Is A Horrible / Evil* Word! I don't want to hurt anyone's feelings with my statement, for example, the words Gay Pride, well my thinking is less pride makes more *love unity / brotherhood*.

I once saw a lawyer, and he asked me if I wanted to water down the manuscript. Well for me, from the beginning of taking on the responsibility of the manuscript, not that long after Anna's transition/death, I started to learn the basics about publishing and no, no, no, no, *I wanted her complete words, her feelings sharply expressed, not altered.*

In the chapter "Wallpaper" Anna describing her mother's eyes, as being "fixated" is very interesting to me. In the western section of the state of Massachusetts USA there is an area where all of the people have this lack of inertia in their eyes, called Dystrophic Depression, which is very predominate in times of duress. The nucleus of this state of mind is in the town of Athol, Massachusetts, where you can particularly see this in the eyes of the children. When I've driven in this town, I noticed that in one area, the majority of the home owners never finished painting their houses, by not painting the eaves (top 2 or 3 feet); I imagine they were emotionally and physically exhausted, whereby completion never took place.

Going west away from the nucleus of this psychological personality trait there are numerous small country towns where many intentional communities, had been peripherally located, during the sixties and seventies. The largest commune on the east coast of America was located in this area. The founder/leader, a triple Leo astrologically, as a teenager went to Florida and rode a motorcycle with the Hell's Angles to learn about Brotherhood first hand.

On the very fringes of this geographical personality trait / vibration Anna had once lived in an upper class alternative community called the Sirius Community. Only seven miles away, as the crow flies, I had once built my old home and huge organic garden in a small radical town within the lack of inertia environment. Personally, I think the people in this lack of inertia personality area basically need to learn the word "moderation."

Oh, Anna and I both loved, at separate times, partaking in the Indian Sweat Lodge gatherings at the Sirius Community.

Again I wish to share my personal comments. I am 67 presently and still have a little touch of the mental defectiveness Dystrophic Depression – my last teacher to help me correct myself was Anna, advising me to slow down in the kitchen one day, saying, lovingly I used to be like you."

Ok look, when I was in the third grade, I was prescribed drugs. U*ppers* and *downers* by my pediatrician with my mother's compliance and her having a fat check book. I remember one month that everyday life got worse and worse; finally, one day pedaling my bike home for lunch exhaustedly blown-out, I tried momentarily to kill myself, letting a city bus run me down. Luckily, I came out of it and then chose to struggle home another block and a half. Anyway, upon arriving home I simply told my mother, "I tried to kill myself." She didn't say a word to me but immediately called my aunt who was a veteran *infantry nurse* from World War Two.

As of that day, all of the drugs were stopped and, as a follow-up later on, my mother took me to a child psychologist. As I edit my writing now, I remember that I believe, on my second visit to the psychologist, it was my aunt who took me. Personally, I think *army infantry nurses* should be given more recognition. Hell, seeing that percentage wise, more American infantry nurses died in the Second World War than the whole of the soldiers. Well, my aunt was deployed from England right after WWII ended to partake in the horrible/pathetic clean-up in Germany. She never talked about it, and she profoundly hated President Truman. She later became the head emergency room nurse in a big city hospital, a post she held until her retirement. I lived with my aunt in the summer in a big lakeside family collective. After the drugs were stopped, my life rapidly got better day by day, thank God.

About 31 years ago, a psychiatrist, off the record some, told me that I was part of the first group of children treated with drugs and was *literally* given *double dosages,* seeing that the treatment procedure was very new to the medical community at that time, about 58 years ago. Along with a couple of tears coming out of my eye as I write this, for the children presently being treated, I must say that, nowadays, I'm doing real good, a lot better than I had previously expected. I wonder what percentage of the children that were given double dosages of uppers and downers ever made it to age twenty!

I've had reservations about printing the materials pertaining to holocaust victims; because a psychic friend once told me that my youngest son in his past life time had previously experienced being cooked in a concentration camp. At that time he was about five years old. Well, I took that statement with a grain of salt, but within the next couple of years, twice he walked in front of the TV and stopped and stared at it that was documenting the holocaust

The second time it happened, I really knew he felt connected to that experience!

Personally, I have only been taught a little about astrology – compared to Anna's twenty-five years at it. Previously she had willed herself not to check out my horoscope, but near the end of her life, she sat right next to me comparing both astrology charts – hers and mine – that were up on a computer screen side-by-side and said to me bewildered, "I don't understand it; I just don't understand."

Then she showed me how she had a lot of planets on one side of the astrological chart. I had a lot of planets on the other side of the chart; and we both had five open houses on opposite sides of our charts. To me, it signifies her purpose in life was to write the book. My part, the nuts and bolts, is to present it to the world.

Pertaining to Anna's grandfather's heroism, Anna had lived in a Hot Springs mountain town in New Mexico for awhile. She observed a pathetic constituency of Vietnam veterans living there wasting away on drugs and alcohol. Her view on American society's attitude was discussed. In German society, people cared about veterans unlike here in America.

A woman I know asked me about heroism. My reply was, "heroes have more fun," and to my surprise she gave me a very dirty look. In America people resort to watching programs where there is a hero, male or female. Personally I refuse to watch the majority of television programs. I have enough problems without letting the auras of actors rub off on me. The reason they are sort of having fun is simple; heroes don't think but act. In essence, be in the moment equals more fun.

Give Credit Where Credit is Due

Recently I went to hear my friend Peggy Shinn give a talk at a Science of Mind Gathering, that the music duo "One Fold" opened. In the middle of her presentation, I overwhelmingly realized that I should express to the world what I had originally communicated *only* to Anna.

I used to, (and may I repeat used to), have this reoccurring dream of a past experience: One evening in Vietnam, in 1966 while in my intoxicated, daring, reckless state of mind I went into an area in the city of Nha Trang, seeking a house of prostitution that was not located in the generally safe areas.

I ended up paying for intercourse with a part-time prostitute who turned out to be a high energy – very sensitive lady. Here is the thing, after the first twenty minutes, (the time I had paid for), we really continued because of changes, - big changes – namely we got intensely into making love. I still have tiny scars on my knees from the bamboo bed that had no mattress. As we were going onward, in our intimacy there was a guy walking back and forth on the other side of this bamboo wall that separated us from the outside alleyway right next to us. The prostitute / lady there spoke with / to this guy walking the alley along with the Mamasan (elderly lady manager). It became evident to us that he was thinking of killing me, seeing that he was actually Viet Cong (the enemy). I was the last person to realize this. As soon as the time was right I was out the door running on adrenaline to get away!

Here is the thing: the two women may very well have saved my life that night. The women had employed what is referred to "Sometime Harmony" – (making temporary harmony) amongst all of us.

The last time I awoke from the dream I got the significant message about women and their Sometime Harmony.

Decades ago I used a book by Edgar Cayce, "The Sleeping Prophet", for guidance. He stated, "If you keep getting the same dream over you have not received/gotten the message yet.

Nowadays I look back at that night as a spiritual experience.

Over the years I've worked in numerous automotive / truck repair facilities and have seen and felt the beneficial benefits of women being the secretary or mechanic or whatever.

One tidbit I'd like to add: In 1965 an American Air Force sergeant recently returned back from Da Nang, (Rocket City) Vietnam. He went way, way, way out of his way one night intoxicated, I believe, going into a security area where he was not authorized to go into, to tell/teach me, "If you talk with someone for ten minutes and you haven't learned something from that person, there isn't something wrong with that person, there is something wrong with you!" It took me a long time, mentally speaking, to get an understanding because of my intellectual arrogance. But I gotten it, thank God; now I learn from everone.

History

The other day my next door neighbor's Mescalero Apache cousin came to visit her with her nine year old daughter. As I was discussing with the mother in the front seat of her car about what my dad and Anna's writings taught me about history, the daughter abruptly spoke up from the rear seat saying, "my history teacher told us history books lie". Well if a good teacher wants to teach Native American children history and not have their concentration going out the window they gotta teach history like it truthfully is.

Oh, when my dad when he was eighty-nine years I would visit him in a rest home and as I walked into his room one day he proceeded to get out of bed saying, "they lied to me" over and over. Immediately I started to work at calming him down and finally he told me that when he was in grammar school 1910 whenever he had to memorize all the battles of the American Revolution and they were <u>lies</u>. When he was a child my Grandparents rented out a room to a Civil War veteran Mr. Murphy for whatever reason at that time they owned a bar in Hartford Connecticut. Reading between the lines my dad learned from Mr. Murphy what he was taught by him and finally at the end of his life learned from Public Television the remaining <u>actual</u> <u>facts</u>.

Hopefully you will have learned some real history from Anna.

Made in the USA
Charleston, SC
25 August 2016